# VITAL SIGNS
## 1994

# VITAL SIGNS 1994

## The Trends That Are Shaping Our Future

Lester R. Brown

Hal Kane

David Malin Roodman

Editor: Linda Starke

with

Ed Ayres
Nancy Chege
Derek Denniston
Christopher Flavin
Hilary F. French
Nicholas Lenssen
Marcia D. Lowe

Anne E. Platt
Sandra Postel
Michael Renner
Megan Ryan
Aaron Sachs
Peter Weber
John E. Young
Howard Youth

W. W. Norton & Company

New York    London

The text of this book is composed in Garth Graphic with the
display set in Industria Alternate.
Composition and manufacturing by the Haddon Craftsmen, Inc.
Book design by Charlotte Staub.

ISBN 0–393–03637–5
ISBN 0–393–31182–1 (pbk)

W. W. Norton & Company, Inc.
500 Fifth Avenue, New York, N.Y. 10110
W. W. Norton & Company Ltd.
10 Coptic Street, London WC1A 1PU

1 2 3 4 5 6 7 8 9 0

This book is printed on recycled paper

# CONTENTS

## Part One: KEY INDICATORS

## Part Two: SPECIAL FEATURES

# ACKNOWLEDGMENTS

Compiling information on a diversity of topics, and keeping it up-to-the-minute and global in scope, has been anything but a neat process. It would have been nearly impossible without the flexible assistance of dozens of people around the world in governments, businesses, academic institutions, and public interest groups—often on unfairly short notice. We would like to thank all who helped.

Several sources provided key data series or set aside time to review early drafts of specific sections. We are therefore indebted to Paul Alaback, Nils Borg, Mary Cesar, Dan Gallik, Paul Gipe, Gerd Hagmeyer-Geverus, Maureen Hinkle, Nels Johnson, Erin Kellogg, Assad Kondakji, Paul Maycock, Mack McFarland, Bob McNally, Maurizio Perotti, Mycle Schneider, Mark E. Whalon, and Helene Wilson.

We would particularly like to thank Paul Sato at the World Health Organization and Daniel Tarantola at the Global AIDS Policy Coalition for providing valuable data on AIDS. The peacekeeping feature would have been impossible without the assistance of Franz Baumann and Amir Dossal at the United Nations. Likewise, Jane Dignon at Lawrence Livermore National Laboratory turned a hope into a reality by bringing up-to-date her calculations of global sulfur and nitrogen emissions.

It fell to our experienced independent editor, Linda Starke, to channel the whirlwind of our work into a coherent final form—the compact book you now hold in your hands. That meant maintaining working relationships with all 18 analysts, as well as with Ross Feldner of New Age Graphics (who prepared all the graphs) and Iva Ashner and Andrew Marasia at W.W. Norton. All this she did while incorporating a long stream of last-minute updates from researchers, with patience and humor.

The *Vital Signs* series owes its existence to the Surdna Foundation, and particularly its executive director Ed Skloot, who has provided enthusiastic support for the project since its inception. The W. Alton Jones Foundation as well has provided direct project support since we began taking the planet's pulse three years ago. This year, we are pleased that the United Nations Population Fund has joined the Surdna and Jones foundations in supporting *Vital Signs*.

Finally, an extensive project like *Vital Signs* draws on the entire staff and resources of the Institute. These in turn are maintained with grants from the Geraldine R. Dodge, MacArthur, Andrew W. Mellon, Edward John Noble, Turner, Wallace Genetic, Frank Weeden, and Joyce Mertz-Gilmore foundations; the Pew Memorial Trust; and the Prickett and Rockefeller Brothers funds. Peter Buckley provided a personal grant for general support. And features related to the health of ocean ecosystems drew on project work funded by the Curtis and Edith Munson Foundation.

Lester R. Brown
Hal Kane
David Malin Roodman

# FOREWORD

One of the most exciting things about doing *Vital Signs* is the addition of new indicators each year. This time, for example, we have added aquacultural output, grainland productivity, roundwood production, gold production, insect species resistant to pesticides, sulfur and nitrogen emissions, AIDS, immunizations, arms trade, peace expenditures, paper recycling, coral reefs, and energy productivity.

Some of the new trends, such as grainland productivity, were relatively easy to develop since data were readily available. But others were far more difficult because the data had never been assembled and published before.

At the top of the list in difficulty was U.N. peacekeeping expenditures. Assembling the data from 1950 onward required working with the United Nations for close to a year. Time-consuming though that was, we think it was worthwhile, enabling us to publish for the first time the historical series of global peacekeeping expenditures—and to compare it with overall global military expenditures.

In a very different field, we are publishing for the first time in *Vital Signs* the historical series on the increasing number of insect species that are resistant to pesticides. Some 520 species of insects and mites are now resistant to one or more of the pesticides that are widely used to control them. Some 17 species are now immune to virtually all pesticides used against them. In many ways, this situation is analogous to that faced by the medical community as more and more species of disease-causing microorganisms become resistant to antibiotics.

Another new indicator is the number of people infected with HIV and the number who have developed AIDS. For this series, we turned to an independent group, an organization that did not have to use the numbers supplied by national governments—the Global AIDS Policy Coalition at the Harvard School of Public Health. We are pleased to publish the HIV and AIDS series compiled by the Coalition.

These data show that despite efforts to control AIDS, the disease is still spreading rapidly in most of the world—indeed, still gaining momentum in many regions. In some urban regions of Africa, 30 percent of all adults now test positive for the HIV virus. Such a high rate of infection among adults increases not only adult mortality, but also child mortality. Last year, more than a million HIV-positive infants were born in Africa.

In this year's *Vital Signs*, several indicators are beginning to convey a sense of limits. This is perhaps most pronounced with oceanic fisheries, where for the fourth year in a row the fish harvest has been static, changing little from the preceding year.

Falling water tables and spreading water scarcity are bringing us face to face with the limits of the hydrological cycle. Water scarcity is beginning to shape the evolution of the global farm economy, altering production patterns and diets in favor of crops that use water more efficiently.

In some countries, farmers are no longer able to raise the productivity of their land. In Japan, rice yields have not increased at all for a decade despite a powerful economic incentive in the form of a support price that is six times the world market level.

The compilation of each year's *Vital Signs* brings with it some surprises. One of these this year was the realization that China has now emerged as the world's leading consumer of red meat, eclipsing the United States. Another surprise in agriculture: developing countries now use more fertilizer than industrial ones do.

Life expectancy, still rising in most of the world, is dropping in some countries. The largest to register a decline is Russia, where a collapsing health care system, high levels of cigarette smoking and alcoholism, and polluted drinking water supplies are taking a heavy toll.

As we publish this, our third *Vital Signs* report, we wish we could share with you our file of letters responding to the new annual series. Comments and suggestions come from people in many walks of life—scholars, environmentalists, foundation and university presidents, former heads of state, and present and past senior government and U.N. officials.

Among the comments in our files is the following from a former senior official in the U.S. Department of State: "a monumental work in terms of research and in terms of boiling down massive amounts of information into readable, digestible form." The head of a public interest group coalition wrote: "a terrific source! I put my copy in my briefcase, and commuted with it for many weeks." The president of one of the world's largest foundations wrote: "Many thanks for the copies of *Vital Signs 1993*. I will be making good use of them by distributing them to our board of directors to enhance their familiarity with world trends."

Responses from outside the United States included one from a senior U.N. official: "When I once again used *Vital Signs* today—after having read and used it many times before—I thought that I should tell you that it is a most interesting and useful publication." A former African head of state took time to write that it was a most "interesting and instructive" volume.

We appreciate the feedback, both the letters indicating how *Vital Signs* is used and those with suggestions for improvements. For example, the addition of traffic fatalities in this year's edition was suggested by a British scientist.

Several readers suggested that we put the data in *Vital Signs* on a diskette so that they would be readily available for use by others. We have now done so. Beginning with *Vital Signs 1993*, we put the data published in the tables and used to chart the graphs on a diskette, marketing it as the *Vital Signs 1993* Diskette. Demand was so strong that we quickly decided to expand it to include data from *State of the World*, the Worldwatch Papers, the Environmental Alert book series, and *World Watch* magazine—in short, all our publications. Information on how to obtain the Worldwatch Database Diskette is found on page 8.

We look forward to your comments on this year's volume and your suggestions for improving *Vital Signs 1995*.

Lester R. Brown
May 1994

Worldwatch Institute
1776 Massachusetts Ave., N.W.
Washington, D.C. 20036

# VITAL
# SIGNS
## 1994

# OVERVIEW
## Charting a Sustainable Future

## Lester R. Brown

When Ed Koch was Mayor of New York, he was fond of asking, "How are we doing?" when he encountered his constituents on the street. *Vital Signs* is designed to answer that question for the world. Specifically, it looks at how we are doing in creating an environmentally sustainable economy, one that satisfies current needs in a way that does not jeopardize the prospects of future generations.

In June 1992, at the Earth Summit in Rio de Janeiro, the world's governments agreed to form the U.N. Commission on Sustainable Development—evidence of the growing concern that the existing economic system is not environmentally sustainable. In July 1993, President Clinton set up the President's Council on Sustainable Development. The launching of similar efforts in some 70 countries, all charting a path to sustainable development, is an encouraging sign.

The term sustainable development, now widely used by national political leaders as well as by environmentalists, is ecological in origin and solidly grounded in science. An environmentally sustainable economy is one that obeys the basic principles or laws of sustainability—principles that are as real as those of aerodynamics or thermodynamics. Anyone designing an aircraft, for example, has to satisfy the principles of aerodynamics, creating a certain amount of thrust and lift or the craft will not fly. Similarly, an environmentally sustainable economic system must also satisfy the principles of sustainability or it will not endure. The basic laws or principles of sustainability are as unyielding as the laws of aerodynamics. A society can violate these laws in the near term, but not in the long term. For example, a fishery can be overfished in the short run without lasting damage if it is permitted to recover in the long run. If overfished indefinitely, however, it will eventually collapse and disappear. Just as an aircraft can lose altitude for a short period without crashing, so can an economy violate the principles of sustainability in the short run without collapsing.

Among the principles of sustainability are the following: Over the long term, species extinction cannot exceed species evolution; soil erosion cannot exceed soil formation; forest destruction cannot exceed forest regeneration; carbon emissions cannot exceed carbon fixation; fish catches cannot exceed the regenerative capacity of fisheries; and human births cannot exceed human deaths.

The consequences of violating these principles are generally self-evident. If species extinction exceeds species evolution, for example, ecosystems eventually collapse. If the catch from a fishery exceeds its regenerative capacity, the fishery will be destroyed. Al-

Units of measure throughout this book are metric unless common usage dictates otherwise. Historical population data used in per capita calculations are from the Center for International Research at the U.S. Bureau of the Census.

though the situation regarding pollution is harder to visualize, if pollutants exceed the capacity of the system to absorb them, then the system is altered. With chlorofluorocarbons (CFCs), this translates into stratospheric ozone depletion. With carbon emissions, it means a buildup of atmospheric carbon dioxide and alterations in the earth's heat balance. With sulfur emissions, it means acid rain and damage to forests, lakes, and crops.

## SPECIES DISAPPEARING

Because of its irreversibility, the loss of species poses a fundamental challenge to governments everywhere. Over long stretches of geologic time, the evolution of new species exceeded extinctions, leading to the extraordinary biological richness of the world we inherited. In recent decades, however, this process has been reversed as habitat destruction and pollution eliminate species at a breakneck pace.

One of the obstacles to monitoring species loss is that there has never been an inventory of the earth's plant and animal species. Not knowing how many species there are, it is difficult to determine precisely how many are being lost.

Lacking this information, we can look at some of the more visible forms of life, such as birds, where there is a complete inventory of species. (See pages 128–29.) Of the 9,600 known species of birds, populations of roughly 3,000 are stable or increasing, but those of 6,600 species are in decline. Of this latter group, the populations of an estimated 1,000 bird species have dropped to the point where they are now threatened with extinction.

The principal reasons for the decline in bird populations are habitat destruction, pollution, and hunting. As rain forests are burned off or wetlands are drained to expand food production, the habitat in which birds must survive is diminished. In North America, the population of 10 common duck species has dropped from 37 million in 1955 to 26 million in 1992. This is partly the result of destruction of half of all U.S. wetlands, the areas ducks use for breeding, resting, and feeding. For birds that migrate long distances—for example, from Europe to Africa—the destruction of the habitat on either end of the migratory path or of rest stops en route can be a threat.

Since the industrial age began, some 150 species and subspecies of birds have disappeared. Among them are North America's passenger pigeon, once one of the world's most abundant birds, which disappeared in 1920; Mexico's imperial woodpecker, last seen in 1958; and Guatemala's Atitlan grebe, which died out in 1987.

Environmental analysts concentrate on the numbers of birds that are threatened because they are among the most easily measured indicators of ecosystem health. Their life-support systems are being destroyed, but they are our life-support systems as well. Of all the available indicators, this may give the clearest sense of the earth's health, of whether the existing economic system is environmentally sustainable or whether it is even now sowing the seeds of its own decline.

## SAVING THE OZONE LAYER

Few recent developments have raised as much alarm within the scientific community as the "hole" in the stratospheric ozone layer. The potential threat to this protective cover from chlorofluorocarbons was first recognized in 1974, when Sherwood Rowland and Mario Molina, two atmospheric scientists at the University of California, warned that the release of these chemicals into the atmosphere could deplete the ozone layer that protects all life on earth from damaging ultraviolet radiation.

In 1985, a team led by Joseph Farman of the British Antarctic Survey reported a recurring hole in the ozone layer over Antarctica that appeared each spring. Scientists knew that if this massive depletion were to spread to other parts of the planet, permitting a corresponding increase in the amount of ultraviolet radiation reaching the earth's surface, it could damage nearly all forms of life on the land and in the sea.

Concern about the potential effects of CFCs led to the international agreement negotiated in Montreal in October 1987 to reduce CFC production. Scientific investigations linking

CFCs and other ozone-depleting substances to the Antarctic ozone hole then led to subsequent agreements in London in 1990 and in Copenhagen in late 1992. These agreements require a complete phaseout of CFCs and other ozone-depleting substances. Between 1988, when CFC production peaked, and 1993, worldwide CFC production fell by 60 percent. (See pages 64–65.) Many industrial countries are committed to discontinuing CFC production by the end of 1994 or 1995. Since the discovery of the hole over Antarctica in 1985, additional research has found a thinning of the ozone layer over all regions outside the tropics, with the heaviest losses concentrated around the poles.

Stratospheric levels of free chlorine, the ozone-depleting agent that develops when CFCs migrate upward in the atmosphere after they are released, appear to be peaking in the mid-nineties at roughly 4 parts per billion by volume (ppbv). If CFC production is phased out as now scheduled, free chlorine levels would increase until around the year 2000 and then should slowly diminish until about 2055, when they will be back at the pre-ozone-hole levels of 2 ppbv. Under this scenario, the most serious damage to plant and animal life from increased ultraviolet radiation would occur around the year 2000, when recovery would begin. However, some level of ozone depletion will continue until about the middle of the next century.

The exact effects of increasing ultraviolet radiation on crop yields and the health of humans and other species over the long term is not known. Although reversing the loss of stratospheric ozone is a long-term proposition, at least the process to do so has been set in motion, making it a model of international environmental cooperation.

STABILIZING CLIMATE

Few things affect the habitability of the earth as directly as the amount of carbon dioxide in the atmosphere. Too much carbon dioxide, and the earth becomes a hothouse, more like Venus; too little, and the earth becomes frigid like Saturn.

From the beginning of the Agricultural Revolution, some 10,000 years ago, until the beginning of the Industrial Revolution, carbon dioxide levels in the atmosphere were remarkably stable. Beginning with the Industrial Revolution, however, they began to rise as the burning of coal, and later other fossil fuels, pushed the level of emissions above the natural rate of carbon dioxide fixation and absorption.

Between the onset of the industrial era and 1959, when the regular sampling of air for carbon dioxide content began, atmospheric carbon dioxide concentrations increased from an estimated 280 parts per million (ppm) to 316 ppm, a rise of 13 percent. (See pages 66–67.) Then from 1959 until 1993, the level increased from 316 ppm to 357 ppm, a gain of another 13 percent. So in just 34 years, atmospheric carbon dioxide concentrations rose as much as they had during the preceding two centuries. If they continue to rise, albeit at a somewhat slower rate, the result will almost certainly be economically disruptive climate change.

The principal source of increasing atmospheric carbon dioxide concentrations, the nearly 6 billion tons of carbon emitted annually from burning fossil fuels, is showing signs of levelling off as energy productivity improves (see pages 126–27), as the world turns to nonfossil sources of energy, and, particularly in the last few years, as energy use has dropped in the former Soviet Union and Eastern Europe. With governments of nearly all industrial countries now committed to holding greenhouse gas emissions in the year 2000 to their 1990 level, there is hope of eventually reversing this trend.

Except for a couple of dips when the price of oil increased, first in the mid-seventies and then in the early eighties, carbon emissions have increased almost every year from mid-century until 1991. (See pages 68–69.) Since 1992, they have actually dropped from 6.03 billion tons to 5.90 billion tons, a decline of 2 percent. This was partly the result of a global recession, including the particularly severe drop in energy use in the former Soviet Union associated with economic reforms. But it also reflects gains in efficiency. Growth in the use

of the highly energy-efficient compact fluorescent bulbs since 1990 has saved enough energy
to close eight large coal-fired power plants
each year. (See pages 60–61.)

The spreading use of bicycles in lieu of cars
for short trips as a way of maintaining mobility
without burning fossil fuels is also helping to
check the rise in carbon emissions. In 1993,
world bicycle production reached a record 108
million, roughly triple the number of automobiles produced. (See Figure 1 and pages 86–
89.) In the world's two most populous countries, China and India, bicycles are the
dominant means of transportation, completely
dwarfing cars, buses, and rail transport.
Densely populated industrial countries, such
as Japan, the Netherlands, and Denmark, rely
heavily on bicycles for local transportation and
as part of a bike-rail commute pattern. In the
United States, where bicycle commuting has
tripled over the last decade, the U.S. Transportation Act of 1991 decreed the establishment of
a bicycle transportation coordinator in each
state.

In addition to the reduction in carbon emissions from gains in efficiency, the pattern of
world energy use is undergoing a radical trans-
formation that is also lowering carbon emissions. (See pages 48–49 and 56–59.) After increasing sixfold between 1950 and 1979, oil
use has levelled off, actually declining 7 percent from 1979 to 1993. Production of coal,
which had been growing rather steadily from
mid-century onward, dropped more than 5
percent from the peak year of 1989. By contrast, the use of natural gas is climbing, its
growth driven both by price and because it is
clean-burning, particularly compared with coal
and oil. Within the next few years, the surging
reliance on natural gas is likely to move it
above coal, making it second only to oil as an
energy source. (See Figure 2.)

For carbon emissions, this shifting pattern is
a major plus, not only in reducing sulfur emissions and acid rain, but also because natural
gas emits much less carbon per unit of energy
produced than either coal or oil.

Beyond this, other nonfossil sources of energy are growing rapidly. For example, wind
electric generation is becoming increasingly
popular both because it is a clean energy
source and because its cost is making it quite
competitive, even with the cheapest coal-fired
plants. (See pages 50–51.) In 1993, global wind-
generating capacity reached nearly 3,000
megawatts. A newfound interest in wind electricity by national governments and utilities is
setting the stage for rapid growth in this energy source in the years ahead.

While increasing the efficiency of energy use
and shifting from coal and oil to natural gas
will help reduce carbon emissions, it will not
stabilize climate. If the world wishes to avoid
economically disruptive global warming, it
will have to phase out the use of
most fossil fuels just as it is now
phasing out the use of CFCs.

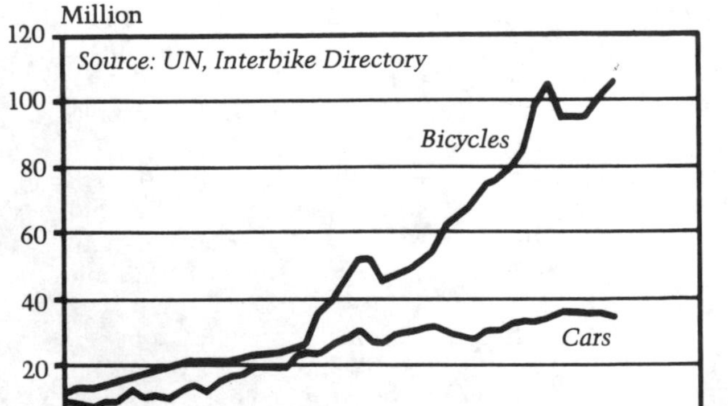

## LAND, WATER, AND FERTILIZER

The dramatic slowdown in world
grain harvest growth over the last
decade is due largely to the limited
availability of productive new cropland and of fresh water for irrigation
expansion, and to the declining response of crops to additional fertilizer use. Growth in the grain harvested area, which slowed
dramatically after mid-century, continued until 1981, when it peaked.

**Figure 1: World Automobile and Bicycle
Production, 1950–93**

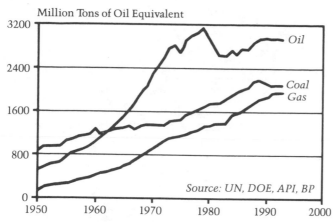

**Figure 2: World Oil and Gas Production, and Coal Use, 1950–93**

use per person dropping, it comes as no surprise that grain production per person is also falling. (See pages 26–27.)

## FOOD SYSTEMS UNDER STRESS

Each of the three food supply systems is under mounting pressure from human demands, demands that are in some situations no longer environmentally sustainable. With fisheries, rising human demands are becoming excessive almost everywhere. After reaching 100 million tons in 1989, the world fish catch has since declined, totalling 98 million tons in 1993. (See pages 32–33.) This drop, combined with continuing population growth, has led to a decline in per capita seafood supplies of 9 percent in five years, a situation that is likely to continue as far as we can see into the future. (See Table 1.)

The U.N. Food and Agriculture Organization, which monitors fish catch and stocks, reports that all 17 major oceanic fishing areas are now being fished at or beyond capacity. Nine are in a state of decline, threatening not only a shrinkage in seafood supplies but jobs in the fishing industry as well. Simply stated, the current level of fishing in many fish-

Since then it has declined slightly. As a result, between 1950 and 1993, the grain area per person dropped from 0.23 hectares to 0.13 hectares. (See Figure 3.)

Meanwhile, from 1950 to 1978 the irrigated area grew rapidly, averaging 2.8 percent per year. (See pages 44–45.) From 1978 to 1991, it grew only 1.4 percent per year, not enough to keep up with population. The result is that the per capita irrigated area dropped more than 5 percent from 1978 to 1991, leaving farmers to face not only a shrinking cropland area per person, but also a dwindling amount of irrigated land per person.

Use of fertilizer, a third major physical input relied on to expand food output, climbed from 14 million tons in 1950 to 146 million tons in 1989. (See pages 42–43.) It then began to decline as governments withdrew subsidies and as crops stopped responding so well to additional fertilizer, falling to an estimated 126 million tons in 1993. In per capita terms, the use of fertilizer fell from 28 kilograms in 1989 to less than 23 kilograms in 1993, a drop of 19 percent.

With the cropland area per person shrinking, with the amount of irrigated land per person declining, and with the amount of fertilizer

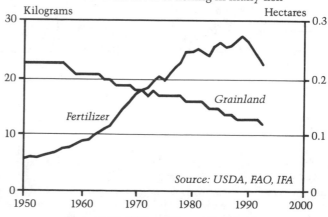

**Figure 3: World Fertilizer and Grainland Per Person, 1950–93**

TABLE 1. PRODUCTION TRENDS PER PERSON OF GRAIN, SEAFOOD, AND BEEF AND MUTTON, 1950–93

| | TREND PER PERSON | | | |
| FOODSTUFF | GROWTH PERIOD | PERCENT GROWTH | DECLINE PERIOD | PERCENT DECLINE |
|---|---|---|---|---|
| Grain | 1950–84 | + 40 | 1984–93 | − 12 |
| Seafood | 1950–88 | + 126 | 1988–93 | − 9 |
| Beef & Mutton | 1950–72 | + 36 | 1972–93 | − 13 |

SOURCE: See pages 26–27 and 30–33.

eries is environmentally unsustainable.

Limits are also beginning to constrain production on the world's rangelands, which support its herds of cattle and flocks of sheep and goats. Like fisheries, rangelands are being grazed at or beyond their sustainable yield almost everywhere. Where cattle and sheep numbers exceed carrying capacity, the rangeland is slowly being converted into wasteland. This is most evident in the pastoral economies of Africa and Central Asia, where rangeland degradation is depriving herdsmen of their livelihood, forcing many of them into cities or food relief camps.

Pressures on the world's croplands, two thirds of which are used to produce grain, are also becoming unsustainable in many countries, leading to extensive soil erosion. Between 1950 and 1984, world grain production expanded 2.6-fold, raising per capita grain consumption some 40 percent. (See pages 26–27.) During the nine years since then, it has expanded by less than one tenth. The result is a fall in per capita grain production of some 12 percent.

Although environmental sustainability is a scientific concept, the failure to abide by its principles has economic and social consequences. For example, the failure to limit growth in the demand for seafood to the sustainable yield of fisheries is leading to their collapse and to a decline in per capita seafood consumption for the world as a whole. The same can be said for rangelands. With crop-

lands, natural constraints imposed by the availability of fertile land to plow, the limited supply of fresh water supplied by the hydrological cycle, and constraints on the yield response to fertilizers are leading to a decline in food consumption per person. For some, food intake has dropped below the survival level.

An economy that is not environmentally sustainable is destined to decline and eventually collapse. Thus, failures to observe the principles of sustainability ultimately exact a human toll.

## GRAIN STOCKS AND PRICES

Between 1993 and 1994, world carryover stocks of grain, the amount in the bin when the new harvest begins, are projected to fall from 351 million to 294 million tons. (See pages 36–37.) This drop of 57 million tons is second only to the 93-million-ton drop in 1989. In days of consumption, stocks are expected to fall from 76 days in 1993 to 62 in 1994, the lowest level since the mid-seventies.

Stocks of all grains have declined, but those of rice have dropped most dramatically, falling to about 41 days of consumption. In each of the last three years, world rice consumption has exceeded production, drawing stocks down. With carryover stocks in 1994 expected to be little more than pipeline supplies, competition for exportable supplies has become intense. The result is that the world rice price doubled between the end of August 1993 and mid-November. For low-income people in rice-importing countries, who were already using 70 percent of their income to buy food, sustainability has become a very personal matter.

The big question for 1994 is whether the rice growers in Asia, where nine tenths of the crop is grown, will be able to raise output enough to not only catch up with the growth in demand, but get far enough ahead of it to rebuild stocks. If they cannot, high rice prices may join high seafood prices as part of the economic landscape.

## A SUSTAINABLE POPULATION

In many ways, the principal threat to an environmentally sustainable future for most countries is the addition of nearly 90 million people a year to the world's population. (See pages 98–99.) This is most evident in the Third World, where some 94 percent of the addition is occurring and where local life-support systems are already deteriorating. Indeed, it is difficult today to find any developing country where human demands have not exceeded the sustainable yield of forests and grasslands.

Water scarcity is becoming commonplace, stirring competition among industrial, residential, and agricultural sectors for increasingly inadequate supplies. In some situations, the diversion of irrigation water to nonfarm uses is reducing food output.

The world is entering a new phase in the era of rapid population growth, one where fishers and farmers can no longer expand output fast enough to keep up with population. This means that the needs of nearly 90 million people added each year are being satisfied only by reducing consumption among those already here. At some point, this new reality will force itself onto the global agenda, translating into much more interest in population policy, family planning, and redistribution and equity than exists today.

## PEACE EXPENDITURES

Recent years have witnessed a rapid expansion of U.N. peacekeeping operations. Expenditures, once measured in millions of dollars, reached $3 billion in 1993, nearly a thirteen-fold increase since 1987. (See pages 112–13.)

During these years, the U.N. peacekeeping role came alive as the number, size, and complexity of U.N. peacekeeping missions grew by leaps and bounds. The three largest peacekeeping interventions (Cambodia, former Yugoslavia, and Somalia) were initiated during this period.

The role of the United Nations in keeping the peace during the nineties is expanding more in line with that envisaged by its founders. Peacekeeping is often politically complex, making it difficult to manage. It is also difficult to finance. And unfortunately, member governments have been slow to pay their assessed costs, leaving the United Nations in arrears in 1993 by some $993 million, a precarious financial situation, to say the least.

The ratio of expenditures by governments on their national military establishment to those on U.N. peacekeeping, which up until a few years ago was roughly 2,000 to 1, is now closer to 250 to 1. The great advantage of a U.N. international security force is that it can make it easier for national governments to reduce military expenditures, freeing up resources to respond to the new threat to security—the environmental degradation of the planet.

# Part ONE

## Key Indicators

# Food

## Trends

# Grain Harvest Plummets                     Lester R. Brown

The 1993 world grain harvest of 1,682 million tons is 86 million tons below the harvest of 1992.[1] (See Figure 1.) This drop of nearly 5 percent is one of the largest on record.

Among the three major grain crops—wheat, corn, and rice—output of wheat and rice changed little: Wheat at 559 million tons was essentially unchanged from the harvest of 1992, while the world rice crop dropped slightly, from 351 million to 344 million tons.[2] It was a 74-million-ton drop in the world corn crop, almost all of it in the United States, that accounted for the dramatic decline.

The drop in the U.S. corn crop, which accounts for over 40 percent of the world corn harvest, was due almost entirely to weather. The area of corn planted in the United States in 1993 fell to 73.6 million acres, down from 79.3 million acres in 1992.[3] Although farmers had intended to plant somewhat less grain in 1993, the uncommonly wet spring reduced the area in corn well below that planned.

Beyond this, flooding during the growing season reduced the harvested area even more. This overall decline from just over 72 million harvested acres to 63 million acres and a drop in the yield from 131 bushels per acre to 103 bushels combined to reduce the corn harvest some 31 percent.[4]

Weather often affects the global harvest, but it is usually drought—hot, dry weather—rather than rainy weather that markedly reduces it. In this sense, the summer of 1993—which saw corn fields on the Mississippi floodplain looking more like rice fields—was unusual.

The drop in the world rice harvest of 2 percent was relatively small, but it did lead to a tightening of world rice supplies. As with corn, it was cool, rainy weather in northeast Asia that reduced the Japanese, Korean, and northeast China rice harvest.

Among the big four grain producers—the United States, China, India, and the former Soviet Union—overall grain production changed little in the latter three. In China, wheat and corn were both up slightly while rice was down some 6 million tons, leading to an overall grain harvest that was essentially unchanged from 1992.[5]

Output in India was remarkably stable: no change at all for wheat, and rice and corn gaining and losing 1 million tons respectively.[6] Similarly in the former Soviet Union, there were no major shifts in output. Wheat did not change at all; corn was up 2 million tons; and barley, the leading coarse grain in the republics, was up 3 million tons.[7]

With 86 million fewer tons of grain harvested worldwide in 1993, and with some 90 million more people to share the harvest, per capita grain output dropped nearly 7 percent. (See Figure 2.) At 303 kilograms per person, it was down 12 percent from the historical high of 346 kilograms reached in 1984.[8] The world average—the lowest level in 20 years—was only slightly higher than that in China.

The challenge in 1994 is to arrest the decline in grain output per person under way since 1984. Getting back even to the 1992 level of per capita grain use—a level that was nutritionally inadequate for close to a billion people—would require a rise in the 1994 harvest of some 115 million tons.[9]

Just keeping up with world population growth for one day requires an additional 83,000 tons of grain.[10] With little opportunity for expanding the area in grain, with irrigation expanding much more slowly than in the past, and with the limited capacity of existing varieties of grain to respond to the application of additional fertilizer, farmers will be hard-pressed to keep up with the projected growth in world population.

To the extent that higher world market prices for grain, including rice selling in early 1994 for twice as much as last year, stimulates production, the 1994 grain harvest could recover strongly from the depressed harvest of 1993.[11] On the other hand, the lower agricultural commodity support prices for some countries that are called for in the 1993 agreement negotiated under the General Agreement on Tariffs and Trade could somewhat offset the effect of higher world grain prices.

## WORLD GRAIN PRODUCTION, 1950–93

| YEAR | TOTAL (mill. tons) | PER CAPITA (kilograms) |
|------|------|------|
| 1950 | 631 | 247 |
| 1955 | 759 | 273 |
| 1960 | 847 | 279 |
| 1961 | 822 | 267 |
| 1962 | 864 | 276 |
| 1963 | 865 | 270 |
| 1964 | 921 | 281 |
| 1965 | 917 | 274 |
| 1966 | 1,005 | 294 |
| 1967 | 1,029 | 295 |
| 1968 | 1,069 | 301 |
| 1969 | 1,078 | 297 |
| 1970 | 1,096 | 296 |
| 1971 | 1,194 | 316 |
| 1972 | 1,156 | 299 |
| 1973 | 1,272 | 323 |
| 1974 | 1,220 | 304 |
| 1975 | 1,250 | 306 |
| 1976 | 1,363 | 328 |
| 1977 | 1,337 | 316 |
| 1978 | 1,467 | 341 |
| 1979 | 1,428 | 326 |
| 1980 | 1,447 | 325 |
| 1981 | 1,499 | 331 |
| 1982 | 1,550 | 336 |
| 1983 | 1,486 | 317 |
| 1984 | 1,649 | 346 |
| 1985 | 1,664 | 343 |
| 1986 | 1,683 | 341 |
| 1987 | 1,612 | 321 |
| 1988 | 1,564 | 306 |
| 1989 | 1,685 | 324 |
| 1990 | 1,780 | 336 |
| 1991 | 1,696 | 315 |
| 1992 | 1,768 | 323 |
| 1993 (prel) | 1,682 | 303 |

SOURCES: USDA, *World Grain Database*
(unpublished printouts) (Washington, D.C.: 1992);
USDA, *World Grain Situation and Outlook*,
Washington, D.C., November 1993.

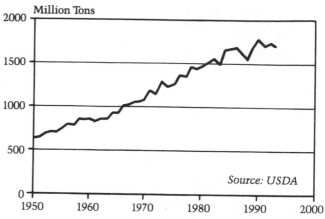

Figure 1: World Grain Production, 1950–93

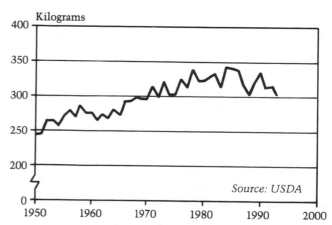

Figure 2: World Grain Production Per Person, 1950–93

# Soybean Crop Down

Lester R. Brown

The 1993 world soybean harvest came in at 111 million tons, down almost 4 percent from 116 million tons in 1992.[1] (See Figure 1.) Worldwide, the area in soybeans increased nearly 4 percent in 1993, but this was more than offset by a yield decline of 8 percent.[2]

Heavy rains and flooding in the U.S. Midwest, the world's principal soybean growing region, accounted for the decline. Many soybeans were planted late, beyond the period when yields are optimal.[3]

Soybean production per person fell more than 5 percent in 1993. (See Figure 2.) Falling from 21 to 20 kilograms, this marked the sixteenth year in which per capita soybean production remained in the 18–21 kilogram range. This plateauing of soybean output per person from 1978 to 1993 contrasts sharply with the period from 1950 to 1978 when soybean output per person climbed from 7 kilograms to 18 kilograms.[4]

Even though the U.S. soybean harvest was down nearly 16 percent, it still accounted for close to half of the world harvest. Brazil, with a harvest of 23 million tons, remained solidly in second place. Argentina again edged out China, further securing its position as the world's number 3 producer.[5] Given the acute land scarcity in China, Argentina may well widen its lead in the years ahead.

Although soybeans originated in China, they have realized their potential far more fully in the western hemisphere. Soybean yield per hectare in the United States, Brazil, and Argentina has consistently ranged between 2 and 2.5 tons per hectare, with the United States and Argentina typically having a slight edge over Brazil.[6] This contrasts sharply with corn, where U.S. corn yields are triple those of Brazil and double those of Argentina.[7] Soybean yields in China are perhaps a third lower than those of the three western producers.[8]

Although soybeans are consumed directly as tofu and soy sauce in many countries, food use accounts for a small fraction of the world harvest. Most of the world's soybeans are grown primarily for the protein meal that is widely used in pork and poultry rations. Wherever the demand for livestock products is growing, so too is the demand for soybean meal.

All three western producers export large quantities of soybeans, either as beans or in the form of soybean meal. The United States regularly exports a third of its crop as beans and enough of the remainder as meal to push the export share of the harvest to nearly one half.[9] Argentina and Brazil, by contrast, crush most of their beans and export them largely as meal, retaining much of the oil for domestic consumption.[10] China exports a small share of its crop as beans, largely for food use in Japan and other Asian countries.[11]

Imports of soybeans are concentrated in Western Europe and East Asia, with each taking roughly half the total. Among the leading importers are Japan, Germany, the Netherlands, and Spain.[12]

Growth in the world demand for soybeans is closely tied to growth in the demand for livestock products and for fish produced on fish farms. In industrial countries, where demand for the former is nearing saturation, the demand for soybeans is not likely to expand much. But in the Third World, where populations are growing and incomes are rising, demand for soybeans is likely to rise for decades to come.

The difficulty in raising soybean yields, even in agriculturally advanced countries, may eventually restrict growth in supply. For example, in the United States, where soybeans and corn are often produced by the same farmers in alternating years, the contrasts in yield trends between the two crops could not be more pronounced. In 1950, the corn yield was 2.4 tons per hectare, 60 percent higher than the 1.5-ton per hectare soybean yield.[13] In the nineties, corn yields are averaging 7.5 tons per hectare, whereas soybeans are still averaging less than 2.3 tons per hectare, a ratio of more than 3 to 1.[14] (See Figure 3.)

With farmers everywhere so dependent on more land to raise output, land scarcity could be the ultimate constraint in the growth in soybean output.

## WORLD SOYBEAN PRODUCTION, 1950–93

| YEAR | TOTAL (mill. tons) | PER CAPITA (kilograms) |
|---|---|---|
| 1950 | 18 | 7 |
| 1955 | 21 | 8 |
| 1960 | 27 | 9 |
| 1961 | 31 | 10 |
| 1962 | 31 | 10 |
| 1963 | 32 | 10 |
| 1964 | 32 | 10 |
| 1965 | 37 | 11 |
| 1966 | 39 | 11 |
| 1967 | 41 | 12 |
| 1968 | 44 | 12 |
| 1969 | 45 | 12 |
| 1970 | 46 | 12 |
| 1971 | 48 | 13 |
| 1972 | 49 | 13 |
| 1973 | 62 | 16 |
| 1974 | 55 | 14 |
| 1975 | 65 | 16 |
| 1976 | 59 | 14 |
| 1977 | 72 | 17 |
| 1978 | 77 | 18 |
| 1979 | 93 | 21 |
| 1980 | 81 | 18 |
| 1981 | 86 | 19 |
| 1982 | 93 | 20 |
| 1983 | 83 | 18 |
| 1984 | 93 | 19 |
| 1985 | 97 | 20 |
| 1986 | 98 | 20 |
| 1987 | 103 | 21 |
| 1988 | 95 | 19 |
| 1989 | 106 | 21 |
| 1990 | 103 | 20 |
| 1991 | 106 | 20 |
| 1992 | 116 | 21 |
| 1993 (prel) | 111 | 20 |

SOURCES: USDA, *World Oilseed Database* (unpublished printouts) (Washington, D.C.: 1992); USDA, *World Oilseed Situation and Outlook Report,* December 1993.

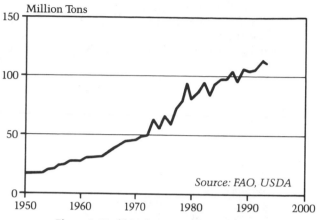

Figure 1: World Soybean Production, 1950–93

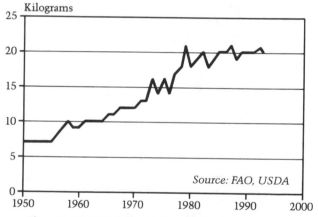

Figure 2: World Soybean Production Per Person, 1950–93

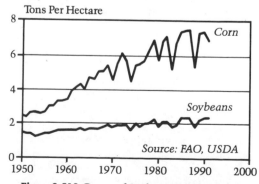

Figure 3: U.S. Corn and Soybean Yields, 1950–91

# Meat Production Increases Slightly    Lester R. Brown

World meat production in 1993, at an estimated 179 million tons, is up slightly from the 1992 figure of 176 million tons.[1] This increase matched the gain in world population, making 1993 the sixth consecutive year in which meat production per person has been essentially unchanged. (See Figures 1 and 2.)

World beef production in 1993 changed little from 1992. Declines in the former Soviet Union, because of reduced feed availability and lowered purchasing power, and in the European Community were offset by gains in North America, South America, and Asia.[2]

By contrast, pork production totalled 72 million tons in 1993, up by a million tons.[3] Production was down about 2 percent in North America and up a bit in Europe; the worldwide rise was due to a 7-percent gain in pork output in China, which now accounts for 41 percent of the world total.

Poultry production registered an impressive 4.3-percent gain, climbing from 43 million tons last year in 1992 to nearly 45 million tons in 1993.[4] The big gains came in the major producers: 5 percent in the United States, 11 percent in China, 8 percent in Brazil, and 3 percent in France.

China and the United States now dominate world meat production. Somewhat surprisingly, surging pork production in China in recent years has made it the world's leading consumer of red meat. Its output of red meat in 1992 totalled 31.6 million tons, compared with 18.6 million tons in the United States.[5] When poultry is included, total meat production in China is nearly 37 million tons versus 31 million tons in the United States.[6]

The pattern of world meat production is changing rapidly. Between 1990 and 1993 world production of beef fell nearly 3 percent, mutton was unchanged, pork went up 6 percent, and poultry climbed 16 percent.[7] (See Figure 3.) In per capita terms, beef production fell nearly 8 percent during this 3-year period, mutton was down 5 percent, pork was up 1 percent, and poultry—the big winner—was up nearly 11 percent.

The growth in beef and mutton production has come to a halt because most of the world's grazing capacity is being fully used or, in some cases, overused. Sizable additions to output can now come only from the feedlot. At this point, the relative conversion efficiencies of different meats come into play. Pork, requiring only 4 kilograms of grain per kilogram of live-weight gain, has a decided advantage over beef, which needs 7 kilograms of grain.[8]

From 1950 into the late seventies, beef and pork production trends moved upward in lockstep, rarely separated by much. But as the seventies ended, pork surged ahead, largely on the strength of rapidly expanding grain supplies in China following the 1978 reforms.

The big winner in the feed efficiency competition, of course, is poultry, where a well-managed broiler operation requires scarcely 2 pounds of grain to produce a pound of weight gain.[9] This helps explain why world poultry production has moved to a new high each year since 1950, setting 43 consecutive records.

The major producers of poultry in 1993 were the United States at 12.5 million tons, China at 5.1 million tons, Brazil at 3.2 million tons, and France at 2 million tons.[10] Together, these four countries accounted for over half of world poultry output.

Beef tends to dominate meat consumption where grazing land is relatively abundant. Among the countries leading beef consumption per person are Argentina (69 kilograms of beef measured in live weight), Uruguay (72 kilograms), the United States (44 kilograms), Australia (38 kilograms), Canada (35 kilograms), New Zealand (34 kilograms), and Brazil (25 kilograms).[11] In some countries with extensive grazing land, mutton looms large in the diet—as in New Zealand (26 kilograms), Australia (20 kilograms), Kyrgyzstan (12 kilograms), and Kazakhstan (11 kilograms).[12]

Although livestock products have not been widely traded traditionally because of difficulty in preservation, modern transport technologies permit meat to be shipped long distances. Densely populated, high-income countries are resorting more and more to imports. Japan has recently crossed a key threshold of import dependency, with its imports of beef (660,000 tons in 1993) climbing above the domestic production of 595,000 tons.[13]

WORLD MEAT PRODUCTION, 1950–93

| YEAR | TOTAL (mill. tons) | PER CAPITA (kilograms) |
|------|------|------|
| 1950 | 46 | 18.0 |
| 1955 | 60 | 21.6 |
| 1960 | 68 | 22.4 |
| 1961 | 70 | 22.7 |
| 1962 | 73 | 23.3 |
| 1963 | 77 | 24.0 |
| 1964 | 78 | 23.8 |
| 1965 | 82 | 24.5 |
| 1966 | 86 | 25.2 |
| 1967 | 90 | 25.8 |
| 1968 | 93 | 26.2 |
| 1969 | 94 | 25.9 |
| 1970 | 98 | 26.5 |
| 1971 | 102 | 27.0 |
| 1972 | 105 | 27.2 |
| 1973 | 106 | 26.9 |
| 1974 | 112 | 27.9 |
| 1975 | 113 | 27.7 |
| 1976 | 116 | 27.9 |
| 1977 | 120 | 28.4 |
| 1978 | 125 | 29.0 |
| 1979 | 129 | 29.5 |
| 1980 | 133 | 29.9 |
| 1981 | 136 | 30.0 |
| 1982 | 137 | 29.7 |
| 1983 | 142 | 30.3 |
| 1984 | 145 | 30.4 |
| 1985 | 150 | 30.9 |
| 1986 | 156 | 31.6 |
| 1987 | 161 | 32.0 |
| 1988 | 164 | 32.1 |
| 1989 | 167 | 32.1 |
| 1990 | 171 | 32.3 |
| 1991 | 174 | 32.3 |
| 1992 | 176 | 32.1 |
| 1993 (prel) | 179 | 32.2 |

SOURCES: FAO, *1948–1985 World Crop and Livestock Statistics* (Rome: 1987); FAO, *FAO Production Yearbooks* (Rome: 1988–91); USDA, *World Agricultural Production,* August 1993; Worldwatch estimates.

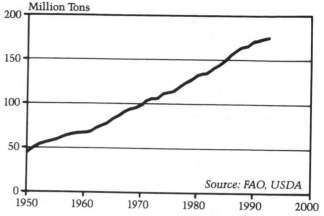

Figure 1: World Meat Production, 1950–93

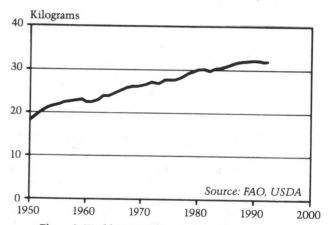

Figure 2: World Meat Production Per Person, 1950–93

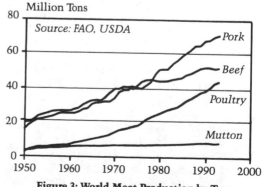

Figure 3: World Meat Production by Type, 1950–93

# Fish Catch Stable                              Anne E. Platt

The 1993 world fish catch is estimated at 98 million tons, the same as in 1992 and 2 percent below the historical high reached in 1989.[1] (See Figure 1.)

Between 1950 and 1970, the world fish catch increased steadily by 6 percent annually, three times the rate of human population growth during those years.[2] In the early seventies, the Peruvian anchovy catch—the largest in the world—collapsed from 12 million to 2 million tons in just three years. Due to overfishing and natural declines, the world fish catch grew by only 2.2 percent a year from 1970 to 1989.[3]

According to the U.N. Food and Agriculture Organization (FAO), all 17 major fishing areas in the world have either reached or exceeded their natural limits.[4] In fact, nine of these areas are in serious decline. FAO marine biologists believe it is unlikely that the global catch can expand, except for possible increases that come from more effective management of stocks.[5]

With fish catch declining in two of the past four years and with population continuing to expand, the per capita catch is falling fast. (See Figure 2.) From a high of 19.4 kilograms in 1988, the per capita catch has fallen to 17.6 kilograms in 1993, a drop of 10 percent.[6]

Despite these trends, some countries have managed to increase their fish catch. For example, the Russian fleet boosted its take with a larger catch of cod and pollack in the North Pacific and the Barents Sea. In the Far East, China has intensified catches and expanded aquaculture (freshwater fish farming) and mariculture (saltwater fish farming) production, which are included in the sum total of marine catch.[7]

Most countries, however—developing and industrial alike—now face the effects of overfishing, overpollution, and coastal habitat destruction. An estimated 200 million people worldwide depend on the fishing industry for their livelihoods.[8] Many of them fear for their jobs. Almost 50,000 Canadian fishers were laid off in 1992 and 1993 due to vanishing cod stocks in the North Atlantic waters.[9]

Although seafood is the world's leading source of animal protein, any increases in supplies are likely to come at a high price. In Africa and Asia, more than 20 percent of the population rely on fish as their primary source of protein.[10] As demand grows and supplies dwindle, seafood prices will continue to increase.

Last year, fishers spent nearly $124 billion to catch $70 billion worth of fish.[11] Governments financed the difference of $54 billion largely with low interest loans and direct subsidies for boats and operations, an expenditure that encouraged overfishing rather than effective management. Governments should reduce these subsidies if they are going to relieve some of the excessive pressure on oceanic fisheries. Already, Peru has limited additions to fleets.[12]

The imposition of fishing quotas and other stock management plans does sometimes work. Cod stocks in the Barents Sea have replenished themselves after quotas on Norwegian and Russian fishers.[13] But the key to quotas is timing and enforcement. To allow stocks to recover, restrictions must be applied before stocks are too depleted, and both governments and fishers need to complement each other's efforts to monitor and enforce restrictions.

To address the issue of bycatch (unwanted fish caught in driftnets), the United Nations passed general resolutions in 1989 and 1990 and an international moratorium in 1991 on the use of driftnets longer than 2.5 kilometers.[14] Since this went into effect on December 31, 1992, only Taiwan and Italy have continued high-seas driftnet fishing: Taiwan in the southern Pacific, Atlantic, and Indian oceans and Italy in the Mediterranean Sea.[15] This moratorium, based on international pressure and coercion, is a model easily applied to other fishing practices.

If fish stocks are given time to replenish themselves, the global catch could stabilize in the future. Even so, the world now faces the prospect of declining seafood catch per person and rising seafood prices for as far as we can see into the future.

## WORLD FISH CATCH, 1950–93

| YEAR | TOTAL (mill. tons) | PER CAPITA (kilograms) |
|------|-------|------------|
| 1950 | 22 | 8.6 |
| 1955 | 29 | 10.4 |
| 1960 | 38 | 12.5 |
| 1961 | 42 | 13.6 |
| 1962 | 45 | 14.4 |
| 1963 | 48 | 15.0 |
| 1964 | 53 | 16.2 |
| 1965 | 54 | 16.1 |
| 1966 | 57 | 16.7 |
| 1967 | 60 | 17.2 |
| 1968 | 64 | 18.0 |
| 1969 | 63 | 17.4 |
| 1970 | 66 | 17.8 |
| 1971 | 66 | 17.5 |
| 1972 | 62 | 16.1 |
| 1973 | 63 | 16.0 |
| 1974 | 67 | 16.7 |
| 1975 | 66 | 16.2 |
| 1976 | 69 | 16.6 |
| 1977 | 70 | 16.5 |
| 1978 | 70 | 16.3 |
| 1979 | 71 | 16.2 |
| 1980 | 72 | 16.2 |
| 1981 | 75 | 16.6 |
| 1982 | 77 | 16.7 |
| 1983 | 77 | 16.4 |
| 1984 | 84 | 17.6 |
| 1985 | 86 | 17.7 |
| 1986 | 93 | 18.8 |
| 1987 | 94 | 18.7 |
| 1988 | 99 | 19.4 |
| 1989 | 100 | 19.2 |
| 1990 | 97 | 18.3 |
| 1991 | 97 | 18.0 |
| 1992 | 98 | 17.9 |
| 1993 (prel) | 98 | 17.6 |

SOURCES: FAO, *Yearbook of Fishery Statistics: Catches and Landings* (Rome: various years); 1992 and 1993, FAO, Rome, private communication, December 20, 1993.

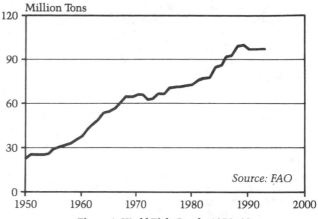

Figure 1: World Fish Catch, 1950–93

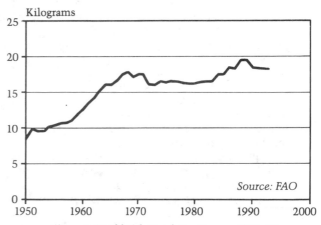

Figure 2: World Fish Catch Per Person, 1950–93

Fish farms produced almost 13 million tons of fish and shellfish in 1991, about double the 6.7 million produced in 1984.[1] (See Figure 1.) That growth stemmed in part from the moribund state of the world's natural fisheries, which can no longer provide increasing amounts of fish. Aquaculture has taken up the slack.

Aquaculture produces 90 percent of all oysters sold on the market; almost half of the tilapia and a third of all salmon are raised by fish farmers; and more than a quarter of all shrimps and prawns are farmed.[2] About two thirds of aquaculture production comes from inland rivers, lakes, ponds, and artificial tanks. The rest is coastal mariculture—grown in bays or the open ocean.[3] Some 70 percent is finfish, such as salmon, flounder, or tilapia; about 24 percent is mollusks, such as oysters and clams; and 6 percent is shrimp and other crustaceans.[4]

China dominates world fish farming, producing almost half the world total.[5] (See Figure 2.) Production from fish farms there is as large as the wild catch. India overtook Japan in 1988 to become the second largest producer.[6] In India, aquaculture production has grown to a quarter the size of its wild fisheries. With those three countries in the lead, Asia produces 80 percent of farmed seafood worldwide. (It also produces almost three quarters of the product of wild fisheries.)

Aquaculture has an advantage over its competitors—the pork, chicken, and beef industries—because fish farming is more efficient. Growing a kilogram of beef in the feedlot typically takes 7 kilograms of feed.[7] A kilogram of pork requires 4 of feed.[8] And although chicken is the most efficient of the land-raised meats, it still takes an estimated 2.2 kilograms of feed to yield a kilogram of chicken.[9] Fish, in contrast, need 2 kilograms or less of feed per kilogram of live-weight gain.[10] Suspended in the water, fish do not have to expend many calories to move about, and since they are cold-blooded, they do not burn calories trying to heat their bodies.

But fish farming shares many of the problems of the livestock and poultry industries. Each depends on the same inputs—feed, water, and land—to grow its produce. For aquaculture, the required land is often expensive coastal, lakefront, or riverfront property. There is competition for the grain used for feed, which could go instead to human consumption. And as with other meats, farmed fish produce wastes that have to be either disposed of or used. A fish farmer, like any other, has to buy supplies and equipment—antibiotics, vaccines, hormones, and equipment for cleaning tanks and oxygenating water.

The technologies fish farmers must buy are needed to fight some of aquaculture's problems. Dense population makes fish, like people, more vulnerable to the spread of disease, a costly problem.[11] Fish that breed among a smaller-than-normal population inbreed, and some occasionally escape, which imperils wild fish populations, whose discrete genetic strains can be disturbed.[12] And organic waste from farmed fish can ruin clam beds and can cause eutrophication, a growth of algae that consumes the water's oxygen, causing fish to suffocate.[13]

Shrimp farming and other aquaculture practiced in coastal areas often requires the clearing of coastal mangrove forests that are the sanctuary, nursery, and breeding grounds of many kinds of life. Without those ecosystems, stocks of wild fish decline, reducing the commercial catch. Hence, some aquacultural production comes at the expense of oceanic fisheries.[14]

Despite those problems, however, there is a strong incentive to grow fish. The world's seafood trade rose from 24 million tons worth $15 billion in 1980 to 37 million tons valued at $36 billion in 1990.[15] Free from the natural constraints of the seas, aquaculture can grow to supply those markets. If it continues to increase at present rates, however, it will require roughly 2 million additional tons of grain every year.[16] That could become too high a cost to pay. In the future, aquaculture will be constrained by the need for feedgrain, as well as the need for land and water.

AQUACULTURAL PRODUCTION, WORLD AND IN CHINA, INDIA, AND JAPAN, 1984–91[1]

| YEAR | WORLD (mill. tons) |
|------|------|
| 1984 | 6.7 |
| 1985 | 7.7 |
| 1986 | 8.8 |
| 1987 | 10.1 |
| 1988 | 11.2 |
| 1989 | 11.4 |
| 1990 | 12.1 |
| 1991 | 12.7 |

| YEAR | CHINA |
|------|------|
| 1984 | 2.2 |
| 1985 | 2.8 |
| 1986 | 3.6 |
| 1987 | 4.4 |
| 1988 | 5.1 |
| 1989 | 5.1 |
| 1990 | 5.5 |
| 1991 | 5.8 |

| YEAR | INDIA |
|------|------|
| 1984 | 0.51 |
| 1985 | 0.64 |
| 1986 | 0.69 |
| 1987 | 0.79 |
| 1988 | 0.90 |
| 1989 | 1.00 |
| 1990 | 1.00 |
| 1991 | 1.20 |

| YEAR | JAPAN |
|------|------|
| 1984 | 0.63 |
| 1985 | 0.66 |
| 1986 | 0.69 |
| 1987 | 1.10 |
| 1988 | 0.81 |
| 1989 | 0.78 |
| 1990 | 0.80 |
| 1991 | 0.80 |

[1]Excludes aquatic plants.
SOURCE: FAO, ''Aquaculture Production 1985–1991,'' Rome, 1993, and ''Aquaculture Production 1984–1990,'' Rome, 1992.

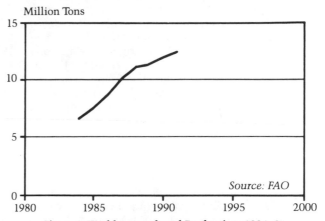

Figure 1: World Aquacultural Production, 1984–91

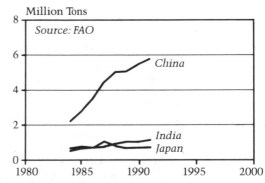

Figure 2: Aquacultural Production in China, India and Japan, 1984–91

# Grain Stocks Drop Lester R. Brown

Between 1993 and 1994, world carryover stocks of grain (the amount in the bins when the new harvest begins) are projected to drop from 351 million to 294 million tons.[1] (See Figure 1.) This drop of 57 million tons will be one of the largest on record, second only to the 93-million-ton drop in 1989 that followed the drought-decimated 1988 grain harvest.

Measured in days of world consumption, stocks are expected to drop from 76 days in 1993 to 62 days in 1994, the lowest level since the mid-seventies. (See Figure 2.) This is far below the record 104 days of consumption in 1987 and getting close to the 55 days in 1973 that led to a doubling of world grain prices.[2]

Among individual grains, there was a wide variation in the decline. Wheat stocks declined little, slipping from 141 million to 139 million tons.[3] Most of the overall drop came in corn, where stocks fell from 101 million to 64 million tons.[4] And most of it occurred in the United States, where the corn crop suffered a near-record drop in 1993. This created some upward pressure on prices, pushing them up roughly one fifth in the fall of 1993.

With rice, stocks dropped from close to 52 million tons to just over 40 million tons, a loss of more than 11 million tons.[5] With world rice consumption averaging roughly 1 million tons a day, the amount in reserve equalled 41 days of consumption. At this level, rice stocks are in a danger zone, an area where prices can rise unpredictably as importing countries compete for scarce supplies.

Even before the end of August 1993, it seemed likely that world rice consumption would exceed production for the third consecutive year, leading to a further drawdown in stocks. But in September, the Japanese government announced that an uncommonly cool, wet summer had reduced its harvest from 9.6 million tons in 1992 to 7.0 million tons, forcing it to consider emergency imports of close to 2 million tons of rice.[6] With the rice market already delicately balanced, these additional Japanese claims on the market, competing with the needs of traditional rice importers, doubled the world export price in little more than two months.[7]

Countries that regularly import rice are the hardest hit: Brazil, Cuba, Iran, Iraq, Peru, and Saudi Arabia. The beneficiaries will be the major rice exporters, including Thailand, the United States, and Vietnam. By November 1993, some exporters in Southeast Asia were trying to get out of long-term rice supply contracts because of the dramatic increase in rice prices.[8]

Between 1984 and 1993, grain production per person worldwide dropped 12 percent.[9] During the late eighties, part of this decline was offset by drawing down stocks. With these much lower during the nineties, however, this is no longer possible without causing dramatic rises in grain prices.

The big question hanging over the world food economy in 1994 is whether rice growers in Asia, where nine tenths of the crop is grown, will be able to raise output enough to not only catch up with population growth but actually get far enough ahead of it to rebuild stocks.[10] If they cannot, rice prices will remain high for at least another year, raising the prospect that scarcity could keep prices high, much as the chronic scarcity of seafood does for seafood prices.

The larger question is whether overall grain stocks will be rebuilt. Given that world grain consumption in 1994 is unlikely to be less than 1,740 million tons, the world grain harvest will need to rebound from 1993's total of 1,682 million tons to at least that level to avoid a further decline.[11] While an increase of 58 million tons—a gain of 3.5 percent—seems large, it is within range, particularly if 1994 is a good weather year.

On the plus side, a return of the U.S. corn yield to near-normal level could restore much of this shortfall. On the minus side, world fertilizer use is expected to decline somewhat further in 1994, making it more difficult to achieve robust gains in output. A severe drought in the United States or a monsoon failure in India would make it almost impossible to rebuild stocks from the 1994 harvest.[12]

## WORLD GRAIN CARRYOVER STOCKS, 1963–94[1]

| YEAR | STOCKS (mill. tons) | (days use) |
|------|------|------|
| 1963 | 190 | 81 |
| 1964 | 193 | 82 |
| 1965 | 194 | 77 |
| 1966 | 159 | 61 |
| 1967 | 190 | 71 |
| 1968 | 213 | 77 |
| 1969 | 244 | 86 |
| 1970 | 228 | 76 |
| 1971 | 193 | 62 |
| 1972 | 217 | 68 |
| 1973 | 180 | 55 |
| 1974 | 192 | 56 |
| 1975 | 200 | 60 |
| 1976 | 220 | 65 |
| 1977 | 280 | 78 |
| 1978 | 278 | 77 |
| 1979 | 328 | 84 |
| 1980 | 315 | 81 |
| 1981 | 288 | 71 |
| 1982 | 309 | 77 |
| 1983 | 357 | 87 |
| 1984 | 304 | 72 |
| 1985 | 366 | 85 |
| 1986 | 434 | 100 |
| 1987 | 465 | 104 |
| 1988 | 409 | 90 |
| 1989 | 316 | 70 |
| 1990 | 301 | 65 |
| 1991 | 342 | 73 |
| 1992 | 317 | 69 |
| 1993 | 351 | 76 |
| 1994 (prel) | 294 | 62 |

[1]Data are for year when new harvest begins.
SOURCE: USDA, *World Grain Situation and Outlook*, November 1993.

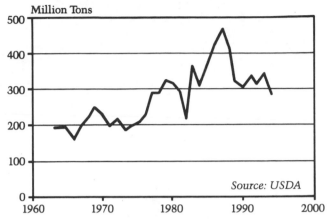

Figure 1: World Grain Carryover Stocks, 1963–94

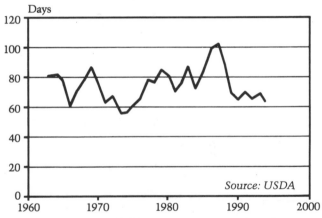

Figure 2: World Grain Carryover Stocks as Days of Consumption, 1963–94

# Agricultural Resource

## Trends

# World Grain Yield Drops

Lester R. Brown

Efforts to raise world cropland productivity were set back in 1993 as grain yield per hectare dropped to 2.48 tons, down 4 percent from the 2.58 tons of 1992.[1] (See Figure 1.) Much of this was due to a 21-percent-drop in the U.S. yield of corn, which accounts for one eighth of the world grain harvest.[2]

Since mid-century the world grain yield has more than doubled, climbing from just over 1 ton per hectare in 1950.[3] This overall trend obscures a dramatic slowdown since 1984: Between 1950 and 1984 grainland productivity climbed by more than 2 percent per year, but from 1984 to 1993 the rise was only 1 percent per year, well below population growth.[4]

The yield of corn, a cereal widely used for feed and food, is highest in the United States, which accounts for 40 percent of the world corn harvest. Between 1950 and 1985, the U.S. corn yield per hectare tripled, but in the eight years since then it has increased little.[5]

A similar situation exists for wheat in the United Kingdom, which has the highest yield of any major wheat-producing country. From 1940 until 1984, the U.K. wheat yield per hectare more than tripled. But in the following nine years it fluctuated around 7.0 tons per hectare, showing little evidence of a continuing rapid rise.[6]

The rise in wheat yields in France, Germany, and other European countries with comparable growing conditions is also slowing as levels approach those in the United Kingdom. A similar slowdown is occurring in the United States and China, the world's two largest wheat exporters.[7] (See Figure 2.) Since wheat in these two countries is grown in low-rainfall regions, the rise in yields is slowing at levels one third to half those in Western Europe. In China, the big jump in wheat production came after the economic reforms in 1978, as yields climbed 81 percent from 1977 to 1984. During the nine years since then, however, they have risen only 16 percent.[8]

After increasing for nearly a century, the increase in rice yields in Japan came to a halt in 1984. Since then they have actually fallen slightly.[9] (See Figure 3.) Yields in China, the world's largest rice producer, now approach Japan's and have been stable since 1990. In India, where less than half the rice crop is irrigated compared with 99 and 93 percent, respectively, in Japan and China, the rise in yields has slowed at a much lower level.[10]

The engine driving the rise in grain yields from mid-century onward was the expanding use of fertilizer—specifically, the synergistic interactions of rising fertilizer use with expanding irrigation and the spread of grain varieties that were responsive to ever heavier applications of fertilizer. This formula was phenomenally successful from 1950 to 1984, when fertilizer use climbed from 14 million to 126 million tons, moving to a new high nearly every year. During this time, each additional ton of fertilizer applied boosted grain output 9 tons.[11]

But 1984 was the last year in which a large increase in fertilizer use led to a comparable gain in world grain output. During the next five years farmers continued to use more fertilizer, but each additional ton raised grain output by less than 2 tons. The combination of this weak response and a cut in fertilizer subsidies in many countries dropped world fertilizer use some 14 percent from 1989 to 1993.[12]

Few countries that have doubled or tripled grain yields during the last several decades can expect to match that record during the next few with existing technologies. Most have either already achieved the easy dramatic rises or lack the natural conditions needed to do so. In semiarid Africa, for example, the prospects for sharply raising output during the next four decades are no better than they were for Australia's farmers, who boosted wheat yields by less than half between 1950 and 1990.[13]

In one sense, it is surprising that the rise in yields is slowing in so many countries at the same time. An analysis of these trends in all countries reveals that the slowdown affects each of the major cereals—wheat, rice, and corn. And it affects rainfed and irrigated crops, temperate and tropical regions, industrial and developing countries. But in another sense, the deceleration is not surprising since farmers everywhere now draw on the same international pool of yield-raising technologies.

WORLD GRAIN YIELD
PER HECTARE, 1950–93

| YEAR | YIELD (tons) |
|------|------|
| 1950 | 1.06 |
| 1955 | 1.18 |
| 1960 | 1.28 |
| 1961 | 1.31 |
| 1962 | 1.26 |
| 1963 | 1.31 |
| 1964 | 1.40 |
| 1965 | 1.40 |
| 1966 | 1.52 |
| 1967 | 1.54 |
| 1968 | 1.59 |
| 1969 | 1.60 |
| 1970 | 1.65 |
| 1971 | 1.77 |
| 1972 | 1.74 |
| 1973 | 1.84 |
| 1974 | 1.76 |
| 1975 | 1.76 |
| 1976 | 1.90 |
| 1977 | 1.87 |
| 1978 | 2.05 |
| 1979 | 2.00 |
| 1980 | 2.00 |
| 1981 | 2.04 |
| 1982 | 2.16 |
| 1983 | 2.10 |
| 1984 | 2.31 |
| 1985 | 2.32 |
| 1986 | 2.38 |
| 1987 | 2.36 |
| 1988 | 2.28 |
| 1989 | 2.43 |
| 1990 | 2.54 |
| 1991 | 2.46 |
| 1992 | 2.58 |
| 1993 (prel) | 2.48 |

SOURCE: USDA, "Production, Supply, and Demand View" (electronic database), Washington, D.C., November 1993; USDA, *World Grain Database* (unpublished printout) (Washington, D.C.: 1992).

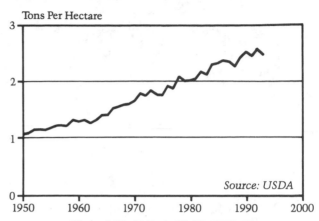

Figure 1: World Grain Yields, 1950–93

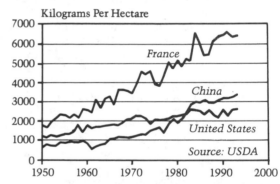

Figure 2: Wheat Yields in United States, France, and China, 1950–93

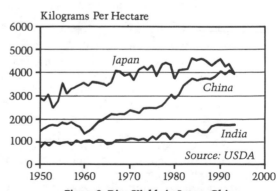

Figure 3: Rice Yields in Japan, China and India, 1950–93

# Fertilizer Use Keeps Dropping                     Lester R. Brown

World fertilizer use in 1993 dropped to 126 million tons, down from 134 million tons in 1992, marking the fourth consecutive annual decline.[1] (See Figure 1.) Since peaking in 1989 at 146 million tons, world fertilizer use has dropped 14 percent. This reverses the long-term trend, which saw fertilizer use climb steadily, moving to a new high almost every year from 1950 to 1989.[2]

Fertilizer use per person worldwide has dropped from the historical high of 28 kilograms in 1989 to less than 23 kilograms in 1993, a drop of 19 percent.[3] This helps explain why grain production per person has been falling in recent years.

The cessation of growth in recent years appears to be largely an agronomic phenomenon. Currently available varieties of grain simply lack the physiological capacity to use effectively much more fertilizer than farmers were applying in 1989. The actual decline in world fertilizer use since 1989 is due largely to the withdrawal of fertilizer subsidies in a number of countries, most importantly the former Soviet Union, for fiscal reasons.[4]

In addition to the decline in use, the early nineties have witnessed another landmark development: fertilizer use in developing countries surpassed that in industrial countries for the first time in 1992. A ranking of countries in terms of fertilizer use in 1993 puts China at the top with 29 million tons, the United States second with 18 million tons, the former Soviet Union third with 13 million tons, and India fourth with 12 million tons.[5]

Regional trends are also enlightening. In Western Europe, where fertilizer use peaked in 1986, there was a particularly sharp fall in 1993, largely because of the decrease in area planted as grainland was shifted into the set-aside programs.[6] In addition, cuts in support prices for cereals, beef, and butter further weakened the demand for fertilizer.[7]

In Central and Eastern Europe, a number of issues associated with economic reforms have been reducing fertilizer use for several years. Among the contributing factors are the reduction or removal of food and fertilizer subsidies, a shortage of credit, and uncertain landownership patterns. In the former Soviet Union, fertilizer use declined in each of the last five years, dropping a total of 48 percent between 1988 and 1993.[8]

In North America, fertilizer use was down 2 percent in 1993.[9] It is projected to rise in 1994, both because of some expansion in planted area as controls are removed on wheat and feedgrains and because it is needed to compensate for the nutrient loss due to heavy rainfall and flooding throughout the U.S. Midwest during the summer of 1993.[10]

In Latin America, fertilizer use rose 4 percent in 1992 and 8 percent in 1993, reflecting economic recovery in key countries such as Brazil and Mexico, which account for two thirds of the region's fertilizer use.[11]

For China, fertilizer use fell from 29.1 million tons in 1992 to 28.6 million tons in 1993, a drop of 2 percent.[12] (See Figure 2.) An additional drop of 9 percent is projected for 1994, largely because of the removal of subsidies. And in India, fertilizer use fell from 12.8 million tons to 12.2 million.[13] (See Figure 3.) This fall of 5 percent—the first in 18 years—reflected a reduction in the fertilizer subsidy.

In Africa (excluding Egypt), where South Africa, Nigeria, and Morocco account for nearly 60 percent of the total, fertilizer use rose 4 percent in 1993.[14] Although the use of this agricultural supplement in the region is rising, it is still quite low compared with other regions.

Even with a small expansion in world grain area likely in 1994, most of it in the United States, world fertilizer use is projected to decline by another 4 million tons as fiscal stingencies lead more governments to cut subsidies.[15] With these largely eliminated, and with the prospect of higher grain prices ahead, the decline in fertilizer use may bottom out in 1994 and be reversed in 1995.

## WORLD FERTILIZER USE, 1950–93

| YEAR | TOTAL (mill. tons) | PER CAPITA (kilograms) |
|---|---|---|
| 1950 | 14 | 5.5 |
| 1955 | 18 | 6.5 |
| 1960 | 27 | 8.9 |
| 1961 | 28 | 9.1 |
| 1962 | 31 | 9.9 |
| 1963 | 34 | 10.6 |
| 1964 | 37 | 11.3 |
| 1965 | 40 | 12.0 |
| 1966 | 45 | 13.2 |
| 1967 | 51 | 14.6 |
| 1968 | 56 | 15.8 |
| 1969 | 60 | 16.5 |
| 1970 | 66 | 17.8 |
| 1971 | 69 | 18.2 |
| 1972 | 73 | 18.9 |
| 1973 | 79 | 20.1 |
| 1974 | 85 | 21.2 |
| 1975 | 82 | 20.1 |
| 1976 | 90 | 21.6 |
| 1977 | 95 | 22.5 |
| 1978 | 100 | 23.2 |
| 1979 | 111 | 25.3 |
| 1980 | 112 | 25.1 |
| 1981 | 117 | 25.8 |
| 1982 | 115 | 25.0 |
| 1983 | 115 | 24.5 |
| 1984 | 126 | 26.4 |
| 1985 | 131 | 27.0 |
| 1986 | 129 | 26.1 |
| 1987 | 132 | 26.3 |
| 1988 | 140 | 27.4 |
| 1989 | 146 | 28.0 |
| 1990 | 143 | 27.0 |
| 1991 | 138 | 25.7 |
| 1992 | 134 | 24.5 |
| 1993 (prel) | 126 | 22.7 |

SOURCES: FAO, *Fertilizer Yearbook* (Rome: various years); International Fertilizer Industry Association; Worldwatch estimates.

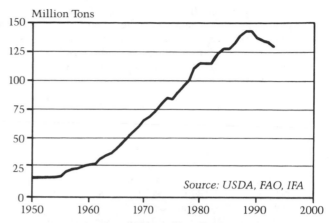

**Figure 1: World Fertilizer Use, 1950–93**

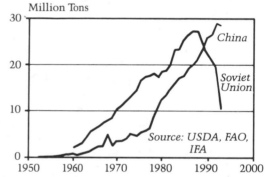

**Figure 2: Fertilizer Use in China and the Soviet Union, 1950–93**

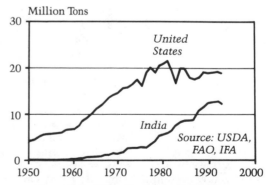

**Figure 3: Fertilizer Use in the United States and India, 1950–93**

# Irrigation Expansion Slowing Sandra Postel

Irrigated area climbed to an estimated 244 million hectares in 1991, the latest year for which global figures are available.[1] (See Figure 1.) Some 4 million hectares were added to the irrigation base, enough to lift per capita irrigated area slightly, to 45.2 hectares per thousand people. (See Figure 2.) Since about a third of the global harvest comes from the 16 percent of world cropland that is artificially watered, irrigated area is an important agricultural indicator.

Despite a slightly higher annual expansion rate during 1988–91, the long-term trend of slower irrigation expansion persists. Between 1961 and 1978, world irrigated area grew an average of 2.8 percent per year, but between 1978 and 1991, it spread by an average of 1.4 percent per year, half as fast.[2] Per capita irrigated area peaked in 1978 and has been falling more or less since then. In 1991, it was 5.4 percent lower than in 1978.

For a number of reasons, global irrigation expansion is unlikely to keep pace with population growth. The cost of adding new irrigation capacity has risen substantially in many regions, making new investments harder to justify economically. Concerns over environmental and social harm also have slowed the pace of investments in some large dam projects, including, for instance, the Sardar Sarovar dam in western India.[3] In the United States, the new Commissioner of the Bureau of Reclamation stated flatly in a recent document that "federally funded irrigation water supply projects will not be initiated in the future." He cited the need to "focus limited Federal funding on increasing efficiency and remediating adverse impacts of existing projects."[4]

The problem of a slowdown in irrigation expansion is compounded by the fact that much existing irrigated land is losing productivity because of waterlogging and salt buildup. When drainage is not adequate, seepage from unlined canals and the overwatering of fields raise the underlying water table. In dry climates, evaporation of water near the soil surface leads to a steady accumulation of salt that at some point begins to reduce crop yields and, if not corrected, can ruin the land.

Between 20 million and 30 million hectares—8–12 percent of world irrigated area—is estimated to suffer from serious salinization, which is costly to remedy, while an additional 60–80 million hectares is believed to be moderately affected.[5] A recent World Bank report finds the problem to be widespread in many important agricultural regions, affecting an estimated 28 percent of the U.S. irrigated area, 23 percent of China's, 21 percent of Pakistan's, 11 percent of India's, and 10 percent of Mexico's.[6] Moreover, salinization may be spreading by as much as 1–1.5 million hectares per year.[7]

Another sign of unsustainable irrigation is the overpumping of groundwater. This problem is pervasive in many important crop-growing regions—including the north China plain, much of the western United States, portions of North Africa and the Middle East, and parts of India.[8] A 1993 study of the Ludhiana district in India's Punjab—the nation's breadbasket—found that groundwater pumping exceeded recharge by one third, causing water tables to drop nearly a meter per year.[9] Since unsustainable use of water cannot continue indefinitely, food produced in this way is not a reliable part of the global harvest over the long term.

Finally, increasing competition for scarce supplies is beginning to pull water out of irrigation in some areas. Around Beijing, for instance, farmers are losing water to urban expansion.[10] In the western United States, where an active water market has developed, 146 water transactions in 14 western states were reported during 1992, with most of the traded water coming from agriculture.[11] California irrigators will likely lose supplies as a result of a late 1992 law requiring that 800,000 acre-feet of federal water be kept in rivers to restore fisheries and wetlands.[12] In addition, recent federal initiatives to restore the environmental integrity of the San Francisco Bay delta could siphon even more water away from farmers.[13]

In sum, irrigation is entering a difficult period. But technologies and methods that increase irrigation efficiency, improve the productivity of existing irrigated lands, and promote more sustainable water use overall can help agriculture adapt to the reality of water scarcity.[14]

### WORLD IRRIGATED AREA, 1961–91

| YEAR | TOTAL (mill. hectares) | PER CAPITA (hectares per thousand population) |
|------|-----------------------|----------------------------------------------|
| 1961 | 139 | 45.3 |
| 1962 | 142 | 45.2 |
| 1963 | 145 | 45.2 |
| 1964 | 148 | 45.1 |
| 1965 | 151 | 45.1 |
| 1966 | 154 | 45.2 |
| 1967 | 157 | 45.1 |
| 1968 | 160 | 45.2 |
| 1969 | 165 | 45.5 |
| 1970 | 169 | 45.5 |
| 1971 | 172 | 45.6 |
| 1972 | 176 | 45.7 |
| 1973 | 181 | 46.3 |
| 1974 | 185 | 46.3 |
| 1975 | 191 | 46.7 |
| 1976 | 196 | 47.2 |
| 1977 | 201 | 47.5 |
| 1978 | 206 | 47.9 |
| 1979 | 209 | 47.8 |
| 1980 | 211 | 47.5 |
| 1981 | 215 | 47.4 |
| 1982 | 216 | 46.9 |
| 1983 | 217 | 46.3 |
| 1984 | 223 | 46.8 |
| 1985 | 225 | 46.4 |
| 1986 | 227 | 46.0 |
| 1987 | 228 | 45.3 |
| 1988 | 230 | 45.0 |
| 1989 | 235 | 45.1 |
| 1990 | 240 | 45.2 |
| 1991 | 244 | 45.2 |

SOURCES: Worldwatch, based on FAO, *Production Yearbook* (Rome: various years); Bill Quimby, USDA, ERS, private communication, December 17, 1993.

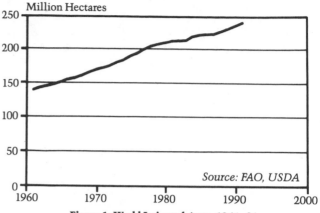

**Figure 1: World Irrigated Area, 1961–91**

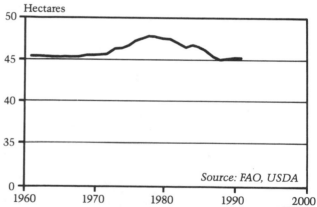

**Figure 2: World Irrigated Area Per Thousand People, 1961–91**

# Energy
## Trends

# Oil Production Flat

World oil production fell slightly in 1993, to 2,910 million tons (58.4 barrels per day), according to preliminary estimates.[1] (See Figure 1.) This leaves it at about the level recorded in 1989, a four-year plateau that reflects both a period of slack demand brought on by widespread recession and the continuing collapse of the energy-intensive economies of central Europe and the former Soviet Union.[2]

By 1992 (the last year for which national data are available), Russia's oil use was down 13 percent compared with 1989, Czechoslovakia's was down 32 percent, and Ukraine's, 41 percent.[3] While oil use is starting to bottom out in some central European nations, declines are still under way in the former Soviet republics, particularly in Russia, where oil subsidies are being withdrawn and many enterprises are likely to collapse in the next few years.

The only regions in which oil use increased significantly in 1992 and 1993 were East Asia and North and South America, all of which enjoyed rapid economic growth. Among the largest increases in 1992 were South Korea's, which rose 21 percent; Indonesia's, which increased 8 percent; and China's, up 9 percent.[4] Oil use in the United States—still higher than anywhere else—increased by a more modest 2 percent in 1992 and less than 1 percent in 1993.[5]

In oil production, as in use, the most striking recent shifts are in the former Eastern bloc countries. Russia, for example, lost its status as the world's largest oil producer when its daily output fell from 11 million barrels in 1988 to about 6.5 million barrels in 1993—larger even than the fall in the country's oil use.[6] This led to a decline in Russia's oil exports, its principal foreign-exchange earner.

U.S. oil production also declined in 1993. For the year as a whole, U.S. oil output averaged less than 7 million barrels daily—its lowest level since 1955.[7] This boosted U.S. oil import dependence to a record figure of 52 percent—higher even than in the late seventies. The decline in U.S. and Russian oil production in the early nineties has been only partly offset by modest increases in Mexico, Nigeria, Norway, and Venezuela.

In late 1993, the world price of oil reached its lowest level since 1986, pulled down by an excess daily production capacity of 3–4 million barrels.[8] Virtually all the excess is in Iraq, sidelined by a U.N. oil embargo since the Gulf War, and Saudi Arabia, which has been the world's "swing producer" for two decades—raising and lowering output to match the needs of the world market. Still, Middle Eastern oil production reached more than 18 million barrels a day in 1993—the highest level in 13 years.[9] (See Figure 2.)

The late nineties is likely to see a tightening of the world oil market, as growing demand—particularly in Asia—presses against limited supplies. Since oil production outside the Middle East is projected to remain roughly flat, the world may need an additional 5–8 million barrels per day of Middle Eastern oil by decade's end.[10] This demand can be met if additional Middle Eastern oil fields are developed (mainly in Saudi Arabia), but the last time the desert kingdom was required to produce all-out—in 1979—a revolution in Iran led to a doubling of prices, and a global recession.

Heavy oil dependence presents environmental risks as well as economic ones. The combustion of oil emitted about 2.4 billion tons of carbon in 1993, accounting for more than 40 percent of total carbon emissions from fossil fuels, as well as huge quantities of sulfur dioxide, nitrogen oxides, and hydrocarbons.[11] Much of the oil is burned by motor vehicles, and the resulting pollutants are major contributors to urban smog.

There may be light at the end of the tunnel of oil dependence, however. More than half the world's oil is used in transportation, and most of the growth is spurred by continued rapid growth in the use of cars and trucks around the world.[12] Although the rapid improvement in automobile efficiency that marked the eighties has recently levelled off, new technologies being developed may lead to a new generation of super-efficient cars fueled by natural gas or electricity. If governments take action to accelerate the commercialization of these technologies, world oil demand could begin to decline soon after the year 2000.

WORLD CRUDE OIL PRODUCTION, 1950–93

| YEAR | WORLD (mill. tons) |
|------|-------|
| 1950 | 518 |
| 1955 | 767 |
| 1960 | 1,049 |
| 1961 | 1,115 |
| 1962 | 1,210 |
| 1963 | 1,300 |
| 1964 | 1,408 |
| 1965 | 1,509 |
| 1966 | 1,638 |
| 1967 | 1,743 |
| 1968 | 1,937 |
| 1969 | 2,050 |
| 1970 | 2,281 |
| 1971 | 2,410 |
| 1972 | 2,547 |
| 1973 | 2,779 |
| 1974 | 2,803 |
| 1975 | 2,659 |
| 1976 | 2,901 |
| 1977 | 2,988 |
| 1978 | 3,023 |
| 1979 | 3,122 |
| 1980 | 2,976 |
| 1981 | 2,779 |
| 1982 | 2,644 |
| 1983 | 2,619 |
| 1984 | 2,701 |
| 1985 | 2,659 |
| 1986 | 2,774 |
| 1987 | 2,754 |
| 1988 | 2,881 |
| 1989 | 2,918 |
| 1990 | 2,963 |
| 1991 | 2,928 |
| 1992 | 2,936 |
| 1993 (prel) | 2,910 |

SOURCE: API, *Basic Petroleum Data Book* (Washington, D.C.: 1993); Worldwatch estimates based on BP and *Oil & Gas Journal*.

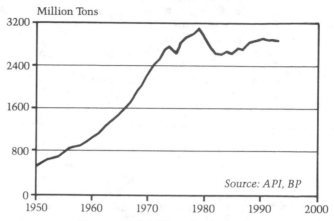

Figure 1: World Oil Production, 1950–93

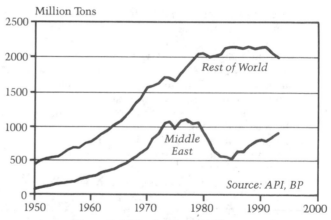

Figure 2: Oil Production, Middle East and Rest of World, 1950–93

# Wind Power Rises                                    Christopher Flavin

Global wind power generating capacity reached 2,976 megawatts in 1993, according to preliminary estimates, up 13 percent from a year earlier.[1] (See Figure 1.) Most of the 1993 growth was in northern Europe, while installed capacity in North America—still the world's largest wind generator—declined slightly. Although wind power still supplies less than 0.1 percent of the world's electricity, it is one of the fastest growing energy sources.[2]

Roughly 20,000 wind turbines are now hooked into the world's electric power systems, 90 percent of them in California and Denmark, which led the world into the modern wind power era during the eighties.[3] The technology that dominates the industry today is a single-speed, upwind turbine with three fiberglass blades 20–30 meters in diameter. Most wind farms are highly automated and have electronic controls.

The early nineties saw a dramatic slowdown in California, which still leads the world in wind power but where virtually no new power capacity of any kind has been ordered since the mid-eighties. In 1993, California was also plagued by poor winds in the Altamont Pass— site of the world's largest wind farms—and growing controversy over the danger that the machines in the pass pose to birds, including the rare golden eagle.[4] In late 1993, the National Audubon Society's chief scientist called for a moratorium on wind power in areas where migratory birds are active until the problem is better understood and mitigated.[5]

Several new California wind projects appear likely to move forward in the mid-nineties, after wind fared well in a power auction conducted by utilities there in 1993.[6] Meanwhile, sizable wind power projects are also being planned in Washington, Montana, Wyoming, Texas, Minnesota, and Maine.[7] Most of the U.S. wind potential is in the Great Plains. It is estimated that all the power needs of the United States could be met by exploiting the potential of just three states—North and South Dakota and Texas.[8]

During the past few years, northern Europe has displaced California as the main locus of wind power activity. In an effort to shift away from fossil fuels and reduce carbon dioxide emissions, some European governments opened their electricity grids to private wind developers in the early nineties, and even provided subsidies for wind energy generation.[9]

According to preliminary figures, European wind generation rose 32 percent in 1993, putting Europe on track to surpass wind generation in North America by 1995 or 1996.[10] (See Figure 2.) Denmark continues to lead the European wind industry, but Germany, the Netherlands, and the United Kingdom all have sizable wind power developments under way, while smaller efforts have begun in France, Italy, Spain, and Poland.[11] Altogether, European countries plan to install 4,000 megawatts of wind power capacity by 2000, more than three times the 1993 figure.[12]

Wind power is being considered as a serious energy option by several other countries in disparate parts of the world, including China, India, Mexico, New Zealand, and Ukraine.[13] As these and other countries open their power grids to private competition (including joint ventures with foreign companies), wind energy is likely to spread rapidly.

The recent expansion in wind power is driven in part by the declining cost of capturing wind energy—from more than 20¢ a kilowatt-hour for the first modern wind turbines installed in 1981 to 7–9¢ a kilowatt-hour for new turbines in the United States in the early nineties.[14] Somewhat higher prices are reported in Europe, where wind power is more heavily subsidized.[15]

Some turbine manufacturers claim to be on the verge of producing power for 5–6¢ per kilowatt-hour, which would make wind power nearly competitive with gas- and coal-fired plants, even before considering wind's environmental advantages.[16]

Experience with other mass-produced technologies suggests that wind power costs should fall to 4¢ per kilowatt-hour by the end of the decade, and perhaps eventually to 3¢. Wind energy appears poised to become a major source of electricity, and one of the largest manufacturing industries in the twenty-first century.[17]

WORLD WIND ENERGY
GENERATING CAPACITY, 1980–93

| YEAR | CAPACITY (megawatts) |
|------|------------|
| 1980 | 4 |
| 1981 | 16 |
| 1982 | 33 |
| 1983 | 97 |
| 1984 | 274 |
| 1985 | 694 |
| 1986 | 1,025 |
| 1987 | 1,401 |
| 1988 | 1,568 |
| 1989 | 1,579 |
| 1990 | 1,789 |
| 1991 | 2,208 |
| 1992 | 2,633 |
| 1993 (est) | 2,976 |

SOURCE: Paul Gipe and Associates, Tehachapi,
Calif., private communication,
January 31, 1994.

Note: These figures differ from those in
earlier *Vital Signs* because of revisions by
Gipe and Associates.

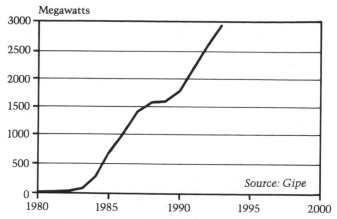

**Figure 1: World Wind Energy Generating Capacity, 1980–93**

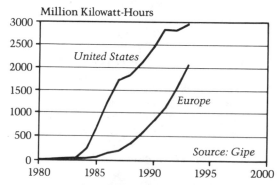

**Figure 2: Wind Energy Generation in
United States and Europe, 1980–93**

# Nuclear Power Climbs                    Nicholas Lenssen

In 1993, total installed nuclear generating capacity increased by nearly 3 percent, from 328,000 megawatts to 337,000 megawatts.[1] This figure surpasses the previous peak of 329,000 megawatts reached in 1990. (See Figure 1.) Yet given the continued decline in plants under construction and the increase in plant closings, worldwide nuclear capacity is still likely to peak before the turn of the century.

Nuclear power now provides less than 17 percent of the world's electricity and 5 percent of its total energy, levels unlikely to be surpassed in the future.[2] In the past three years, construction has started on only six new reactors. (See Figure 2.) Worldwide, some 40 plants (with a combined capacity of 32,000 megawatts) are believed to be under active construction, the fewest in more than a quarter-century.[3] Most are scheduled to be completed in the next three years.

Eighty-one reactors, with a total generating capacity of 19,000 megawatts, have already been taken out of service. On average they were in use less than 17 years.[4] The number retired each year is likely to increase as technical problems in older reactors continue to appear. Dozens of larger plants could be shut down in the next few years in North America and Western Europe, exceeding the number coming on-line elsewhere and causing the total amount of generating capacity to decline.[5]

In 1992, for the first time ever, the total generation of nuclear electricity fell, by 0.5 percent.[6] This is but one symptom of the aging of reactors. The decline was largely concentrated in the former Soviet Union, but six countries outside the former Eastern bloc also saw output dwindle.

The gain in global nuclear capacity in 1993 came from the completion of four reactors in Japan as well as single units in Canada, France, Russia, and the United States. At the same time, only two reactors were closed down in 1993.[7]

Governments in Russia and Ukraine resisted western nations' calls for the closure of some two dozen older, unsafe reactors. Indeed, the Ukrainian government repealed its earlier decision to close the remaining two Chernobyl units permanently. Both countries announced plans to resume stalled construction programs, though it remains unclear how many of the 21 planned reactors are being worked on actively there.[8]

East Asia accounts for nearly half the nuclear plants still being built, but most programs continue to lose steam. Japan's construction program appears to be winding down, with just six reactors left in the pipeline, down from 12 just three years ago.[9] South Korea has five reactors currently being built.[10]

Northern reactor vendors have moved aggressively to sell plants in China, Indonesia, Taiwan, and Thailand, touting the supposedly modest cost of atomic power. Taiwan's effort to resume a project delayed for more than a decade faced continuing difficulties and postponements.[11] In China, the government is planning to build nuclear power plants at several sites.[12] And Thailand is considering ordering as many as six nuclear plants despite the World Bank's opposition to the plan on economic grounds.[13]

In Western Europe, nuclear expansion plans have been stopped everywhere but in France, where only four reactors remain under construction.[14] And Canada's final nuclear plant was completed in 1993.[15]

In the United States, one reactor is under active construction; it has been more than 20 years since a reactor order was placed there that was not subsequently cancelled.[16] A 1993 analysis by the investment firm Shearson Lehman concluded that as many as 25 aging U.S. reactors could close during the next decade as the cost of operating and maintaining them exceeds that of replacing them. The report, as well as one issued by Moody's Investors Services, stated that the cost of decommissioning retired plants and handling radioactive wastes would continue to escalate, causing financial problems for electric utilities.[17]

Most electric utilities have concluded that nuclear power is no longer competitive with other power sources. Not only coal plants, but also new, highly efficient natural gas plants and new technologies such as wind turbines and geothermal energy are less expensive than new nuclear plants.

WORLD NET INSTALLED ELECTRICAL
GENERATING CAPACITY OF
NUCLEAR POWER PLANTS, 1960–93

| YEAR | CAPACITY (gigawatts) |
|------|----------------------|
| 1960 | 0.8 |
| 1961 | 0.9 |
| 1962 | 1.8 |
| 1963 | 2.1 |
| 1964 | 3.1 |
| 1965 | 4.8 |
| 1966 | 6.2 |
| 1967 | 8.3 |
| 1968 | 9.2 |
| 1969 | 13.0 |
| 1970 | 16.0 |
| 1971 | 24.0 |
| 1972 | 32.0 |
| 1973 | 45.0 |
| 1974 | 61.0 |
| 1975 | 71.0 |
| 1976 | 85.0 |
| 1977 | 99.0 |
| 1978 | 114.0 |
| 1979 | 121.0 |
| 1980 | 135.0 |
| 1981 | 155.0 |
| 1982 | 170.0 |
| 1983 | 189.0 |
| 1984 | 219.0 |
| 1985 | 250.0 |
| 1986 | 276.0 |
| 1987 | 297.0 |
| 1988 | 311.0 |
| 1989 | 321.0 |
| 1990 | 329.0 |
| 1991 | 326.0 |
| 1992 | 328.0 |
| 1993 (prel) | 337.0 |

SOURCES: Worldwatch Institute database,
compiled from the International Atomic
Energy Agency, and press reports.

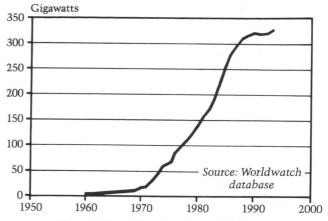

Figure 1: World Electrical Generating Capacity
of Nuclear Power Plants, 1960–93

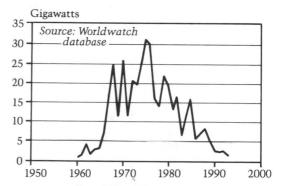

Figure 2: World Nuclear Reactor
Construction Starts, 1960–93

# Solar Cell Growth Slows                    Nicholas Lenssen

Global shipments of photovoltaic (PV) cells—thin silicon wafers that convert sunlight directly into electricity—increased 4 percent in 1993, to 60.1 megawatts.[1] (See Figure 1.) This is slower than the 10-year average growth rate of 11 percent a year, probably because of the economic recessions still plaguing Europe and Japan.

The United States regained the position it last held in 1984 as the world's largest shipper of PV cells, overtaking Japan, which has seen its output fall 16 percent in the past two years.[2] U.S. shipments rose nearly 24 percent in 1993 alone, with virtually all the increase coming from U.S.-based (though German-owned) Siemens Solar, a company formerly owned by ARCO.[3] Meanwhile, European output remained flat in 1993.[4] Together, the United States, Japan, and Europe account for 93 percent of world sales.

PV cells have the advantage of being able to work anywhere there is sunshine, which is more widely distributed around the globe than any other energy source. They are also easy to transport because they come in small, modular panels that can be connected together to produce any amount of power needed. Thus they can supply electricity to remote areas less expensively than central power plants and associated power lines would.

Thousands of villagers in remote regions now use PV cells to light their homes, run their radios, pump their water, and meet myriad other household needs. PVs are also useful in rural health and immunization facilities. More than 200,000 photovoltaic residential lighting units have been installed in recent years in Colombia, the Dominican Republic, India, Mexico, Sri Lanka, and South Africa.[5]

Price is still the largest obstacle to the proliferation of solar power generation. Future price cuts are expected, spawned by more efficient cells and lower-cost manufacturing. Historically, each time production of PVs doubled, prices fell 20 percent. (See Figure 2.) Unlike the labor-intensive batch processes still used today by most PV manufacturers, future production lines will incorporate "smart automation" and assembly-line techniques that will lower overall costs.[6]

Since reaching its nadir in the late eighties, research and development funding for PVs by governments has increased substantially, nearly doubling in the four years up to 1992.[7] To spur the solar cell industry, governments (led by those in Europe) also have initiated commercialization programs. The German government's plan led to PVs on 2,500 rooftops over the past three years, and Switzerland launched a program in 1991 aimed at placing at least one PV system in each of the country's 3,029 villages by the end of the decade.[8]

Japan is set to launch an ambitious commercialization effort by installing some 62,000 units, with a combined capacity of 185 megawatts, by the turn of the century.[9] Government support takes the form of a subsidy that initially will cover half the cost of the system, declining gradually until it reaches zero after seven years.[10]

In the United States, a coalition of more than 60 utilities plans to install 50 megawatts of solar cells between 1994 and 2000—much of them at the household level.[11] The total cost of the plan will be more than $500 million; the utilities have offered to pay 70 percent of the total and the federal government has been asked to cover the remainder.[12]

The Sacramento Municipal Utility District initiated its own program last year, and has plans to purchase more than 1 megawatt of solar cells on average each year until the end of the decade, kicking off its effort with a 1993 procurement of 640 kilowatts for 108 residential rooftops and an electrical substation.[13]

The prospect of growing sales has led a few manufacturers to begin building larger factories, including ones that can produce as much as 10 megawatts of solar cells a year. Plants like these are believed capable of bringing PV prices to less than half the current figure.[14] Such costs would bring PV electricity prices down to around 12–15¢ a kilowatt-hour, allowing it to be cost-effectively integrated into existing power grids.

## WORLD PHOTOVOLTAIC SHIPMENTS, 1971–93

| YEAR | SHIPMENTS (megawatts) |
|------|-----------------------|
| 1971 | 0.1 |
| 1975 | 1.8 |
| 1976 | 2.0 |
| 1977 | 2.2 |
| 1978 | 2.5 |
| 1979 | 4.0 |
| 1980 | 6.5 |
| 1981 | 7.8 |
| 1982 | 9.1 |
| 1983 | 21.7 |
| 1984 | 25.0 |
| 1985 | 22.8 |
| 1986 | 26.0 |
| 1987 | 29.2 |
| 1988 | 33.8 |
| 1989 | 40.2 |
| 1990 | 46.5 |
| 1991 | 55.3 |
| 1992 | 57.9 |
| 1993 (prel) | 60.1 |

SOURCES: Paul Maycock, *PV News* (February 1994, February 1992, February 1985, and February 1982) and private communication, December 1993.

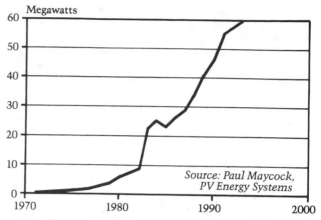

**Figure 1: World Photovoltaic Shipments, 1971–93**

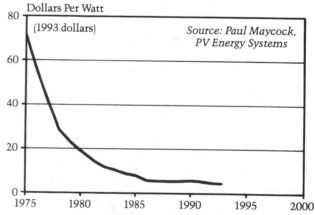

**Figure 2: Average Factory Prices for Photovoltaic Modules, 1975–93**

# Natural Gas Production Expands          Christopher Flavin

World production of natural gas, the world's third largest energy source, reached a record 1,974 million tons of oil equivalent in 1993, according to preliminary estimates.[1] (See Figure 1.) Natural gas now provides 21 percent of the world's primary energy. The recession of the early nineties and the collapse of the Russian economy caused a slowdown in the use of gas, but long-term growth of 3–4 percent per year is likely to reemerge soon.

The late eighties and early nineties were marked by expanding use of natural gas throughout most of the world. In Europe, major new pipelines are being extended from Norway, Russia, and northern Africa; demand is rising rapidly, particularly in eastern Europe, which is switching from dirtier fuels.[2] In Germany, gas use has increased 12 percent since the Berlin Wall fell in 1989, while overall energy use has fallen 5 percent.[3]

Reliance on natural gas is also expanding rapidly in the developing world, including Argentina, Mexico, Egypt, and the former Soviet republics of Kazakhstan and Turkmenistan.[4] Soon, new pipelines will allow Bolivia to sell gas to Brazil, and Myanmar to sell it to Thailand.[5] China, which relies minimally on natural gas today, is also stepping up its exploration efforts, and building major new pipelines in Guangdong and Szechuan.[6]

Elsewhere in Asia, trade in liquefied natural gas is expanding rapidly, and may soon reach countries such as India and Pakistan.[7] Plans are also being made to extend an undersea pipeline from the rich gas reserves of the Middle East to the one fifth of humanity living on the Indian subcontinent.[8] Japan, meanwhile, is considering a domestic pipeline system, including undersea connections to Russian oil fields off Sakhalin Island and to southeast Asia, which would open the way for a Far Eastern pipeline network.[9]

Natural gas is a more versatile fuel than coal or oil. Until recently, however, its main role was as a source of heat in industry and buildings. Efficient new technologies such as natural gas-powered cooling systems and heat pumps are challenging electricity's dominance of some of the fastest-growing energy uses.

This source of energy has also begun to find its way into markets from which it was excluded in the past. Its use for electric power generation, for example, is growing rapidly in many countries, spurred by the fact that gas produces less pollution than coal does. Most of the new natural gas "combined cycle" plants use a gas turbine—an adapted jet engine—and a steam turbine that is driven by the waste heat from the first.[10]

Natural gas is also attracting attention as a vehicle fuel, as cities struggle to cope with air pollution. In the United States, many local governments have began to promote these vehicles in public and private fleets. Manufacturers have developed a new generation of lightweight all-composite gas cylinders that will make it possible to build natural gas vehicles—even the smallest passenger cars—with a range similar to their gasoline-powered equivalents.[11] An industry study estimates that as many as 4 million natural gas vehicles could be on U.S. roads by 2005.[12]

This is not an entirely benign energy source, of course. Leaking methane is a powerful greenhouse gas in its own right, and further efforts are needed to reduce these emissions, particularly in Russia, where the leakage rate of the Moscow city system is estimated at 17 percent (compared with less than 1 percent in most U.S. cities).[13] At the same time, concern is growing about the impact of an uncontrolled "gas rush" that is disrupting pristine sections of the Canadian Rockies and other regions with exploratory drilling efforts.

As the nineties progress, natural gas continues to close in on oil, the world's most important energy source. (See Figure 2.) Based on new, higher estimates of the natural gas resource base, and assuming that the fuel's economic and environmental advantages stimulate demand, use of natural gas can be expected to double or even triple during the next few decades.[14] Since world oil production is likely to grow only modestly from the current level, and then decline, natural gas could become the most important fossil fuel by 2010—building a long-term bridge to an energy economy that is fueled by hydrogen gas generated from solar energy.

WORLD NATURAL GAS PRODUCTION, 1950–93[1]

| YEAR | PRODUCTION (mill. tons of oil equivalent) |
|---|---|
| 1950 | 168 |
| 1955 | 267 |
| 1960 | 411 |
| 1961 | 446 |
| 1962 | 486 |
| 1963 | 511 |
| 1964 | 556 |
| 1965 | 595 |
| 1966 | 642 |
| 1967 | 691 |
| 1968 | 763 |
| 1969 | 833 |
| 1970 | 920 |
| 1971 | 992 |
| 1972 | 1,049 |
| 1973 | 1,112 |
| 1974 | 1,126 |
| 1975 | 1,129 |
| 1976 | 1,174 |
| 1977 | 1,205 |
| 1978 | 1,239 |
| 1979 | 1,324 |
| 1980 | 1,357 |
| 1981 | 1,398 |
| 1982 | 1,385 |
| 1983 | 1,393 |
| 1984 | 1,520 |
| 1985 | 1,573 |
| 1986 | 1,608 |
| 1987 | 1,685 |
| 1988 | 1,768 |
| 1989 | 1,828 |
| 1990 | 1,865 |
| 1991 | 1,920 |
| 1992 | 1,936 |
| 1993 (prel) | 1,974 |

[1]Includes natural gas liquids production.
SOURCES: U.S. Department of Energy, *Annual Energy Review 1992* (electronic database); Worldwatch estimates based on DOE, API, UN, and government sources.

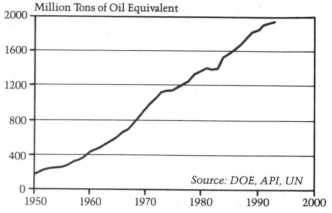

Source: DOE, API, UN

**Figure 1: World Natural Gas Production, 1950–93**

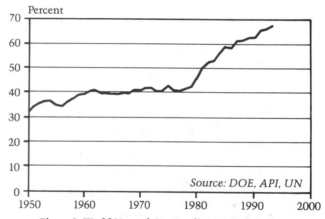

Source: DOE, API, UN

**Figure 2: World Natural Gas Production in Relation to Crude Oil Production, 1950–93**

# Coal Use Declines David Malin Roodman

Ending a steep four-decade increase, the use of coal has fallen four years in a row. The 1993 level of 2,081 million tons of oil equivalent (MTOE) was 5 percent below the peak reached in 1989, according to preliminary estimates.[1] (See Figure 1.) Rapidly expanding coal use in developing countries, however, may eventually drive the total upward again.

During the last 10 years, coal consumption has grown in developing countries at about 5 percent annually, fast enough to double every 15 years.[2] Use in industrial nations has essentially stabilized at around 820 MTOE per year since the late eighties in the face of competition from natural gas and nuclear power as sources for electricity, and with the onset of the economic recession.[3] (See Figure 2.)

Coal use has fallen abruptly in the former Eastern bloc, down 35 percent in just four years, to 410 MTOE in 1992.[4] This downward trend will slow as economic activity picks up again, but many older, inefficient coal-fueled factories there will never reopen since they will be unable to compete with cleaner, more-efficient plants that run on natural gas, a fuel plentiful in the former Soviet Union.

Coal provides 23 percent of the world's energy, down from at least twice that level in 1950, despite a doubling in total use over the same period.[5] In industrial nations, higher-quality energy sources such as oil, natural gas, and electricity have taken over the roles that coal once played in powering the Industrial Revolution—heating homes and fueling trains, ships, and factories. Today, almost all the coal used in these countries is devoted either to generating electricity or making steel. In the United States, for example, electric utilities accounted for 87 percent of coal use in 1992, up from 17 percent in 1949.[6]

Coal plays a much more dominant role in some developing countries, such as India and China, where there are large domestic reserves. China uses coal for three quarters of its commercial energy, making it the world's leading consumer.[7] But it uses just 24 percent of this in power plants, burning the remainder directly in factories and buildings.[8]

Perhaps no other mineral resource offers humanity a Faustian bargain as dangerous as coal does. It is at once the world's most abundant and its dirtiest fossil fuel. While supplies of oil and gas will probably last another century at most, 200–300 years' worth of coal lies within easy reach of miners.[9] But these vast supplies contain a variety of naturally occurring trace chemicals that threaten human health and the environment when they are liberated into the air and water in large quantities.

Coal combustion generates substantial amounts of sulfur dioxide and particulates, for example, as well as nitrogen oxides. These create severe air pollution and cause acid rain, leading to crop and forest damage in scores of countries.[10] Trace elements such as mercury, lead, and arsenic are also released in minute quantities, and these can build up over time in distant ecosystems, eventually endangering species at the top of the food chain—including, for instance, fish and the people who eat them.[11]

Because of the large-scale, mechanical nature of the work, coal mining has historically been hard on local ecosystems and on miners. Strip mining has destroyed hundreds of square kilometers of landscape in some countries, often displacing residents and polluting nearby water supplies.[12] Meanwhile, underground mining has left many thousands of workers with black lung disease.

New pollution control technologies and better regulation can prevent many of these problems, but not coal's threat to the global climate. Coal contains 80 percent more carbon per unit of energy than natural gas does, and 30 percent more than oil.[13] Burning it released 2.3 billion tons of carbon into the atmosphere in 1993, or about 40 percent of all energy-related carbon emissions.[14] Schemes for trapping carbon—for example, by pumping it deep into the oceans—would probably be extraordinarily expensive.[15]

As recessions come to an end in industrial nations, and as growth continues in developing countries, world coal use may begin to climb again, but probably not as rapidly as before. Overall, coal's role in the global economy is likely to shrink as humanity confronts the Faustian bargain, and turns to less environmentally damaging energy sources.

## WORLD COAL USE, 1950–93

| YEAR | USE (mill. tons of oil equivalent) |
|------|------|
| 1950 | 884 |
| 1955 | 1,045 |
| 1960 | 1,271 |
| 1961 | 1,174 |
| 1962 | 1,199 |
| 1963 | 1,251 |
| 1964 | 1,280 |
| 1965 | 1,299 |
| 1966 | 1,321 |
| 1967 | 1,255 |
| 1968 | 1,317 |
| 1969 | 1,357 |
| 1970 | 1,359 |
| 1971 | 1,355 |
| 1972 | 1,355 |
| 1973 | 1,413 |
| 1974 | 1,434 |
| 1975 | 1,450 |
| 1976 | 1,525 |
| 1977 | 1,581 |
| 1978 | 1,615 |
| 1979 | 1,681 |
| 1980 | 1,708 |
| 1981 | 1,732 |
| 1982 | 1,751 |
| 1983 | 1,804 |
| 1984 | 1,877 |
| 1985 | 1,980 |
| 1986 | 2,001 |
| 1987 | 2,062 |
| 1988 | 2,183 |
| 1989 | 2,195 |
| 1990 | 2,115 |
| 1991 | 2,088 |
| 1992 | 2,087 |
| 1993 (prel) | 2,081 |

SOURCES: UN, *World Energy Supplies* and *Energy Statistics Yearbook* (New York: various years); UN, *Yearbook of World Energy Statistics* (New York: 1983); Worldwatch estimates based on UN, BP, government sources, and press reports.

Note: This series disagrees somewhat with the one printed in *Vital Signs 1993* due to the use of a different technique for dealing with discrepencies among various U.N. data series.

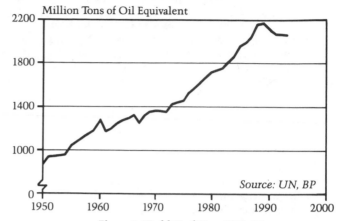

Figure 1: World Coal Use, 1950–93

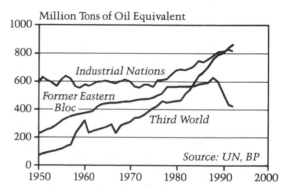

Figure 2: Coal Use in Industrial Nations, Former Eastern Bloc, and Third World, 1950–92

# Compact Fluorescents Flourish    David Malin Roodman

Sales of the compact fluorescent lamp (CFL)—an efficient substitute for the century-old incandescent bulb—increased to 200 million in 1993, according to preliminary estimates, and have quadrupled over the last five years.[1] (See Figure 1.) All told, some 400 million CFLs are probably now in use. By replacing incandescents, these are together saving enough electricity to match the output of about 18 large coal plants, or 18,000 megawatts.[2]

Old-fashioned but low-priced incandescent bulbs still outsell CFLs nearly 50 to 1.[3] But since the fluorescents last 10 times as long, they actually claimed a surprisingly large share of the lighting market in 1993—about one sixth, in terms of hours of lighting capacity sold.[4] Western Europe accounted for nearly half of CFL sales in 1992, and North America claimed about half the rest. (See Figure 2.)

The incandescent bulb is inefficient because more than 90 percent of the energy it draws is needed to heat its filament enough for it to glow.[5] The CFL, in contrast, makes use of recent advances in fluorescent lighting technologies to achieve efficiencies four times greater. Unfortunately, the very advances that make CFLs efficient also make them more complicated and expensive to produce, resulting in a retail price tag of $15–20.

But a CFL is almost always cost-effective when considered over its 10,000-hour lifetime, since each one can eliminate the need to purchase 10 incandescents and 450 kilowatt-hours of electricity. In the United States, this means using a CFL can save $20, despite the high cost of the lamp itself. In Japan, where electricity costs 60 percent more, net savings average about $40 per bulb.[6] It is not surprising, then, that CFLs now provide more than 80 percent of home lighting in Japan.[7]

In most other parts of the world, the high initial cost of CFLs has been a major obstacle to sales, despite their long-term cost-effectiveness. Many governments have adopted aggressive policies to encourage the use of energy-efficient technologies, however, primarily through cash rebates and high-profile consumer education campaigns.[8] The CFL sales trend thus demonstrates the success not just of a new technology, but also of a new technology policy.

In the United States, utilities now spend nearly $3 billion a year encouraging energy efficiency, much of it devoted to lighting programs.[9] Many of these encourage customers to buy CFLs by offering substantial rebates—enough to make the lights easy to buy. They then pass the costs of the rebates, along with a profit margin, back to consumers through slightly higher electricity prices. Participants in the programs still profit, since they are buying much less electricity for lighting. Similar efforts are now under way in Western Europe, Canada, Mexico, Brazil, and Thailand.[10]

By requiring less electricity, the CFL helps reduce many pollution problems associated with electricity generation, including acid rain and global warming. And thanks to the longer life and higher efficiency of CFLs, using these bulbs also reduces solid and toxic wastes. Generating electricity from fossil or nuclear fuels involves the construction and maintenance of large infrastructures to mine, deliver, and use the energy, all of which generate waste. As a result, it has been estimated that each CFL in use cuts solid waste by 90 kilograms over its lifetime compared with standard incandescents.[11]

In addition, coal burning, which now provides 39 percent of the world's electricity, releases small, toxic amounts of mercury, arsenic, and lead into the air, which can collect in downwind lakes, farmlands, and cities.[12] So even though CFL tubes do contain 5 milligrams of mercury each (one one-hundredth of the amount in a household thermometer), overall mercury generation can still be cut in half by using the more efficient lights, while arsenic and lead emissions drop by 75 percent.[13]

Likewise, "magnetic" ballasts (the components that regulate the electric current to the fluorescent tubes) do contain very small amounts of radioactive isotopes, but they are becoming less common, and the avoided radioactive wastes from nuclear power (source of some 17 percent of global electricity) are a million times greater.[14]

WORLD SALES OF COMPACT
FLUORESCENT BULBS, 1988–93

| YEAR | WORLD (million) |
| --- | --- |
| 1988 | 45 |
| 1989 | 59 |
| 1990 | 83 |
| 1991 | 109 |
| 1992 | 134 |
| 1993 (prel) | 200 |

SOURCE: Evan Mills, Lawrence Berkeley
Laboratory, private communication,
February 3, 1993; 1993 from Nils Borg, National
Board for Industrial and Technical Development,
Stockholm, Sweden, private communication,
March 14, 1994.

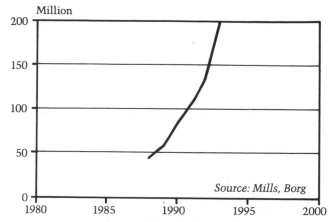

Figure 1: World Sales of Compact Fluorescent Bulbs, 1988–93

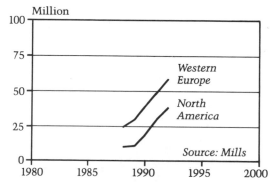

Figure 2: Sales of Compact Fluorescent Bulbs,
North America and Western Europe, 1988–92

# Atmospheric
## Trends

# CFC Production Continues to Drop  Megan Ryan

Global chlorofluorocarbon (CFC) production decreased 20 percent in 1993, falling for the fifth consecutive year and bringing total production levels down 60 percent from their peak in 1988.[1] (See Figure 1.) This continuing reduction is the result of the international community's firm commitment to a rapid phaseout of the family of chemicals depleting the stratospheric ozone layer.

International efforts to protect stratospheric ozone began in October 1987, when many of the world's nations—galvanized by the threat posed by increased exposure to ultraviolet radiation—signed the Montreal Protocol, pledging to cut CFC production in half over 10 years.[2] This unprecedented accord followed the release of data indicating a growing "hole" in the ozone layer over Antarctica.[3]

Since the Montreal Protocol was drafted, new evidence linking ozone depletion to CFCs and other ozone-depleting substances as well as evidence of additional ozone loss has spurred the world to further action. The agreement has been strengthened twice—in London in 1990 and in Copenhagen in 1992—in order to achieve a more rapid and complete phaseout of CFCs. The London amendments called for a total CFC ban by 2000, and then the Copenhagen amendments moved the phaseout date to January 1, 1996, with a 75-percent reduction by 1994.[4]

If all the 120 nations that ratified the Montreal Protocol comply with the terms of the Copenhagen amendments, atmospheric concentrations of chlorine (a measure of the ozone-depletion potential of the stratosphere) will be measurably declining by the end of the decade, having peaked at around 4 parts per billion by volume.[5] (See Figure 2.)

Some nations are taking action to accomplish the phaseout of ozone-depleting substances even quicker than they have committed to through international agreements. Most notably, the 12-member European Union has pledged to stop producing CFCs by the end of 1994, a year ahead of schedule.[6]

Despite these encouraging initiatives, however, many developing nations may have difficulty meeting their commitments under the Montreal Protocol. In 1991, signatories of the agreement from the developing world increased their use of CFCs by 53 percent.[7] These countries are not violating the agreement, as the accord gave them a 10-year grace period to move to less damaging technologies. But their ability to make this shift will be vital to international efforts to protect the ozone layer.

To aid in this transition, 43 countries set up a multilateral fund as part of the Montreal Protocol, pledging financial contributions to assist with the development of substitutes and the acquisition of recycling equipment. Although these nations pledged $240 million for 1991–93, by the end of 1993 they had only put $135 million into the fund.[8] At the Copenhagen meeting, governments pledged an additional $455 million for 1994–96.[9]

The link between CFCs, halons, and other ozone-depleting substances and the destruction of the stratospheric ozone layer has been well established. Stratospheric ozone over Antarctica is depleted in the Antarctic spring, when cloud particles convert the chlorine generated by the breakdown of CFCs in the upper stratosphere to an active form that destroys ozone, weakening the shield it provides. In recent years, this depletion has been more pronounced than usual, with the remaining stratospheric ozone measured over Antarctica in October 1993 at an all-time low of 90 Dobson units, down from the previous year's record low of 105 Dobson units.[10] In 1993 the hole was 15 percent larger than it has been in recent years.[11]

Similar chemical reactions take place at other latitudes as well, but the effect varies greatly by region. According to data gathered by NASA's Nimbus 7 satellite, the biggest decreases have been in the northern midlatitudes, including most of North America, Europe, and Asia.[12] Averaged over the earth as a whole, from 1979 to 1991 stratospheric ozone thinned by about 3 percent.[13] In April 1993, NASA scientists reported that global ozone levels for the second half of 1992 and early 1993 were the lowest observed in the 14 years the agency had been monitoring the stratosphere from space, falling by 13–14 percent below normal over the midlatitudes.[14]

ESTIMATED GLOBAL CFC PRODUCTION, 1950–93, AND ATMOSPHERIC CHLORINE, 1975–93

| YEAR | TOTAL[1] (thousand tons) | ATMOSPHERIC CHLORINE (parts per bill. by vol.) |
|---|---|---|
| 1950 | 42 | — |
| 1955 | 86 | — |
| 1960 | 150 | — |
| 1961 | 170 | — |
| 1962 | 210 | — |
| 1963 | 250 | — |
| 1964 | 290 | — |
| 1965 | 330 | — |
| 1966 | 390 | — |
| 1967 | 440 | — |
| 1968 | 510 | — |
| 1969 | 580 | — |
| 1970 | 640 | — |
| 1971 | 690 | — |
| 1972 | 790 | — |
| 1973 | 900 | — |
| 1974 | 970 | — |
| 1975 | 860 | 2.0 |
| 1976 | 920 | 2.1 |
| 1977 | 880 | 2.2 |
| 1978 | 880 | 2.3 |
| 1979 | 850 | 2.4 |
| 1980 | 880 | 2.5 |
| 1981 | 890 | 2.6 |
| 1982 | 870 | 2.7 |
| 1983 | 950 | 2.8 |
| 1984 | 1,050 | 2.9 |
| 1985 | 1,090 | 3.0 |
| 1986 | 1,130 | 3.1 |
| 1987 | 1,250 | 3.2 |
| 1988 | 1,260 | 3.4 |
| 1989 | 1,150 | 3.5 |
| 1990 | 820 | 3.7 |
| 1991 | 720 | 3.8 |
| 1992 (prel) | 630 | 3.9 |
| 1993 (prel) | 510 | 4.0 |

[1]Includes all CFCs (CFC-11, CFC-12, CFC-113, CFC-114, and CFC-115). The totals are increasingly uncertain because a growing percentage of use occurs in regions where data are not readily available.
SOURCE: 1950 and 1955, Worldwatch estimates based on Chemical Manufacturers Association; 1960–93 from E.I. Du Pont de Nemours, Wilmington, Del., private communication, March 9, 1994.

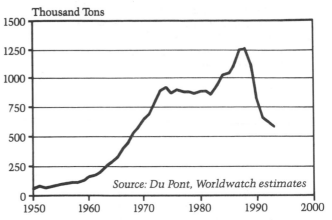

Figure 1: World Production of Chlorofluorocarbons, 1950–93

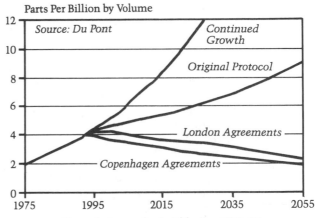

Figure 2: Atmospheric Chlorine, 1975–93, with Projections to 2055 Under Four Scenarios

# Global Temperature Rises Slightly David Malin Roodman

The average air temperature at the surface of the earth rose slightly in 1993, from 15.13 to 15.20 degrees Celsius. Though cooler than some of the record-setting years of the previous decade, 1993 was still warmer than the 1951–80 average that meteorologists use as a reference.[1] (See Figure 1.)

Year-to-year changes in the average temperature of the lower atmosphere, like day-to-day temperature changes in particular locations, are quite erratic. Just a thin layer of gases, the atmosphere is easily perturbed by such outside forces as solar cycles, ocean currents, and volcanoes.

The long-term historical record of sea- and land-based measurements shows, however, that the global temperature has climbed over the last century by a total of about 0.5 degrees Celsius. The nine warmest years ever recorded have all occurred since 1980.[2] Satellites started collecting global temperature data in 1979, too recently to detect the latest warming trend, although they have so far corroborated the overall accuracy of the older, ground-based record.[3]

It took the largest volcanic eruption in a century to end the latest string of warm years. In June 1991, Mount Pinatubo exploded in the Philippines, spewing millions of tons of sulfur particles into the upper atmosphere. Slowly spreading to a thin pall over much of the planet, the particles filtered out some of the sunlight that normally reaches the surface.[4] The resulting cooling effect took hold late in 1991, lowering the annual average temperature slightly, to 15.41 degrees Celsius, from 15.47 the year before.[5] (Temperatures in 1991 had been well on their way to another record before the eruption.) The cooling effect registered more fully in 1992, with a temperature drop of 0.28 degrees Celsius.[6]

Detailed month-to-month data reveal an even steeper drop. Between the summers of 1991 and 1992, the global temperature plummeted about 0.5 degrees Celsius, mostly attributable to the volcano's effects.[7] Global temperatures then recovered somewhat as the sulfur particles precipitated to earth over the course of 1992 and 1993.[8] (See Figure 2.)

The same computer models that climatolo-gists use to forecast global warming succeeded in predicting the temperature changes experienced after Mount Pinatubo erupted. This unexpected natural test of the models validated certain assumptions about the short-term dynamics of atmospheric behavior. For the hundreds of scientists on the Intergovernmental Panel on Climate Change (IPCC) sponsored by the United Nations and the World Meteorological Organization, the recent cooling episode has actually strengthened confidence in the likelihood of global warming.[9]

Many key variables remain uncertain, however. Scientists are still unsure about important effects such as cloud formation rates and the evolution of the ocean's ability to absorb carbon.[10] What is indisputable is that by altering the chemical composition of the atmosphere, we are in effect staking our fate on a vast and irreversible experiment.

The atmospheric concentration of the principal greenhouse gas, carbon dioxide ($CO_2$), has continued to rise as a result of fossil fuel burning and deforestation. In 1993 there was 13 percent more $CO_2$ in the air—357 parts per million—than in 1959, the first year in which it was systematically measured.[11] (See Figure 3.) The carbon emissions driving this rise constitute about two thirds of all the greenhouse gases added to the atmosphere each year as a result of human activities.[12]

The concentration of methane from rice paddies, the digestive tracts of grazing livestock, coal mines, gas pipelines, and other sources is also growing. Likewise, nitrous oxide from deforestation and certain industrial processes also continues to build up.[13]

The IPCC projects that global temperatures will reach between 16 and 19 degrees Celsius by 2050 as a result of the effective doubling of $CO_2$ concentrations.[14] Such a rapid warming could disrupt water and food supplies for millions of people, cause sea levels to rise, and threaten the survival of many plant and animal species.

GLOBAL AVERAGE TEMPERATURE AND ATMOSPHERIC CONCENTRATION OF CARBON DIOXIDE, 1950–93

| YEAR | TEMPERATURE (degrees Celsius) | CARBON DIOXIDE (parts per mill.) |
|------|------------|----------------|
| 1950 | 14.86 | |
| 1955 | 14.94 | |
| 1960 | 14.98 | 316.8 |
| 1961 | 15.08 | 317.5 |
| 1962 | 15.02 | 318.3 |
| 1963 | 15.02 | 318.8 |
| 1964 | 14.74 | — |
| 1965 | 14.85 | 319.9 |
| 1966 | 14.91 | 321.2 |
| 1967 | 14.98 | 322.0 |
| 1968 | 14.88 | 322.8 |
| 1969 | 15.03 | 323.9 |
| 1970 | 15.04 | 325.3 |
| 1971 | 14.89 | 326.2 |
| 1972 | 14.93 | 327.3 |
| 1973 | 15.19 | 329.5 |
| 1974 | 14.93 | 330.1 |
| 1975 | 14.95 | 331.0 |
| 1976 | 14.79 | 332.0 |
| 1977 | 15.16 | 333.7 |
| 1978 | 15.09 | 335.3 |
| 1979 | 15.14 | 336.7 |
| 1980 | 15.28 | 338.5 |
| 1981 | 15.39 | 339.8 |
| 1982 | 15.07 | 341.0 |
| 1983 | 15.29 | 342.6 |
| 1984 | 15.11 | 344.3 |
| 1985 | 15.11 | 345.7 |
| 1986 | 15.16 | 347.0 |
| 1987 | 15.32 | 348.8 |
| 1988 | 15.35 | 351.4 |
| 1989 | 15.25 | 352.8 |
| 1990 | 15.47 | 354.0 |
| 1991 | 15.41 | 355.4 |
| 1992 | 15.13 | 356.2 |
| 1993 (prel) | 15.20 | 357.0 |

SOURCES: Temperature from James Hansen and Sergej Lebedeff, "Global Trends of Measured Surface Air Temperature," *Journal of Geophysical Research,* November 1987, and from Helene Wilson and James Hansen, Goddard Institute for Space Studies; carbon dioxide from Charles D. Keeling and Timothy Whorf, Scripps Institute of Oceanography.

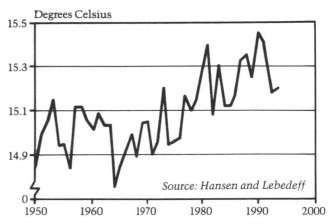

Figure 1: Global Average Temperature, 1950–93

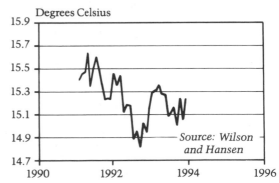

Figure 2: Global Average Temperature, January 1991 – December 1993

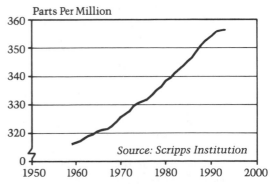

Figure 3: Atmospheric Concentrations of Carbon Dioxide, 1959–93

# Carbon Emissions Unchanged
## David Malin Roodman

In 1993, the burning of fossil fuels around the world released 5.9 billion tons of carbon into the atmosphere as carbon dioxide, according to preliminary esimates.[1] (See Figure 1.) This represents a slight fall from 1992 and essentially continues the flat trend seen since 1989. (Oil-field fires set by the retreating Iraqi army in the final days of the Persian Gulf War caused a temporary spike in 1991.)

Deforestation supplemented the carbon from fossil fuel burning by releasing an estimated 1–2 billion additional tons.[2] As a result, total emissions of carbon, the major greenhouse gas, now occur faster than the world's oceans and forests can absorb them— leading to steady increases in overall atmospheric concentrations of carbon dioxide.[3] (Emissions of other greenhouse gases— chlorofluorocarbons, methane, nitrous oxide— are thought to add the equivalent of another 4 billion tons of carbon to the atmosphere each year in global warming potential.)[4]

Carbon emissions have risen throughout the twentieth century, posting a greater than threefold rise since 1950, and an elevenfold increase since 1900. Yet emission growth has slowed since the fifties and sixties—from an average 4.6 percent annually between 1950 and 1973 to just 1.6 percent between 1973 and 1988.[5] Higher oil prices after 1973 encouraged energy conservation efforts, led to the development of efficient energy technologies, and contributed to slower economic expansion in most parts of the world. At the same time, maturing industrial economies shifted away from energy-intensive industries such as mining and toward less energy-intensive service businesses such as computer software.[6]

Two short-term trends explain the current plateau, however: the economic recession in industrial countries, and an even deeper contraction in the former Soviet bloc. In the former Soviet Union, carbon emissions fell to 810 million tons in 1993, a 26-percent decline from the 1988 high of 1,099.[7]

Meanwhile, in the rapidly industrializing countries of Asia, emissions have continued to press skyward, sometimes at double-digit rates. For example, emissions in China grew 7 percent in 1992; in India, 17 percent; and in South Korea, 28 percent.[8] Because of China's size, however, its 43-million-ton increase actually outweighed those of the other two combined. Rapid increases in coal use in China and the breakup of the Soviet Union have combined to make China the world's second-largest carbon emitter, between the United States and Russia.[9] At current growth rates, it could pass the United States within a few decades. (See Figure 2.)

The East European free fall in emissions cannot continue indefinitely, and emissions are projected to continue increasing modestly in western industrial economies—under current policies—and more than modestly in developing countries. As a result, the global rise is expected to resume soon, at a rate of 1–2 percent per year for the remainder of the decade.[10]

Carbon emission rates continue to vary widely among countries. Per capita emissions in the United States were 5.4 tons in 1992, ahead of Canada at 4.2, Russia at 4.0, Germany at 3.1, Japan at 2.4, and China at 0.6 tons.[11] Although China's energy planners hold a wild card in terms of the world's struggle to minimize global warming, most of the responsibility rests with industrial and former Eastern bloc nations—with 68 percent of the emissions and just 22 percent of the world's people.[12] Transitional use of low-carbon natural gas and the exploitation of energy efficiency and carbon- free sources such as wind, sunlight, and biomass could all play major roles.

The Framework Convention on Climate Change signed at the Earth Summit in 1992 provides a start in this direction. It requires industrial nations to formulate climate policies with the avowed intention of turning emissions downward by the end of the decade— though there is no penalty if the policies fail.[13] Several countries, including Denmark, the Netherlands, and the United States, have come up with innovative climate plans in the spirit of the Convention, but none has yet faced the test of time.[14] And since global emissions will have to fall at least 60 percent to stabilize atmospheric concentrations, today's carbon-intensive nations will have to cut even more than that in order to allow limited growth in emissions in developing countries.[15]

WORLD CARBON EMISSIONS FROM
FOSSIL FUEL BURNING, 1950–93

| YEAR | EMISSIONS (mill. tons of carbon) |
|------|---------------------------------|
| 1950 | 1,620 |
| 1955 | 2,020 |
| 1960 | 2,543 |
| 1961 | 2,557 |
| 1962 | 2,659 |
| 1963 | 2,804 |
| 1964 | 2,959 |
| 1965 | 3,095 |
| 1966 | 3,251 |
| 1967 | 3,355 |
| 1968 | 3,526 |
| 1969 | 3,735 |
| 1970 | 4,006 |
| 1971 | 4,151 |
| 1972 | 4,314 |
| 1973 | 4,546 |
| 1974 | 4,553 |
| 1975 | 4,527 |
| 1976 | 4,786 |
| 1977 | 4,920 |
| 1978 | 4,960 |
| 1979 | 5,239 |
| 1980 | 5,172 |
| 1981 | 5,000 |
| 1982 | 4,960 |
| 1983 | 4,947 |
| 1984 | 5,109 |
| 1985 | 5,282 |
| 1986 | 5,464 |
| 1987 | 5,584 |
| 1988 | 5,801 |
| 1989 | 5,912 |
| 1990 | 5,941 |
| 1991 | 6,026 |
| 1992 (est) | 5,910 |
| 1993 (prel) | 5,904 |

SOURCES: Thomas A. Boden, Oak Ridge
National Laboratory, private communication
and printout, September 20, 1993; 1992 and
1993, Worldwatch estimates based on Boden
and on BP.

Note: This series differs from the one in
*Vital Signs 1992* because Oak Ridge National
Laboratory has revised its estimates back to
1970.

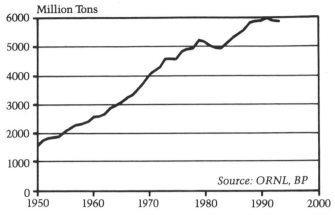

**Figure 1: World Carbon Emissions from
Fossil Fuel Burning, 1950–93**

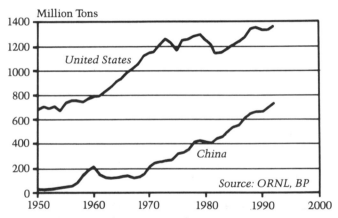

**Figure 2: Carbon Emissions from Fossil Fuel Burning
in China and the United States, 1950–92**

# Economic Trends

# World Economy Expanding

**Lester R. Brown**

In 1993, the world output of goods and services expanded by 2.2 percent, the largest gain in three years.[1] This past year was also the first in the last three in which the growth in output exceeded that of population, raising per capita output by 0.5 percent.[2] (See Figures 1 and 2.)

Last year's economic expansion obscures a wide difference between industrial countries, which grew at 1.1 percent, and developing ones, which expanded by an impressive 6.1 percent. Among the three largest industrial economies, only the United States actually expanded during 1993, boosting its growth in output from 2.6 in 1992 to 2.7 percent.[3] Japan, meanwhile, dropped from 1.3 to –0.1 percent.[4] Germany dropped even more, going from a growth of 1.9 percent in 1992 to a contraction of –1.6 percent in 1993.[5]

For developing countries, the growth achieved in 1993 was the largest on record, led by 8.7-percent growth in Asia.[6] At the other end of the scale, the African economy expanded 1.6 percent in 1993, up from 0.4 percent the preceding year but still scarcely half as fast as the population.[7]

Developing countries in the western hemisphere registered a growth in 1993 of 3.4 percent, up from 2.5 percent in 1992.[8] This expansion—the largest since 1986—was led by Chile, Mexico, and Argentina. Each of these has grown substantially in recent years following economic reforms, including a reduction in inflation and the privatization of public-sector enterprises.[9]

By far the most interesting performance in 1993 was the 13-percent growth of the Chinese economy. For China, which is rapidly privatizing its economy, this was the second consecutive year of 13-percent growth. In 1992, the economy there returned to double-digit growth after three years when growth ranged between 4 and 8 percent annually.[10]

For India, 1993 was a year of recovery, with economic growth estimated at close to 5 percent, up from 3.3 percent in 1992 and 2.3 percent in 1991.[11] In 1991, the Indian government faced a deteriorating economic situation and an overall lack of confidence, and it acted decisively to alter the outlook. High on the list was a reduction of the fiscal deficit by cutting both fertilizer subsidies and transfer payments to inefficient state enterprises. Steps were also taken to encourage industrial investment from abroad.[12]

In Central Europe, Poland—the first country to restore growth after economic reforms—expanded its economy by 1 percent in 1992. This was followed by a more robust expansion of 4 percent in 1993.[13] Joining Poland in the post-reform growth club were the Czech Republic, which achieved a growth of 1 percent, and Albania, at 3.4 percent.[14] Hungary's economic output in 1993 was the same as in 1992, suggesting that its decline is bottoming out.[15]

In the former Soviet Union, economic output was down an estimated 14 percent in 1993. Although painful, this was less than the 18-percent drop of 1992. Output in 1993 was down in every republic except Turkmenistan, where economic activity was up 3.9 percent over 1992. In nearly all the republics, the decline in 1993 was less than in 1992. Two exceptions were Ukraine and Belarus, where it was actually greater.[16]

In October 1993, the International Monetary Fund estimated that the global economy would expand by 3.2 percent in 1994, up from 2.2 in 1993.[17] This is largely because of changes in the outlook for industrial economies. Growth in the United States is expected to continue at roughly the same pace. For Japan, it is expected to go from 0.1 percent to 2.0 percent.[18] The turnaround in Germany is anticipated to be even greater, going from –1.6 percent in 1993 to an expansion of 1.2 percent.[19]

At a time when light is visible at the end of the tunnel of economic reform in Central and Eastern Europe, and when some developing countries are boosting living standards at record rates, some clouds remain on the horizon. One, quite visible, is the high level of structural unemployment in many countries, industrial and developing. Another is the ominous slowdown in output from each of the world's three food systems—fisheries, rangelands, and croplands. If rapid, sustained growth in food output cannot be restored, it will eventually diminish the prospect for raising living standards everywhere.

## GROSS WORLD PRODUCT, 1950–93

| YEAR | TOTAL (trill. 1987 dollars) | PER CAPITA (1987 dollars) |
|------|------|------|
| 1950 | 3.8 | 1,487 |
| 1955 | 4.9 | 1,763 |
| 1960 | 6.1 | 2,008 |
| 1961 | 6.4 | 2,079 |
| 1962 | 6.7 | 2,137 |
| 1963 | 7.0 | 2,184 |
| 1964 | 7.5 | 2,289 |
| 1965 | 7.9 | 2,362 |
| 1966 | 8.3 | 2,430 |
| 1967 | 8.6 | 2,468 |
| 1968 | 9.1 | 2,560 |
| 1969 | 9.7 | 2,673 |
| 1970 | 10.1 | 2,727 |
| 1971 | 10.5 | 2,776 |
| 1972 | 11.0 | 2,850 |
| 1973 | 11.7 | 2,973 |
| 1974 | 11.8 | 2,941 |
| 1975 | 11.9 | 2,912 |
| 1976 | 12.5 | 3,006 |
| 1977 | 13.0 | 3,073 |
| 1978 | 13.5 | 3,137 |
| 1979 | 14.0 | 3,197 |
| 1980 | 14.1 | 3,165 |
| 1981 | 14.3 | 3,156 |
| 1982 | 14.4 | 3,124 |
| 1983 | 14.8 | 3,156 |
| 1984 | 15.4 | 3,228 |
| 1985 | 16.0 | 3,297 |
| 1986 | 16.4 | 3,321 |
| 1987 | 17.0 | 3,382 |
| 1988 | 17.8 | 3,480 |
| 1989 | 18.4 | 3,534 |
| 1990 | 18.8 | 3,549 |
| 1991 | 18.7 | 3,471 |
| 1992 | 18.9 | 3,448 |
| 1993 (prel) | 19.3 | 3,464 |

SOURCES: World Bank and International Monetary Fund tables.

Note: As a result of a different method of calculation, this per capita GWP series is somewhat lower than the one published in *Vital Signs 1993*.

Figure 1: Gross World Product, 1950–93

Figure 2: Gross World Product Per Person, 1950–93

# Third World Debt Still Rising                    Hal Kane

The indebtedness of the world's developing countries rose again slightly in 1993, to $1.77 trillion.[1] (See Figure 1.) Developing countries spend more each year servicing their debt than they do on the military, a notorious drain on resources. Debt servicing takes more than four times as much from their budgets as health care, and almost twice as much as education.[2] Despite recent attempts to correct those imbalances by reducing indebtedness, developing countries still carry a burden that stifles attempts to fight poverty.

Most Third World debt is not likely to be paid back anytime soon. The countries that owe it are not earning enough money to repay it. Instead, they make occasional payments of the interest that has come due, rather than paying off the principal. Taken as a whole, the Third World owes an amount equal to about half of its yearly income.[3] (See Figure 2.)

One bright spot has been the recent fall in world interest rates, which has meant that borrower countries have paid less interest on their loans.[4] Debt service has not grown since the mid-eighties, and now stands slightly below its 1987 peak. Nevertheless, developing countries pay $180 billion every year in debt service.[5] (See Figure 3.) Another bright spot has been an economic growth of 6.1 percent among developing countries.[6] That is not enough to pay back the debt quickly, but it is better than it has been.

Another way to measure the severity of indebtedness is to compare it with the value of a nation's exports, because the foreign income from exports is needed to pay off debt. From this perspective, many of the Latin American countries have improved their situation since the early eighties. Brazil, Ecuador, and Chile in particular are better able to confront their debts than they were around 1981 and 1982 when the debt ''crisis'' began.[7]

Many of the countries of sub-Saharan Africa, however, have become less able. Uganda, Burundi, Zimbabwe, and Ethiopia are among the nations where the debt-to-export ratios have become worse.[8] The situation in Asia varies. Some countries, notably India and Indonesia, have also seen their debt-to-export ratios deteriorate, while others, including Thailand and the Philippines, have done somewhat better.[9] Among all developing nations, the debt-to-export ratio rose from the late seventies to 1986, but since then has fallen from 178 percent down to 116 percent.[10] On the whole, developing countries owe more than they earn from exports in a year.

Debt reschedulings, which try to reduce the burden on some of the poorest countries, will help. But despite repeated reschedulings during the late eighties and early nineties, the sums of money paid to service debt have not fallen for the Third World.[11] Although reschedulings are constructive and welcome, they need to be augmented with even stronger action.

Creditors like the World Bank and the International Monetary Fund have tried to put indebted countries on the track to repayment through structural adjustment programs. These modify indebted countries' interest rates, exchange rates, wages, trade policies, and other economic variables in an effort to help them earn cash. To date, their record has been mixed at best, and many countries that accepted adjustment programs are worse off than they were before. Moreover, these programs have been particularly hard on the poorest people in the poorest countries by cutting government subsidies for food and health care.[12]

Because structural adjustment itself places a burden on impoverished countries, in its present form it may not be adequate for fighting the burdens associated with debt. In the meantime, traditional lending continues. It must take countries whose economies stagnated during the eighties and start them off toward industrialization and high incomes. The hope is that the loans will do better this time.

EXTERNAL DEBT AND DEBT SERVICE
OF ALL DEVELOPING COUNTRIES,
1970–93

| YEAR | DEBT | SERVICE |
|------|------|---------|
| | (bill. 1992 dollars) | |
| 1970 | 247 | 31 |
| 1971 | 274 | 33 |
| 1972 | 305 | 34 |
| 1973 | 345 | 44 |
| 1974 | 399 | 51 |
| 1975 | 499 | 54 |
| 1976 | 573 | 60 |
| 1977 | 712 | 74 |
| 1978 | 828 | 100 |
| 1979 | 976 | 133 |
| 1980 | 971 | 157 |
| 1981 | 1,027 | 165 |
| 1982 | 1,098 | 169 |
| 1983 | 1,149 | 153 |
| 1984 | 1,169 | 159 |
| 1985 | 1,267 | 170 |
| 1986 | 1,356 | 176 |
| 1987 | 1,485 | 185 |
| 1988 | 1,418 | 193 |
| 1989 | 1,391 | 175 |
| 1990 | 1,621 | 188 |
| 1991 | 1,648 | 181 |
| 1992 | 1,662 | 178 |
| 1993 (prel) | 1,766 | 183 |

SOURCE: World Bank, unpublished printouts,
various dates; 1993, Worldwatch calculations
based on data from IMF and World Bank.

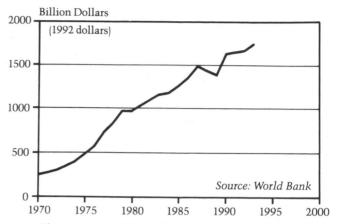

Figure 1: External Debt of Developing Countries, 1970–93

Figure 2: Third World Debt Service, 1970–93

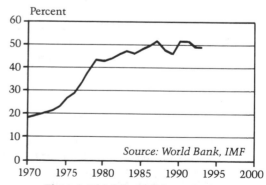

Figure 3: Third World Debt as Share of
Gross Domestic Product, 1970–93

In 1993, the value of internationally traded goods approached an estimated $3.8 trillion (in 1990 dollars), up some 3 percent from 1992. (See Figure 1.) This marked the eleventh year of consecutive growth, though at a rate significantly reduced from those of the late eighties.[1] World trade has increased almost yearly since 1950, when it stood at $308 billion; the share of gross world product represented by trade has increased even more steeply, reaching almost 20 percent in 1993.[2] The only times this did not happen were during the deep recessions after the two oil shocks of the seventies and eighties.

Trade continues to rise both because commercial activity in general is expanding and because governments that view free trade as an engine of economic growth have deliberately removed trade barriers. When the General Agreement on Tariffs and Trade (GATT) was established in 1947, tariffs worldwide added an average of almost 40 percent to the price of imported products; today, in contrast, that figure is about 5 percent.[3] The recently concluded Uruguay Round of the GATT will cut tariffs and other trade barriers further, leading to projected gains in economic output of $270 billion by 2002, according to the Organisation for Economic Co-operation and Development.[4]

Freer trade has also been aggressively promoted through regional trade pacts. The European Union, the world's largest trading bloc, has eliminated tariffs completely within its borders, and North America is set to follow under the North American Free Trade Agreement (NAFTA), which took effect on January 1, 1994.[5] In the years ahead, several Latin American nations will likely join the NAFTA pact. In addition, Asian countries are moving toward economic integration through the Association of Southeast Asian Nations and the Asian-Pacific Economic Council, which held its first summit meeting in November 1993.[6]

With the strong encouragement of organizations like the International Monetary Fund and World Bank, many developing countries have recently embraced exports and open economies, reversing some of the inward-oriented strategies of the sixties and seventies. As a result, exports from these nations have been on an upward course.[7] (See Figure 2.)

Much of the growth has come from the newly industrializing tigers of Asia—at first mainly South Korea, Hong Kong, Singapore, and Taiwan, but now broadening to include other countries such as China, Indonesia, Malaysia, and Thailand, where export growth rates have often exceeded 10 percent annually.[8] Other regions, notably Africa, have seen exports stagnate in response to adverse economic conditions, including declining commodity prices.[9] Developing countries continue to face many barriers to penetrating industrial-country markets, with agricultural protectionism alone estimated to cost developing countries $100 billion in lost revenue annually.[10]

The rapid expansion of world trade poses complicated questions for environmental policymakers. In the absence of environmental safeguards, access to global markets can magnify the damaging effects of unsustainable production practices, and can transfer the environmental impacts of a country's consumption patterns to someone else's backyard. On the other hand, trade helps diffuse environmentally beneficial technologies worldwide, and creates wealth that could make environmental investments more likely.[11]

Though trade and environmental policymaking have been carried on for decades as though they were entirely separate affairs, the last year has seen growing recognition of their interconnections. Environmental issues became pivotal in the debate over NAFTA, leading to the negotiation of a side agreement that can subject a country to possible trade sanctions if it fails to enforce its own environmental laws.[12] In November 1993, the Maastricht treaty took effect in Europe, which enshrines environmental protection and sustainable development as priorities of the European Union.[13]

This progress at the regional level has yet to be reflected in the GATT. But governments are now discussing the post-Uruguay Round negotiating agenda, and environmental questions are expected to be high on the list. A Trade and Environment committee charged with moving the process forward will likely be established as part of the newly created World Trade Organization.[14]

WORLD EXPORTS, 1950–93

| YEAR | EXPORTS (bill. 1990 dollars) |
|------|------|
| 1950 | 308 |
| 1955 | 459 |
| 1960 | 620 |
| 1961 | 644 |
| 1962 | 691 |
| 1963 | 744 |
| 1964 | 816 |
| 1965 | 869 |
| 1966 | 933 |
| 1967 | 977 |
| 1968 | 1,100 |
| 1969 | 1,222 |
| 1970 | 1,336 |
| 1971 | 1,417 |
| 1972 | 1,549 |
| 1973 | 1,755 |
| 1974 | 1,869 |
| 1975 | 1,769 |
| 1976 | 1,972 |
| 1977 | 2,048 |
| 1978 | 2,158 |
| 1979 | 2,340 |
| 1980 | 2,353 |
| 1981 | 2,331 |
| 1982 | 2,231 |
| 1983 | 2,302 |
| 1984 | 2,518 |
| 1985 | 2,585 |
| 1986 | 2,594 |
| 1987 | 2,761 |
| 1988 | 2,988 |
| 1989 | 3,200 |
| 1990 | 3,340 |
| 1991 | 3,542 |
| 1992 (prel) | 3,675 |
| 1993 (prel) | 3,785 |

SOURCE: Worldwatch calculations based on IMF data and deflators.

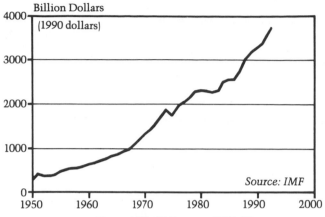

Figure 1: World Exports, 1950–93

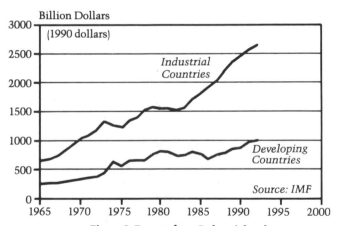

Figure 2: Exports from Industrial and Developing Countries, 1965–92

# Global Paper Production Keeps Growing　　Nancy Chege

In 1993—despite a year of poor profitability as a result of oversupplied markets, depressed prices, and continuing environmental pressure—an increase of about 1 percent brought the world's paper production to 247 million tons.[1] (See Figures 1 and 2.) Since 1950, production of paper has expanded sixfold, and the industry currently has a world trade value of about $50 billion.[2]

The United States, Japan, China, and Canada are the four largest paper-producing countries, accounting for over half the world total. In per capita terms, the United States uses 20 times more paper per person a year than the average Chinese does.[3]

In industrial countries, the growth of advertising and the automation of office equipment have driven the growth of paper consumption. Sixty percent of space in American magazines and newspapers is reserved for ads, while some 52 billion assorted advertising pieces—including 14 billion mail-order catalogs that often go straight into the trash—clog up the U.S. post office every year.[4] Rising literacy trends have also contributed to the increase in paper use. In 1950, 56 percent of the world was literate; by 1992, the figure had risen to 74 percent.[5]

In 1948, the first photocopier was produced. Just four-and-a-half decades later, there are more than 19 million photocopiers worldwide.[6] And because fast copiers, printers, and word processing programs have made it possible to produce paper documents effortlessly and rapidly, multiple drafts are being generated in large quantities.

Pulp and paper production causes significant degradation of the environment. The use of chemicals in pulping and bleaching dumps into rivers at least 950,000 tons of effluent, including troublesome quantities of toxic organochlorine compounds, and pumps into the air roughly 100,000 tons of acid rain-producing sulfur dioxide.[7] In addition, pulp and paper mills use large amounts of fossil fuel energy and fresh water.

Around the world, as studies reveal the negative effects of industrial use of elemental chlorine, environmentalists are urging that chlorine be phased out of the paper-making industry. U.S. mills have been slower than European ones to use chlorine substitutes, although interest in such alternatives is growing.[8] In Germany, Austria, Switzerland, and the Nordic nations, hydrogen peroxide and ozone are increasingly being used as bleaching agents to produce totally chlorine free (TCF) paper.[9] It is estimated that European demand for TCF paper will grow from 1.8 million tons in 1993, a 15-percent market share, to 3.2 million tons in 1996, a 25-percent share.[10]

The percentage of wood in pulp production is dropping significantly worldwide due to increased paper recycling and use of nonwood pulp. Asian countries have traditionally relied on wastepaper imported from industrial countries, and have in addition developed alternatives to wood pulp.[11] Meanwhile, industrial countries are expanding their programs to enhance recovery rates, which currently stand at around 40 percent.[12]

Increasingly, the wood pulp industry may have to resort to processes that use nonwood sources, which currently account for 10 percent of all paper produced worldwide.[13] Agricultural wastes, such as cereal straw and bagasse (sugarcane stalks), and fiber crops such as kenaf and hemp (which is illegal in the United States) are examples of pulp sources for treeless paper.[14] Sixty percent of Chinese paper is manufactured with nonwood pulp.[15] Not only do these sources need substantially less energy than wood does, it takes a lot less land to produce the same amount of paper.

The newsprint market (13 percent of total world paper consumption) has been experiencing a glut for the last three years, partly because of the growing number of North Americans and Europeans who have turned to television and video for news and entertainment, and partly because of a large increase in capacity.[16] As the economies of industrial countries revive, consumption is likely to rise slightly. But the most promising markets are those of Eastern Europe, Latin America, and Asia, where improved living standards, a flourishing business sector, and emerging democratic forces will enhance demand for newspapers.

WORLD PAPER AND PAPERBOARD PRODUCTION, 1950–93

| YEAR | PRODUCTION (mill. tons) | PER CAPITA (kilograms) |
|------|------|------|
| 1950 | 38 | 15 |
| 1955 | 57 | 21 |
| 1960 | 74 | 24 |
| 1961 | 77 | 25 |
| 1962 | 81 | 26 |
| 1963 | 86 | 27 |
| 1964 | 92 | 28 |
| 1965 | 98 | 29 |
| 1966 | 105 | 31 |
| 1967 | 107 | 31 |
| 1968 | 115 | 32 |
| 1969 | 124 | 34 |
| 1970 | 128 | 35 |
| 1971 | 129 | 34 |
| 1972 | 138 | 36 |
| 1973 | 148 | 38 |
| 1974 | 151 | 38 |
| 1975 | 131 | 32 |
| 1976 | 147 | 35 |
| 1977 | 152 | 36 |
| 1978 | 160 | 37 |
| 1979 | 169 | 39 |
| 1980 | 170 | 38 |
| 1981 | 171 | 38 |
| 1982 | 167 | 36 |
| 1983 | 177 | 38 |
| 1984 | 190 | 40 |
| 1985 | 193 | 38 |
| 1986 | 203 | 41 |
| 1987 | 215 | 43 |
| 1988 | 227 | 45 |
| 1989 | 232 | 44 |
| 1990 | 240 | 45 |
| 1991 | 243 | 45 |
| 1992 | 245 | 45 |
| 1993 (prel) | 247 | 45 |

SOURCES: FAO, *Forest Products Yearbook*, 1950 through 1992; *Pulp and Paper*, January 1994.

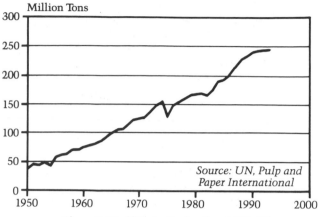

Million Tons

Source: UN, Pulp and Paper International

Figure 1: World Paper Production, 1950–93

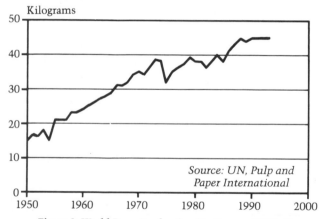

Kilograms

Source: UN, Pulp and Paper International

Figure 2: World Paper Production Per Person, 1950–93

In 1992, total roundwood production increased by 1.5 percent over the previous year, reaching 3.5 billion cubic meters.[1] (See Figure 1.) The previous year, it had declined by 2.6 percent, after increasing steadily from the mid-seventies until 1990. The world used about two-and-a-half times as much wood at the beginning of the nineties as it did in 1950.[2]

About half the roundwood consumed globally is used as the primary source of energy in developing countries in the form of fuelwood and charcoal. Industrial roundwood, used to manufacture lumber, paper, and other materials, accounts for the other half of global wood demand.[3] (See Figures 2 and 3.)

The production of fuelwood and charcoal totalled 1.9 billion cubic meters in 1992, a 2.5-fold increase since 1950, and it is expected to continue rising.[4] As the population in the Third World continues to increase, and as modern forms of energy such as electricity and liquefied petroleum gas remain out of financial reach for billions of people, fuelwood consumption will continue to rise in absolute terms.[5]

The use of charcoal, which is made by burning wood in airtight kilns, is on the rise. As Third World urban centers expand and nearby trees are cut for firewood, lumber, or real estate development, charcoal becomes the preferred fuel because it is light in weight, less bulky, and easier to transport than firewood.[6] During the last decade, charcoal use rose by 26 percent, while fuelwood consumption grew by 19 percent.[7]

Widespread use of charcoal puts even greater stress than firewood on the environment because converting wood to charcoal requires twice as much timber to yield the same cooking energy. When the conversion, transportation, and combustion processes are included, charcoal emerges as leading producer of carbon dioxide—the most prevalent greenhouse gas.[8]

Industrial roundwood is cut as timber and processed into veneer, sawnwood, fiberboard, paper and paperboard, and plywood, mainly in industrial countries. The world's consumption of timber has risen from 0.7 billion cubic meters in 1950 to 1.6 billion cubic meters in 1992.[9] Great regional disparities lie behind such global figures. For example, India—which ranks thirteenth in world production—used 25 million cubic meters of timber in 1991, approximately 0.03 cubic meters per person.[10] The equivalent figure in the United States, the world's leading timber producer, was 1.6 cubic meters, roughly 53 times as much.[11] Although individual usage is high now in the industrial world, most of the future growth in wood use is expected to occur in developing countries.

A little over half of industrial roundwood is produced by the United States, the former Soviet Union, and Canada, and it is used primarily in the building industry.[12] In North America and Europe, the construction of new houses claims more lumber than any other timber-industrial activity.[13]

The paper industry is another major consumer. Approximately one quarter of harvested wood is turned into pulp for paper and other products.[14] During the twentieth century, per capita consumption rates have grown rapidly, and they are expected to continue rising. This can be attributed not only to the increasing literacy rates worldwide, but also to the automation of office equipment and the rise of the consumer culture. Photocopiers, computers, and fax machines have made it a lot easier to make multiple copies of documents. Personal computers are estimated to consume 115 billion individual sheets of paper annually.[15]

Logging, mining, ranching, and farming all contribute to the degradation of primary forests, but logging in particular plays a significant role. The aggressive buying of timber pursued by countries in East Asia, such as Japan, is a major cause of primary rain forest destruction in Central Africa and Southeast Asia.[16]

In their attempt to acquire the most commercially viable trees, logging companies build a dense network of roads. In some areas of West Africa, 10 kilometers of road are constructed for every 10 square kilometers of forest harvested.[17] The roads expose forests to exotic pests, diseases, and wildlife; in the steeper regions, they sharply increase soil erosion. But the greatest and most serious effect of roads on the forests is that they open the once impenetrable ecosystem to fortune seekers.

## WORLD PRODUCTION OF ROUNDWOOD, 1950–92

| YEAR | TOTAL (mill. cubic meters) |
|------|------|
| 1950 | 1,421 |
| 1955 | 1,496 |
| 1960 | 1,753 |
| 1961 | 2,049 |
| 1962 | 2,073 |
| 1963 | 2,106 |
| 1964 | 2,185 |
| 1965 | 2,214 |
| 1966 | 2,189 |
| 1967 | 2,238 |
| 1968 | 2,505 |
| 1969 | 2,561 |
| 1970 | 2,640 |
| 1971 | 2,534 |
| 1972 | 2,532 |
| 1973 | 2,586 |
| 1974 | 2,628 |
| 1975 | 2,579 |
| 1976 | 2,687 |
| 1977 | 2,712 |
| 1978 | 2,795 |
| 1979 | 2,880 |
| 1980 | 2,929 |
| 1981 | 2,926 |
| 1982 | 2,928 |
| 1983 | 3,039 |
| 1984 | 3,153 |
| 1985 | 3,180 |
| 1986 | 3,267 |
| 1987 | 3,338 |
| 1988 | 3,386 |
| 1989 | 3,451 |
| 1990 | 3,507 |
| 1991 | 3,429 |
| 1992 | 3,476 |

SOURCE: FAO, *Forest Products Yearbook, 1950–1960* (Rome: 1952–1962); FAO, AGROSTAT-PC 1993 (electronic database), Rome, 1993; 1992 from Philip Wardle, FAO, Rome, private communication, February 17, 1994.

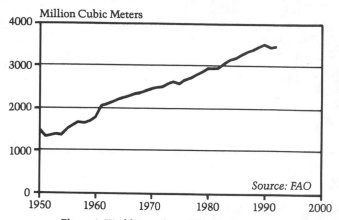

Figure 1: World Roundwood Production, 1950–92

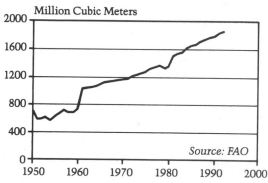

Figure 2: World Fuelwood and Charcoal Production, 1950–92

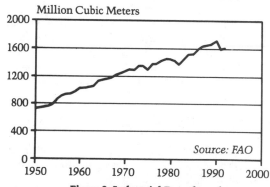

Figure 3: Industrial Roundwood Production, 1950–92

# Gold Production at Record High

John E. Young

In 1993, world gold production reached 2,290 tons, a new high.[1] (See Figure 1.) Although no official statistics were kept, a new record was almost certainly set in gold mining waste as well: an estimated 690 million tons, about 9 tons per ounce of gold. The waste generated each year by gold mining could fill enough 218-ton dump trucks to form a bumper-to-bumper convoy around the equator.[2]

Mining waste is not merely an eyesore. It is often contaminated with other metals, acid-forming chemicals, and solvents used to extract gold from ore. These can cause acid drainage, heavy metal contamination, and other problems for centuries.[3]

Since 1980—when the price of gold soared to an all-time high three times its current level (in constant dollars)—world gold production has gone up by 89 percent.[4] Although in 1980 South Africa and the Soviet Union produced more than three fourths of the world's gold, virtually all the increase occurred in other areas. Low ore grades and rising labor costs in South Africa and political turmoil and inefficient operations in the Soviet Union and its successor states have limited output. By 1993, South Africa and the former Soviet states were producing just over a third of the world total.[5]

Meanwhile, production grew explosively in the United States, Australia, and Canada. Since 1980, U.S. gold production has increased elevenfold, Australia's fourteenfold, and Canada's threefold.[6] The three countries now account for nearly a third of world gold output.

Developing countries produce much of the remainder. After the price of gold skyrocketed in 1980, millions of small-time miners fanned out into remote areas of the Third World. Major gold rushes broke out in Brazil and other Amazonian countries, China, Indonesia, the Philippines, and various African countries, most of which also host large mines.[7]

The global gold rush appears to be slowing, however, as gold prices remain relatively low. (See Figure 2.) The 2-percent production increase in 1993 was less than half the average annual growth since 1980.[8]

A new technology—cyanide heap leaching—has been a major factor in increased gold output in North America and Australia. Miners use cyanide solution to extract gold from huge piles of crushed ore. The use of the new technique has made it economically attractive for large mining companies to level entire mountains of low-grade ore that contain as little as a hundredth of an ounce of gold per ton.[9]

Heap leaching creates enormous amounts of waste. U.S. miners now generate, on average, about 3 million kilograms of waste for each kilogram of gold, triple the figure in 1980.[10] And the high toxicity of heap leaching's active agent can cause major problems: reservoirs used to collect cyanide solution often attract and kill waterfowl, and leaks can threaten lakes, streams, and underground drinking-water supplies.[11]

Third World gold rushes have had severe impacts as well. In Brazil, for example, the arrival of as many as a million prospectors in the Amazon Basin in the eighties brought epidemics of disease to indigenous tribes, eroded soils, clogged streams with silt, and contaminated ecosystems and people with an estimated 90–120 tons per year of mercury, a highly toxic metal commonly used by small-scale miners to capture and purify gold.[12]

Jewelry is the dominant use of gold, taking about 80 percent of annual consumption. The amount of gold used for jewelry soared from 851 tons in 1983 to 2,461 tons in 1992.[13] In the United States, Japan, and Western Europe, where most of what is sold is made from lower-grade gold alloys, jewelry is mainly an adornment.[14] Investors in those countries usually buy gold in the form of bars and coins. In Asia and the Middle East, however, jewelry with high gold content is a common investment.[15]

Oddly enough, the largest potential gold mine in the world lies in state bank vaults and private hoards. An estimated 97,000 tons—85 percent of all the gold ever mined—are circulating in the world economy.[16] Of this, about 35,000 tons are held by governments and some 62,000 tons by companies and private citizens.[17] In the unlikely event that consumer demand for gold jewelry were largely eliminated, industrial needs could be met for centuries by the gold now in government and private hoards.

WORLD GOLD PRODUCTION, 1950–93

| YEAR | TOTAL (tons) | PER CAPITA (grams) |
|---|---|---|
| 1950 | 1,016 | 0.40 |
| 1955 | 1,118 | 0.40 |
| 1960 | 1,160 | 0.38 |
| 1961 | 1,222 | 0.40 |
| 1962 | 1,281 | 0.41 |
| 1963 | 1,342 | 0.42 |
| 1964 | 1,395 | 0.43 |
| 1965 | 1,438 | 0.43 |
| 1966 | 1,449 | 0.42 |
| 1967 | 1,423 | 0.41 |
| 1968 | 1,436 | 0.40 |
| 1969 | 1,450 | 0.40 |
| 1970 | 1,478 | 0.40 |
| 1971 | 1,446 | 0.38 |
| 1972 | 1,395 | 0.36 |
| 1973 | 1,347 | 0.34 |
| 1974 | 1,248 | 0.31 |
| 1975 | 1,197 | 0.29 |
| 1976 | 1,214 | 0.29 |
| 1977 | 1,210 | 0.29 |
| 1978 | 1,212 | 0.28 |
| 1979 | 1,207 | 0.28 |
| 1980 | 1,209 | 0.27 |
| 1981 | 1,283 | 0.28 |
| 1982 | 1,341 | 0.29 |
| 1983 | 1,405 | 0.30 |
| 1984 | 1,460 | 0.31 |
| 1985 | 1,532 | 0.32 |
| 1986 | 1,602 | 0.32 |
| 1987 | 1,658 | 0.33 |
| 1988 | 1,848 | 0.36 |
| 1989 | 1,971 | 0.38 |
| 1990 | 2,050 | 0.39 |
| 1991 | 2,110 | 0.39 |
| 1992 | 2,248 | 0.41 |
| 1993 (prel) | 2,290 | 0.41 |

SOURCE: U.S. Bureau of Mines, *Mineral Commodity Summaries 1994* (Washington, D.C.: U.S. Government Printing Office, 1994).

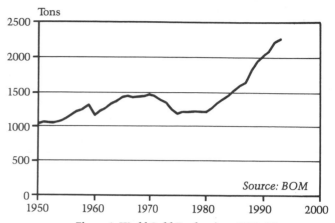

Figure 1: World Gold Production, 1950–93

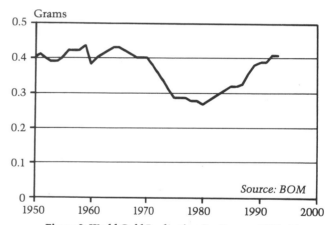

Figure 2: World Gold Production Per Person, 1950–93

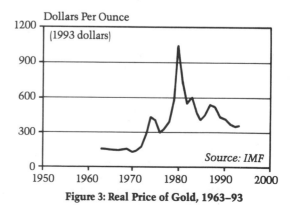

Figure 3: Real Price of Gold, 1963–93

# Transportation
## Trends

# Bicycle Production Rises Again       Marcia D. Lowe

Some 108 million bicycles were produced worldwide in 1993, outstripping global automobile output by a factor of nearly three to one.[1] (See Figure 1.) Since the mid-seventies, the trend in world bicycle production has roughly paralleled that of China, which, as the largest producer, accounts for more than a third of the total. The resumed climb in global output since 1990 largely reflects China's recovery following a 1988 surplus that forced the bike industry to stockpile some 13 million bicycles and to scale back production for two years.[2] (See Figure 2.)

China's image as the Bicycle Kingdom suffered a jolt in 1993, as officials in Guangzhou and Shanghai announced their intention to ban bicycles from certain thoroughfares in order to make way for cars and trucks.[3] But in a country with some 250 bicycles for every automobile and with precious little space for roads, such decrees are hard to justify, let alone enforce. At least in Guangzhou, the mayor—blasted by an immediate public outcry—was forced to alter his proposed ban.[4]

In other developing countries, a long history of government discrimination has failed to dislodge the bicycle as the most widely used vehicle for private transport. Despite decades of scorn and bias in transport policy, people in much of Africa, Asia, and Latin America depend heavily on bikes and load-carrying three-wheelers to commute to work, reach remote rural communities, and haul vegetables to market. In many cities in Asia, pedal power—including cycle rickshaws—accounts for 20–60 percent of people's trips.[5]

In countries with high automobile ownership, by contrast, the extent of bicycle use has been heavily influenced by swings in both public policy and popular attitudes. Particularly in North America and Australia, heavy government spending on highways and a rush to acquire cars meant bicycles were neglected in the fifties and sixties. But oil shocks and unprecedented environmental awareness in the seventies inspired renewed respect for bicycling from industrial-country governments and citizens alike. The bicycle's nonpolluting and energy-saving advantages helped stimulate a surge in world bike production in the early to mid-seventies.

During the past two decades, railway passengers in Japan and Europe have increasingly relied on bicycles as a convenient, affordable way to reach train stations. On a typical weekday, nearly 3 million bicycles are parked at rail stations throughout Japan.[6] In Denmark, 25–30 percent of commuter rail passengers set out from home on a bicycle.[7] And the Netherlands National Railway noted in a recent policy report that "on average, the bicycle is regarded as by far the most important means of transport to the station."[8]

Although a growing number of bus and rail systems in the United States are providing bicycle racks and lockers, "bike-and-ride" remains far below its potential. Pedaling all the way to work is more popular; the number of U.S. commuters who do so regularly has roughly tripled during the past 10 years, to an estimated 3 million.[9] In what is perhaps the clearest sign that bicycles are increasingly considered "serious" transportation, police officers are now using them in more than 300 bike patrols nationwide.[10]

Recent changes in government policy mean the bicycle is gaining ground even where it has long been ignored. In the United States, federal law now requires every state to appoint a bicycle coordinator and each state and metropolitan area to have a long-range bicycle plan; state and local governments also have new flexibility to provide bicycling facilities with much of the federal funding formerly reserved for highways.[11]

Cuba suddenly discovered bicycles to be indispensable in the early nineties when the demise of the Soviet Union cut the nation's motor vehicle and oil imports to a trickle. Today one out of three trips in Havana is made by bicycle, and the government is busy trying to retrofit the roads to cater to cyclists' needs.[12]

In Lima, Peru, and Rio de Janeiro, Brazil, officials have not waited for an economic crisis to force them to promote bicycling. Both cities are aiming to reduce smog and improve transport efficiency by building bikeways, subsidizing purchases for low-income workers, and educating people about the advantages of cycling.[13]

WORLD BICYCLE PRODUCTION, 1950–93

| YEAR | PRODUCTION (million) |
|---|---|
| 1950 | 11 |
| 1955 | 15 |
| 1960 | 20 |
| 1961 | 20 |
| 1962 | 20 |
| 1963 | 20 |
| 1964 | 21 |
| 1965 | 21 |
| 1966 | 22 |
| 1967 | 23 |
| 1968 | 24 |
| 1969 | 25 |
| 1970 | 36 |
| 1971 | 39 |
| 1972 | 46 |
| 1973 | 52 |
| 1974 | 52 |
| 1975 | 43 |
| 1976 | 47 |
| 1977 | 49 |
| 1978 | 51 |
| 1979 | 54 |
| 1980 | 62 |
| 1981 | 65 |
| 1982 | 69 |
| 1983 | 74 |
| 1984 | 76 |
| 1985 | 79 |
| 1986 | 84 |
| 1987 | 98 |
| 1988 | 105 |
| 1989 | 95 |
| 1990 | 90 |
| 1991 | 96 |
| 1992 | 103 |
| 1993 (prel) | 108 |

SOURCES: 1950 and 1955, Worldwatch estimates; UN, *The Growth of World Industry 1969 Edition,* Vol. II and *Yearbooks of Industrial Statistics 1979 and 1989 Editions,* Vol. II; 1990–93, Worldwatch estimates based on *Interbike Directory 1994.*

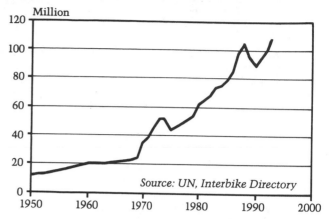

Figure 1: World Bicycle Production, 1950–93

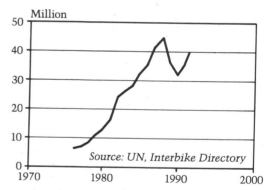

Figure 2: Bicycle Production in China, 1976–92

# Auto Production Falls                    Ed Ayres

World automobile production declined again in 1993—the fourth consecutive year it has failed to grow. Output dropped below 34 million cars, about the same number built in 1988.[1] (See Figure 1.) Thus there has been no net increase in the annual output of cars during a half-decade in which world population has increased by nearly a half-billion.[2] (See Figure 2.) The growth curve has remained basically flat for nearly a decade.

In Europe, new car purchases dropped by 17 percent in 1993.[3] As a result, production plummeted by 2 million units—more than the total decline for the world as a whole. In Japan, production remained at about the same depressed level as in 1992, when it fell significantly for the first time.[4] U.S. production, which had been declining for two decades (shrinking by more than 40 percent between 1973 and 1991), continued the modest recovery begun in 1992. Production also increased in the developing and newly developed countries of South America and Asia.[5]

The global pattern continued two concurrent trends. On the one hand, industrial countries, with their slow population growth and saturated markets (two to five people per car), have levelled out in their production of new cars and show few signs of being able to accommodate much more growth in the remainder of the century.[6]

On the other hand, the developing world—with faster population growth and far larger "untapped" markets (more than 12 people per car overall, and more than 200 per car in China)—has generated rapidly growing demand with only modest or scattered increases in purchasing power. One analysis, for example, suggests that when the average income in a Chinese community rises by 25 percent, the number of people who can afford a car there may increase by 250 percent.[7]

The rising Asian demand for cars has led to a striking division of opinion among experts trying to assess the world's automotive future. Some industry forecasters see huge growth potential in China and other developing nations—based on the assumption that these markets will follow the historic pattern of explosive growth experienced in the United States after World War II.[8] Others, however, note that Asia faces constraints unheard of in the American automotive heyday. The land required for automotive infrastructure, for example, is far less available in today's China or India. With the world's per capita food production declining, much of the land that would be required for extensive highway networks is now needed for crops.[9]

Moreover, most countries are far less able to afford the enormous capital cost of such systems—and the large "hidden" costs. In the United States, for example, the public cost of automobiles, even with an infrastructure already largely in place, has been estimated at more than $1,000 per person a year—more than the annual incomes of most Asians.[10]

Environmental considerations, too, will probably limit the growth of these markets. Third World urbanization has created cities so polluted that health concerns will inevitably push governments toward greater investment in public transit and other alternatives to private cars.[11] The international treaty on climate change, with its limitations on carbon emissions, adds further urgency to this pursuit of alternatives.

Even in the United States, where the "Big Three" auto makers optimistically speak of recapturing industry leadership from the slumping Japanese, the resurgence—fueled by economic recovery and aggressive adoption of Japanese "lean production" techniques—may have a limited future.[12]

Because many Americans have switched from conventional cars to lightweight pickup trucks and vans that are not included in automobile statistics, the actual figures for U.S. personal-vehicle production are stronger than they appear—but they may also be inflated by the artificially low prices of gasoline in the country. The vans and pickup trucks that have given U.S. manufacturers their greatest profitability have poorer fuel efficiency than cars and take up more space in city streets.

In its overall mix of vehicle designs, the U.S. industry is still responding to short-term consumer appetites rather than developing long-term strategies consistent with the world's changing social and environmental priorities.

WORLD AUTOMOBILE
PRODUCTION, 1950–93

| YEAR | PRODUCTION (million) |
|---|---|
| 1950 | 8 |
| 1955 | 11 |
| 1960 | 13 |
| 1961 | 11 |
| 1962 | 14 |
| 1963 | 16 |
| 1964 | 17 |
| 1965 | 19 |
| 1966 | 19 |
| 1967 | 19 |
| 1968 | 22 |
| 1969 | 23 |
| 1970 | 22 |
| 1971 | 26 |
| 1972 | 28 |
| 1973 | 30 |
| 1974 | 26 |
| 1975 | 25 |
| 1976 | 29 |
| 1977 | 30 |
| 1978 | 31 |
| 1979 | 31 |
| 1980 | 29 |
| 1981 | 28 |
| 1982 | 27 |
| 1983 | 30 |
| 1984 | 30 |
| 1985 | 32 |
| 1986 | 33 |
| 1987 | 33 |
| 1988 | 34 |
| 1989 | 36 |
| 1990 | 36 |
| 1991 | 35 |
| 1992 | 35 |
| 1993 (prel) | 34 |

SOURCES: Motor Vehicle Manufacturers
Association; Worldwatch estimates based on
*Automotive News* and other press reports.

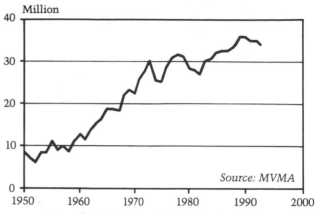

**Figure 1: World Automobile Production, 1950–93**

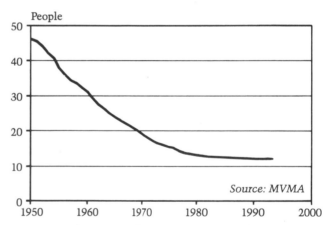

**Figure 2: People Per Automobile, 1950–93**

# Environmental
## Trends

# Resistance to Pesticides Growing                    Peter Weber

Pesticides continue to lose their effectiveness against crop-destroying pests as a result of genetic selection. At least 520 insects and mites, 150 plant diseases, and 113 weeds have developed resistance to one or more pesticides meant to control them.[1] (See Figure 1.) In addition, at least 17 insect species are resistant to all major classes of insecticides, and several plant diseases are immune to most fungicides used against them.[2]

Resistance to pesticides is as natural as evolution. In fact, it is natural selection in fast forward, provoked by the very chemicals meant to control the pest. Resistant strains develop particularly quickly when farmers overuse pesticides and try to eliminate pests rather than control them. Kill 99.9 percent of the insects in a field, and the survivors are a superstrain.

Because insecticides were the first class of pesticides to be heavily used, the selection pressure led insects to show resistance first. Starting with DDT, insecticides caused crop losses to fall in the United States, but over time the pests rebounded despite increasing doses. Insecticides also kill off beneficial insects, unleashing potentially crop-destroying pests that were previously held in check. Of the 300 most destructive insects in the United States, about 100 are such secondary pests.[3]

The number of reported new cases of resistant insects has decreased in recent years for two reasons, according to Mark Whalon, an applied ecologist at Michigan State University.[4] One is a reporting problem that applies to all classes of pesticides: information is hard to come by for developing countries, where pesticide use is increasing and selection pressure for resistance is currently higher. (See Figures 2 and 3.) The second factor is that insecticide formulas have not changed since the latest generation of synthetic pyrethroids was introduced in 1988. Therefore, many of the strains potentially resistant to existing insecticides have already emerged. Multiple resistance, however, continues to develop, with the most disturbing trend being international outbreaks of highly resistant pests, such as palm thrips and poinsettia whiteflies, that are immune to all synthetic pesticides.[5]

Pesticide resistance in plant diseases came after insects, but with new formulas of fungicides still coming on the market, resistance continues to increase, and multiple resistance is taking hold. In a testament to the adaptability of plant diseases, the potato late blight—the fungal disease of the Irish potato famine—has developed a highly aggressive strain that is threatening potato crops worldwide. New strains of the late blight fungus have shown resistance to metalaxyl, one of the major fungicides used to protect potatoes.[6]

Rapidly increasing herbicide use and significant residues have created the selection pressure that has led to the recent rise in weed resistance. Herbicides now account for 46 percent of world pesticide use.[7] In Australia, some weeds that compete with wheat are now immune to a broad array of herbicides.[8] New data from the Weed Science Society of America is expected to show that more weeds have developed multiple resistance to herbicides.[9]

Crop pests do not just develop resistance to synthetic pesticides, however. The diamondback moth—a major crop pest worldwide—has developed resistance to *Bacillus thuringiensis* (*Bt*), a naturally occurring insect toxin that has been used extensively in place of more-harmful synthetic pesticides. Increased use of *Bt* is likely to accelerate this resistance.[10]

To slow resistance, farmers can use integrated pest management (IPM) and biological controls. Under these methods, farmers use preventative measures to control crop pests and apply pesticides sparingly and selectively, which reduces selection pressure and can improve both yields and profits. Indonesia rice farmers, who suffered extreme pest outbreaks resulting from overuse of insecticides, actually had their rice yields rise by 15 percent between 1987 and 1991 after the government banned the use of 57 insecticides and promoted IPM practices. Pesticide use dropped by 65 percent, saving the government $120 million annually on pesticides.[11] Judicious use of pesticides not only reduces their environmental threats, it actually increases the effectiveness of pest control.

### PESTICIDE-RESISTANT SPECIES, SELECTED YEARS

| YEAR | INSECTS AND MITES (number of resistant species) |
|------|------|
| 1908 | 1 |
| 1938 | 7 |
| 1948 | 13 |
| 1954 | 25 |
| 1957 | 75 |
| 1960 | 138 |
| 1963 | 156 |
| 1965 | 187 |
| 1967 | 225 |
| 1975 | 362 |
| 1978 | 400 |
| 1980 | 429 |
| 1984 | 449 |
| 1989 | 504 |
| 1993 (est) | 520 |

| YEAR | PLANT DISEASES | WEEDS |
|------|------|------|
| 1940 | 1 | |
| 1953 | 6 | |
| 1960 | 10 | |
| 1963 | 16 | |
| 1965 | 20 | |
| 1967 | 22 | |
| 1970 | 29 | 4 |
| 1972 | 40 | |
| 1973 | 51 | 4 |
| 1975 | 74 | |
| 1976 | 82 | 6 |
| 1977 | 86 | |
| 1978 | 92 | 7 |
| 1980 | | 8 |
| 1984 | | 50 |
| 1986 | 150 | |
| 1989 | | 113 |

SOURCE: Jodie S. Holt and George P. Georghiou, University of California at Riverside, private communication, March 9, 1992; update on insects from Mark E. Whalon, Michigan State University, East Lansing, private communication, February 14, 1994.

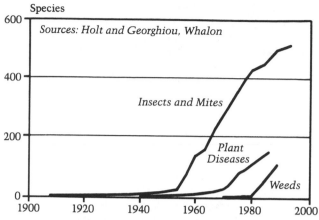

**Figure 1: Pesticide-Resistant Species Since 1908**

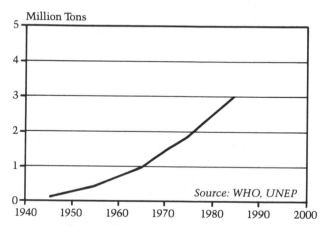

**Figure 2: World Production of Formulated Pesticide, 1945–85**

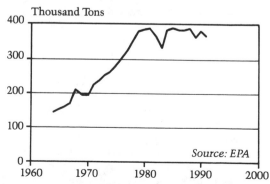

**Figure 3: Pesticide Use, U.S. Agricultural Sector, 1964–91***

*\* Measured in active ingredients, which is only a fraction of the formulated pesticide.*

# Sulfur and Nitrogen Emissions Resume Rise    Hal Kane

World emissions of sulfur and nitrogen from the burning of fossil fuels resumed their historical climbs in 1991 after a rare drop during 1990. Some 70 million tons of sulfur were released into the atmosphere in 1991 in the form of sulfur dioxide, along with 27 million tons of nitrogen in the form of nitrogen oxides.[1] (See Figures 1 and 2.) In addition, roughly 10 million tons of sulfur were released through other industrial processes, and some 6–12 million tons of nitrogen were added to the atmosphere through the burning of forests and other biomass.[2]

As a result, emissions from all sources were probably closer to 80 million tons of sulfur and 33–39 million tons of nitrogen. All figures are unofficial estimates, however, because no comprehensive official data gathering system exists to measure international nitrogen or sulfur pollution.

Sulfur and nitrogen pollution damage natural resources, reduce economic potential, and harm human health. Both sulfur and nitrogen emissions cause acid rain. Nitrogen oxide also contributes to smog, to other urban air pollution, and to climate change. One study found that 75 percent of Europe's forests, for example, suffer from damaging sulfur deposition, at an economic loss of $30.4 billion a year.[3] Adding damage from nitrogen oxides would bring the figure even higher.

According to the World Health Organization and the U.N. Environment Programme, 625 million people are exposed to unhealthy levels of sulfur dioxide from fossil fuel burning.[4] A study for the United States estimates that air pollution of all kinds may cost the nation as much as $40 billion annually in health care and lost productivity.[5]

The largest source of sulfur emissions is the burning of coal, but it also comes from burning oil, smelting metal, and other industrial processes. Nitrogen emissions mainly come from cars, power stations, and industrial engines.

Cleaner technologies and fuels have slowed the rise in both pollutants. Coal washing and stack "scrubbers" have achieved impressive results where they have been used; so has switching to a lower sulfur coal or to natural gas, which is much cleaner.[6] These approaches have been particularly successful for sulfur emissions. For example, Japan's power plants cut their output of sulfur dioxide from almost seven grams a kilowatt-hour in 1970 to less than one gram by 1980.[7] With nitrogen emissions, however, progress has been considerably slower. The concentration of nitrogen oxides in the atmosphere over Japan was as high at the end of the eighties as it was at the end of the seventies.[8] Industrial countries as a whole were able to cut sulfur oxide emissions almost in half since 1970, but nitrogen oxide emissions have risen, and are about 15 percent higher now.[9]

Increased energy consumption due to economic growth in developing countries is likely to more than offset the improvement in sulfur emissions, however, particularly because these countries often lack clean technologies and rely heavily on coal. China's current rapid economic growth and emphasis on coal, for example, will release a substantial amount of sulfur into the atmosphere, along with smaller additional amounts of nitrogen.

China's sulfur emissions have risen steadily since the early seventies, while those of the United States have decreased. In 1970, the United States emitted 15 million tons of sulfur to China's 5 million tons, but in about 1990 the two countries converged at some 11 million tons.[10] The Soviet Union's sulfur emissions rose to about 13 million tons before its breakup, and have probably fallen since.[11] No other countries approach the sulfur emissions of those three giants. India and Poland are the next largest emitters, with 2.5–3 million tons each.[12]

The United States is the largest producer of nitrogen pollution. Emissions there rose to about 6.5 million tons by the mid-seventies but have fallen since to under 6 million tons.[13] The Soviet Union had reached about 5.5 million tons before the country split up, but that may be down with declining economic activity.[14] China is a distant third, at about 3 million tons of nitrogen a year, but growing.[15] Germany and Japan are next, with around 1 million tons a year.[16]

WORLD NITROGEN AND SULFUR
EMISSIONS FROM FOSSIL FUEL
BURNING, 1950–91

| YEAR | NITROGEN | SULFUR |
|------|----------|--------|
|      | (mill. tons) | |
| 1950 | 6.8  | 30.1 |
| 1960 | 11.8 | 46.2 |
| 1970 | 18.1 | 57.0 |
| 1971 | 18.6 | 56.9 |
| 1972 | 19.5 | 58.2 |
| 1973 | 20.6 | 60.9 |
| 1974 | 20.8 | 60.9 |
| 1975 | 19.9 | 56.4 |
| 1976 | 21.0 | 58.6 |
| 1977 | 20.8 | 60.1 |
| 1978 | 22.3 | 61.0 |
| 1979 | 22.4 | 62.6 |
| 1980 | 22.3 | 62.9 |
| 1981 | 22.1 | 61.9 |
| 1982 | 22.2 | 62.1 |
| 1983 | 22.5 | 63.0 |
| 1984 | 23.3 | 64.5 |
| 1985 | 23.4 | 64.2 |
| 1986 | 23.6 | 65.2 |
| 1987 | 24.3 | 66.5 |
| 1988 | 25.3 | 68.4 |
| 1989 | 26.6 | 70.3 |
| 1990 | 26.5 | 68.4 |
| 1991 | 26.8 | 69.7 |

SOURCES: J. Dignon, Lawrence Livermore
Laboratory, unpublished data series, private
communication, February 23, 1994; Sultan
Hameed, SUNY Stony Brook, Stony Brook, N.Y.

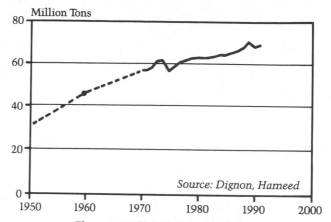

**Figure 1: World Sulfur Emissions from
Fossil Fuel Burning, 1950–91**

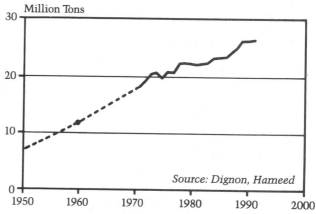

**Figure 2: World Nitrogen Emissions from
Fossil Fuel Burning, 1950–91**

# Social
## Trends

# Population Increase Drops Slightly   Aaron Sachs

In 1993, the world added 87 million people to its numbers, slightly fewer than in 1992.[1] Total population now stands at nearly 5.6 billion. (See Figures 1 and 2.) During each month of the year the world gained the demographic equivalent of a new Switzerland.[2]

Last year's population growth turned out to be slightly less than expected, thanks largely to a startling fertility decline in China, home to more than one fifth of the world's population. Taking this into account, demographers have revised downward their estimates of the last five years' worth of world population growth. Previous estimates for the annual addition stood at more than 90 million people. But now the all-time high is estimated to have been 89 million, in 1989.[3]

Net annual population growth has remained relatively stable over the past few years. Expressed as a percentage, then, population growth is slowing down. Since 1986, the average annual growth rate has declined from 1.75 percent to 1.56 percent.[4] (See Figure 3.) A smaller share of the world's women are bearing children each year, and the average woman is bearing fewer children during her lifetime.

Despite these recent developments, however, the slowdown in the world's population growth rate is happening much more gradually than was expected just a few years ago. In 1982, the United Nations projected that world population would stabilize in the year 2100 at 10.2 billion. The U.N. now projects that population will continue to grow until after 2200, and that it will reach 11.6 billion.[5] Fertility declines have hit a plateau in several countries where population growth slowed dramatically in the seventies, and few declines in fertility levels have begun in other countries.

Of last year's population growth, 94 percent occurred in developing nations, which are now home to about 4.3 billion people—78 percent of the world total.[6] Parents in the Third World often want large families because so many children there are claimed by disease, war, and famine. But burgeoning populations are likely to make life even harder in many nations. Only significant donations of resources from wealthier nations and serious attempts to improve the status of women and the general quality of life will have a major influence on fertility rates in most of the developing world.

Asia, home of the world's two demographic giants, China and India, dominates the population picture in terms of total numbers. India's 1993 population increase of almost 17 million surpassed the combined increases of the United States, Europe, Latin America, and the former Soviet Union.[7]

Africa, however, is the world's fastest-growing region. In some nations south of the Sahara, women on average still have more than seven children. In addition, 45 percent of Africans are under the age of 15, so the demographic rise is still building momentum.[8]

Even in Africa, however, fertility is generally declining, albeit quite slowly in some places. In Kenya, the total fertility rate—the number of children the average woman has in her lifetime—has fallen from 7.9 to 6.5 in just 12 years.[9]

In China, according to the new data, the total fertility rate plummeted from 2.3 to 1.9 between 1991 and 1993.[10] Government officials attributed the drop to the nation's one-couple, one-child policy, to improvements in birth control services, and to a rising standard of living. Unfortunately, there is also evidence that government agents are using coercive tactics on childbearing couples—that China is buying slower population growth with intolerable violations of human rights.[11]

In 1994, the international community has an important opportunity to rethink population issues at the U.N. International Conference on Population and Development (ICPD), being held in September in Cairo. Momentum for the ICPD got a significant boost in 1993 when the Clinton administration restored U.S. funding to the U.N. Population Fund and the International Planned Parenthood Federation.[12]

Although the ICPD's resolutions will likely guide the world's population policies and programs for years to come, U.N. delegates intend to limit the meeting itself to nine days. If they keep to that schedule, the world's population will grow by only about 2.2 million during their deliberations.

WORLD POPULATION, TOTAL AND
ANNUAL ADDITION, 1950–93

| YEAR | POPULATION (billion) | ANNUAL ADDITION (million) |
|---|---|---|
| 1950 | 2.555 | 37 |
| 1955 | 2.779 | 53 |
| 1960 | 3.038 | 41 |
| 1961 | 3.079 | 56 |
| 1962 | 3.135 | 70 |
| 1963 | 3.204 | 71 |
| 1964 | 3.276 | 69 |
| 1965 | 3.345 | 70 |
| 1966 | 3.414 | 69 |
| 1967 | 3.484 | 71 |
| 1968 | 3.555 | 74 |
| 1969 | 3.629 | 75 |
| 1970 | 3.704 | 78 |
| 1971 | 3.782 | 77 |
| 1972 | 3.859 | 77 |
| 1973 | 3.936 | 76 |
| 1974 | 4.012 | 74 |
| 1975 | 4.086 | 73 |
| 1976 | 4.159 | 73 |
| 1977 | 4.232 | 73 |
| 1978 | 4.304 | 76 |
| 1979 | 4.380 | 77 |
| 1980 | 4.457 | 77 |
| 1981 | 4.534 | 81 |
| 1982 | 4.614 | 81 |
| 1983 | 4.695 | 80 |
| 1984 | 4.775 | 81 |
| 1985 | 4.856 | 86 |
| 1986 | 4.942 | 87 |
| 1987 | 5.029 | 88 |
| 1988 | 5.117 | 88 |
| 1989 | 5.206 | 89 |
| 1990 | 5.295 | 86 |
| 1991 | 5.381 | 88 |
| 1992 | 5.469 | 88 |
| 1993 (prel) | 5.557 | 87 |

SOURCE: U.S. Bureau of the Census, Center for
International Research, private communication,
November 2, 1993.

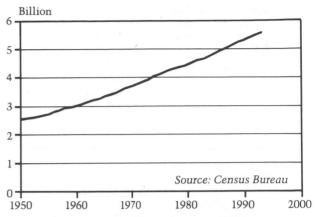

Figure 1: World Population, 1950–93

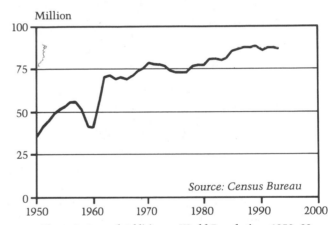

Figure 2: Annual Addition to World Population, 1950–93

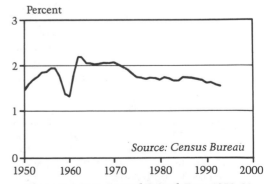

Figure 3: Average Annual Growth Rate, 1950–93

# Overall Cigarette Production Rises Hal Kane

World cigarette production per person was about flat in 1993, at 982 cigarettes. Total production rose, however, to more than 5.45 trillion pieces, up from 5.38 trillion in 1992.[1] (See Figures 1 and 2.)

At 4.6 percent below its 1988 peak of 1,029 cigarettes per person worldwide, smoking rates are no longer growing and may be falling. The United States is leading the industrial countries' trend away from the habit: its cigarette consumption per adult has fallen by 40 percent since the 1966 peak of 4,287 cigarettes a year.[2] (See Figure 3.) China represents the other side of the coin, however. Consumption there rose from fewer than 500 billion cigarettes in 1976 to almost 1,700 billion in 1993.[3]

The largest increase in production in 1993 occurred in China, just as it had in 1992. Some 56 billion additional cigarettes were manufactured there last year, more than all the cigarettes produced in France or Italy. China makes two and a half times more cigarettes than the next largest producer, the United States.[4]

The second largest increase in production in 1993 occurred in Russia, where rates had fallen from the late eighties until 1991. A jump of 13 billion cigarettes in 1993 to 161 billion brought output back to the 1989 level.[5] That production was supported by takeovers of factories in Russia and neighboring republics by Western tobacco companies, especially Philip Morris, RJR Nabisco, and the Liggett Group.[6]

Production also increased in some East Asian countries where the economies have been growing. Indonesia boosted output by 3 billion pieces, South Korea by 2 billion, and the Philippines by 4.5 billion.[7] Turkey added more than 10 billion additional cigarettes to its output and now makes one third more cigarettes than it did just three years ago.[8] Morocco added 3 billion pieces and Egypt added 2 billion.[9]

Cigarette production dropped slightly in several European countries that manufacture large amounts of tobacco. Germany's output fell by almost 7 billion pieces, Bulgaria's fell by 5 billion, and output in Romania and Spain fell by 3.5 billion each.[10]

To understand the relationship between smoking and health, data from the United States are among the most comprehensive. Testimony to the U.S. Congress by scientists from the Office of Technology Assessment (OTA) in 1993 put the average number of years of life lost per smoking death at 15.[11] That translates into more than 6 million years of life lost every year in the United States. Some 417,000 people die there from smoking each year, at a cost of $68 billion, or $2.59 per pack of cigarettes. That includes $20.8 billion in direct health care costs and $47.2 billion in lost productivity and foregone earnings, according to OTA. The cost to the economy per smoker is $1,078 a year.[12] Those numbers indicate what other countries can expect if they follow the same path as the United States. And during 1993, additional connections between smoking and illness were reported by medical researchers.[13]

In developing countries, tobacco is already responsible for 30 percent of all cancer deaths and a larger, but unknown, number of deaths from cardiovascular disease.[14] Those rates are rising. The World Bank predicts that tobacco consumption in developing countries will increase by about 12 percent between 1990 and 2000.[15] China alone is expected to eventually register 2 million tobacco-related deaths a year.[16] If smoking rates in developing countries rise to those of industrial ones—where about a third of young adults smoke—then some 12 million people in the Third World will die prematurely every year as a result.[17]

Noting those catastrophic trends in developing countries, the World Bank recently pledged to stop lending funds to support tobacco production, processing, or marketing (with exceptions), and to help countries diversify away from tobacco. It also said that in some cases it would not try to lower import taxes on tobacco products.[18] It has been joined by a slowly growing group of Southern governments that have started fighting tobacco with cigarette taxes, educational campaigns, and limited bans.[19]

WORLD CIGARETTE PRODUCTION,
TOTAL AND PER PERSON, 1950–93

| YEAR | PRODUCTION (billion) | PER PERSON (number of cigarettes) |
|---|---|---|
| 1950 | 1,686 | 660 |
| 1955 | 1,921 | 691 |
| 1960 | 2,150 | 708 |
| 1961 | 2,140 | 695 |
| 1962 | 2,191 | 699 |
| 1963 | 2,300 | 718 |
| 1964 | 2,402 | 733 |
| 1965 | 2,564 | 767 |
| 1966 | 2,678 | 784 |
| 1967 | 2,689 | 772 |
| 1968 | 2,790 | 785 |
| 1969 | 2,924 | 806 |
| 1970 | 3,112 | 840 |
| 1971 | 3,165 | 837 |
| 1972 | 3,295 | 854 |
| 1973 | 3,481 | 884 |
| 1974 | 3,590 | 895 |
| 1975 | 3,742 | 916 |
| 1976 | 3,852 | 926 |
| 1977 | 4,019 | 950 |
| 1978 | 4,072 | 946 |
| 1979 | 4,214 | 962 |
| 1980 | 4,388 | 985 |
| 1981 | 4,541 | 1,002 |
| 1982 | 4,550 | 986 |
| 1983 | 4,547 | 968 |
| 1984 | 4,689 | 982 |
| 1985 | 4,855 | 1,000 |
| 1986 | 4,987 | 1,009 |
| 1987 | 5,128 | 1,020 |
| 1988 | 5,266 | 1,029 |
| 1989 | 5,295 | 1,017 |
| 1990 | 5,440 | 1,027 |
| 1991 | 5,373 | 999 |
| 1992 | 5,383 | 984 |
| 1993 (prel) | 5,455 | 982 |

SOURCE: USDA, FAS, unpublished printouts,
various dates; data for 1950 and 1955, estimates
based on U.S. data.

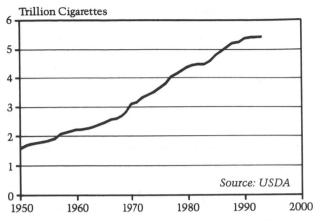

**Figure 1: World Cigarette Production, 1950–93**

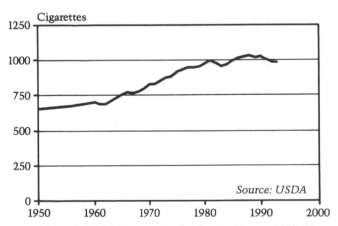

**Figure 2: World Cigarette Production Per Person, 1950–93**

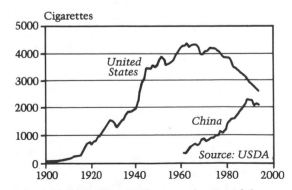

**Figure 3: Cigarette Consumption Per Adult,
United States, 1900–93, and China, 1960–93**

# HIV/AIDS Cases Rising Steadily

### Aaron Sachs

In 1993, between 2 million and 3 million people around the world contracted the human immunodeficiency virus (HIV), which causes AIDS.[1] Since the beginning of the HIV/AIDS pandemic, in the late seventies, 15–23 million people have been infected.[2] (See Figure 1.) It is quite likely that 1 of every 100 people worldwide will have HIV by the end of this decade.[3]

Current medical theory holds that almost all HIV infections eventually result in cases of full-blown AIDS and that AIDS is almost 100 percent fatal. So far, of the 15–23 million infected people, some 3–5 million have developed AIDS, two thirds of whom have already died.[4] (See Figure 2.)

HIV/AIDS statistics are so rough because they are by necessity estimates: accurate data are simply not available in many parts of the world. Actual AIDS cases are especially difficult to count, since they tend to go both unrecognized and unreported in many developing nations. Even if doctors have the requisite training and equipment to make conclusive AIDS diagnoses, they may be unable to communicate their findings to recordkeeping institutions. While Africa, for instance, accounts for only 36 percent of the AIDS cases that do get reported, the best estimates place the continent's actual share at about 67 percent.[5]

Levels of HIV infection are slightly easier to track: by testing the blood of randomly selected people, medical researchers can tell with reasonable accuracy what percentage of a given population has HIV. But such tests are still not available in many regions.

The one clear global trend is that HIV/AIDS is continuing to spread unabated. Despite increased awareness of the disease in most regions, there were just as many new HIV infections last year as in 1992.[6]

The AIDS cases that these infections will translate into during the next decade could bankrupt health care systems in many countries. By the year 2000, more than 90 percent of all HIV/AIDS cases will be in developing nations, the poorest of which currently spend only about $1 annually on each person's medical services.[7]

From the beginning, sub-Saharan Africa has been at the center of the HIV/AIDS pandemic.

Some 4,000 to 5,000 Africans acquired HIV every day in 1993.[8] The virus is now present in more than 2 percent of the region's adult population, with rates getting as high as 30 percent in some urban areas.[9] According to some projections, AIDS mortality could reduce urban life expectancy in this region by about 19 years during the next decade or so.[10]

HIV/AIDS has already begun to cripple social and economic systems in sub-Saharan Africa. The virus is almost always passed heterosexually in this region, and most often between men and women in their most productive years. Sixty percent of last year's new infections in Africa occurred among people between the ages of 15 and 24.[11] The virus can also be passed from a mother to her fetus, and current research indicates a 30-percent inheritance rate in children born to HIV-positive mothers.[12] The 70 percent who do not inherit the virus will likely find themselves without parents by the time they are 10. Already, more than a million children have been born with HIV in sub-Saharan Africa, and several million more have been orphaned by the disease.[13]

Unfortunately, many other regions of the developing world could quickly follow this path. In South and Southeast Asia, the HIV/AIDS pandemic is currently growing at a rate much like that in Central Africa in the early eighties.[14] The annual number of new HIV infections in Asia may surpass those in Africa during this decade.[15] And the potential for the spread of HIV/AIDS in South and Southeast Asia could be even greater than in sub-Saharan Africa, since this region's adult population is about twice as large.[16]

In most parts of the industrial world, about 90 percent of HIV/AIDS cases have been homosexual males or users of injectable drugs.[17] Although the disease has indeed been devastating in these high-risk groups, HIV prevalence rates have remained well under 1 percent in the general population.[18] The less threatening situation in these richer countries still calls out for urgent action, however, and must not obscure the fact that HIV/AIDS is one of the worst pandemics in world history.

GLOBAL ESTIMATES OF
CUMULATIVE HIV/AIDS
CASES, 1980–93

| YEAR | HIV INFECTIONS (million) |
|------|---------------------------|
| 1980 | 0.1 |
| 1981 | 0.3 |
| 1982 | 0.7 |
| 1983 | 1.3 |
| 1984 | 2.2 |
| 1985 | 3.2 |
| 1986 | 4.9 |
| 1987 | 6.9 |
| 1988 | 9.1 |
| 1989 | 11.4 |
| 1990 | 14.0 |
| 1991 | 16.7 |
| 1992 | 19.5 |
| 1993 | 22.4 |

| YEAR | AIDS CASES (thousand) |
|------|------------------------|
| 1980 | — |
| 1981 | 1 |
| 1982 | 7 |
| 1983 | 21 |
| 1984 | 65 |
| 1985 | 143 |
| 1986 | 279 |
| 1987 | 493 |
| 1988 | 813 |
| 1989 | 1,275 |
| 1990 | 1,892 |
| 1991 | 2,701 |
| 1992 | 3,657 |
| 1993 | 4,820 |

SOURCE: Global AIDS Policy Coalition, Harvard
School of Public Health, Boston, Mass., private
communication, February 24, 1994.

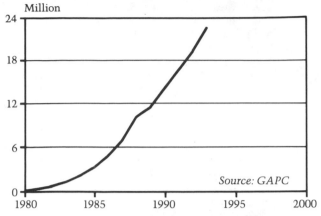

Figure 1: Estimates of HIV Infections Worldwide, 1980–93

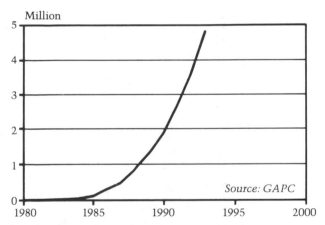

Figure 2: Estimates of AIDS Cases Worldwide, 1980–93

A dramatic worldwide push beginning in the mid-eighties to extend immunizations to four fifths of all infants has succeeded. Immunizations that in the early eighties reached only about a quarter of infants in developing countries in less than a decade were reaching 80 percent.[1] (See Figures 1 and 2.)

By the end of 1990, vaccines administered under the United Nations Expanded Programme for Immunizations—protecting against tuberculosis, tetanus, diphtheria, pertussis, measles, and polio—had dramatically reduced illness from diseases that accounted for about 16 percent of all child deaths. The push to reach the 1990 goal led to a slight relaxation, however, and a fall-off in 1991.[2]

Although such a fall had been anticipated, it was fortunately smaller than expected for the developing world, at about 3 percent.[3] In 101 developing countries, immunization levels were maintained or increased in 1991, and in 28 countries they fell.[4] Asia had little or no fall-off, nor did the Middle East or North Africa. Most of the Americas remained stable, though rates dropped in Brazil and Venezuela. But sub-Saharan Africa's immunization rates fell about 10 percent in 1991.

In 1992, rates remained about constant except for the vaccine given to pregnant women to protect infants from tetanus, which fell. All vaccination rates are expected to rise during the nineties, however.

Vaccines administered in 1992 saved 3 million lives.[5] They are now delivered to 100 million infants on four or five separate occasions each year, one of the international community's more outstanding achievements.[6] At the same time, extending the service even more remains one of the greatest opportunities, as the deaths of another 1.7 million children could have been prevented in 1992.[7]

The cost of fully immunizing a child in low-income countries ranges from $6 to more than $20, with an average of about $15. Total annual costs are $2.2–2.4 billion for the Expanded Programme on Immunization, less than 2 percent of the public health expenditure of developing countries.[8]

The payoffs are difficult to measure, since they largely take the form of avoided costs of health care and expanded productive potential of people. The measles vaccine alone cut death rates from about 2.5 million a year in 1980 to fewer than 900,000 in 1990, and nonfatal measles episodes from about 75 million a year to 25 million.[9] The money saved from not having to treat those 50 million incidents and the productive potential of the 1.6 million people who did not die cannot be measured.

In 1796, Edward Jenner developed the first vaccine, for smallpox, which launched the work on immunizations that is only now reaching most of the people in the world.[10] Even in the seventies, only around 5 percent of the children in developing countries were vaccinated against most diseases.[11] In 1979, nearly two centuries after smallpox could be prevented, the World Health Organization declared that the disease had been eradicated.[12]

There is now hope that more diseases will go the way of smallpox, as eradication is the most cost-effective way of fighting disease. Once a disease is extinct, no additional money ever need be spent on it. Attempts to eradicate polio will cost about $1.4 billion over 10 years, and then the savings on treatment no longer needed would be $500 million a year in the early twenty-first century and would rise thereafter.[13]

Immunizing people in remote areas while maintaining the potency of vaccines is difficult. Currently, for example, vaccines must be kept in refrigerators, freezers, and then cold boxes as they travel from manufacturers to distant villages. That journey has been compared to "the challenge of keeping cold an ice cream cone purchased in Paris for consumption by a child in northeastern Laos."[14]

Attempts are being made to relieve that burden by developing vaccines that require one or two rather than multiple doses, that keep their potency in tropical temperatures, and that can be combined with other inoculations. Vaccines for other major killers are also needed, as 1–2 million deaths from hepatitis B infection every year demonstrate.[15] The ultimate goal is to have a single oral immunization to be given shortly after birth that will protect the world's infants against all major childhood diseases.

## IMMUNIZATIONS OF INFANTS IN DEVELOPING COUNTRIES, 1981–92[1]

| YEAR | TUBERCULOSIS | DIPHTHERIA, PERTUSSIS, AND TETANUS |
|---|---|---|
| | | (percent) |
| 1981 | 31 | 27 |
| 1984 | 36 | 37 |
| 1985 | 40 | 38 |
| 1986 | 51 | 49 |
| 1987 | 69 | 60 |
| 1988 | 75 | 68 |
| 1989 | 85 | 77 |
| 1990 | 90 | 83 |
| 1991 | 85 | 78 |
| 1992 | 86 | 78 |

| YEAR | MEASLES | POLIO |
|---|---|---|
| 1981 | 18 | 24 |
| 1984 | 25 | 36 |
| 1985 | 28 | 38 |
| 1986 | 37 | 50 |
| 1987 | 53 | 60 |
| 1988 | 60 | 69 |
| 1989 | 73 | 79 |
| 1990 | 79 | 85 |
| 1991 | 77 | 80 |
| 1992 | 77 | 78 |

| YEAR | TETANUS TYPHOID[2] |
|---|---|
| 1981 | 14 |
| 1984 | 14 |
| 1985 | 17 |
| 1986 | 19 |
| 1987 | 27 |
| 1988 | 39 |
| 1989 | 44 |
| 1990 | 56 |
| 1991 | 54 |
| 1992 | 38 |

[1]1981–85 exclude data for China.  [2]For pregnant women, not children.
SOURCE: WHO and UNICEF, private communication, February 17, 1994.

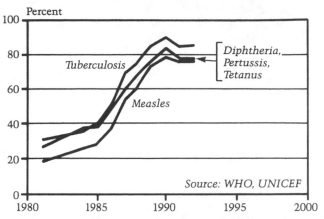

**Figure 1: Immunization of Infants in Developing Countries for Common Childhood Diseases, 1981–92**

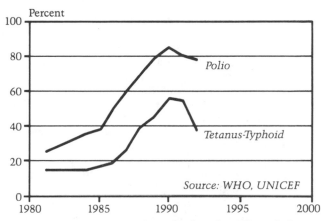

**Figure 2: Immunizations of Infants for Polio and of Mothers for Tetanus-Typhoid, Developing Countries, 1981–92**

# Refugee Flows Swelling                                 Hal Kane

At about 19 million, the number of people seeking asylum is larger now than ever before.[1] (See Figures 1 and 2.) The number has risen almost every year since the mid-seventies, when the United Nations counted some 2.5 million refugees. Before that, the number had fluctuated less and was much smaller, with fewer than 2 million official refugees at mid-century.[2]

Afghanistan has produced the highest number of exiles from a homeland. About 6 million refugees—a third of the world total—have fled Afghanistan, almost all to Iran and Pakistan, though some have now returned.[3] At the end of 1992, Asia accounted for about 7 million refugees total, the most of any continent. Africa was second, with 5.4 million.[4] With the collapse of Yugoslavia and the former Soviet Union, Europe suddenly had 3.6 million people living outside their home country at the end of 1992.[5] And Latin America and North America each had about 1 million.[6]

Officially defined by the United Nations High Commission for Refugees as people who flee their countries because of fear of political, religious, or ethnic persecution or of war, refugees have been called "the human barometer of political stability, of justice and order."[7] Their numbers are often an indicator of things that are otherwise difficult to measure, such as human rights and safe places to live.

Ethnic upheavals continue to overtake new lands and to rage further out of control in existing hot spots. By September 1993, almost 1 million Azerbaijanis had fled their new country, as fighting spilled into previously safe areas.[8] Nearby, Armenia's energy grid and food and water supplies have collapsed, and the Republic of Georgia is disintegrating into a guerilla war. In Tajikistan, Russian troops there to keep foreign fighters, weapons, and drugs out have fought with Afghan troops. More than a half-million people are thought to have fled that new country.[9]

The worst could lie ahead. The number of Russians living outside their home country increased from 5 million to 24 million during 1926–79, as the Soviet government moved people to suit its plans.[10] The same trend occurred for Ukrainians, Belarussians, Georgians, and Moldovans. If ethnic or social hostilities continue to ignite in regions of mixed ethnic heritage, then those demographic patterns will unravel, and disintegration will reach new limits.

Once such fuses have been lit, little success has been realized in stopping the blasts. One analyst called recent efforts "collective failures of our species."[11] For many parts of the world—such as Myanmar (formerly Burma), Guatemala, Angola, Sudan, and Mozambique—few of the world's most educated people have taken the time to understand what is happening to millions of uprooted people. In Somalia, the countries that eventually proved themselves capable of saving lives and at least partially calming a conflict spent more than a year procrastinating. And having said "never again" 40 years earlier, after World War II, the rest of the world found itself unable or unwilling to take action in the former Yugoslavia.

Many other pressures are building that are likely to create the tinder boxes that in turn create refugees. In Africa, 45 percent of the total population is under 15 years old. In Iraq, Iran, and Syria, the figure is 47–49 percent. And in Honduras, El Salvador, Guatemala, and Nicaragua, it stands at more than 45 percent.[12] Large populations of young people who lack jobs, homes, health care, and even clean water have the explosive needs and dim futures that have already disrupted Soviet Central Asian republics, Egypt, and Algeria, among other places.

Those growing populations will survive in part by consuming the environmental resource base that will be needed to support future activities. Every year an area of agricultural land almost the size of Ireland is lost to degradation.[13] The people who formerly survived by farming that area mostly will have to leave. They may go, first, to a nearby city. But finding only a squatter settlement with few prospects for employment or safety, they may have to look for a livelihood elsewhere.

## WORLD REFUGEES, 1960–93

| YEAR | TOTAL (million) |
|------|-----------------|
| 1960 | 1.4 |
| 1961 | 1.3 |
| 1962 | 1.3 |
| 1963 | 1.3 |
| 1970 | 2.5 |
| 1974 | 2.4 |
| 1976 | 2.8 |
| 1977 | 3.3 |
| 1978 | 4.6 |
| 1979 | 5.7 |
| 1980 | 8.2 |
| 1981 | 9.8 |
| 1982 | 10.4 |
| 1983 | 10.9 |
| 1984 | 10.5 |
| 1985 | 11.6 |
| 1986 | 12.4 |
| 1987 | 13.3 |
| 1988 | 14.8 |
| 1989 | 14.9 |
| 1990 | 17.2 |
| 1991 | 17.0 |
| 1992 | 18.2 |
| 1993 | 19.0 |

SOURCE: U.N. High Commissioner for Refugees, *The State of the World's Refugees* (New York: Penguin Books, 1993); 1993, Worldwatch estimate based on UNHCR, private communication, March 16, 1994.

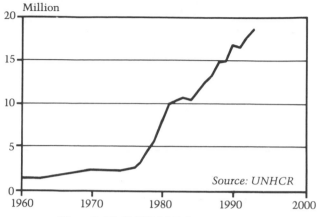

**Figure 1: World Official Refugees, 1960–93**

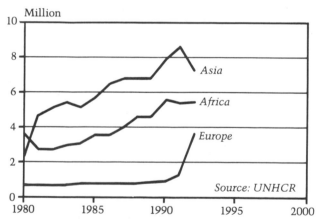

**Figure 2: Official Refugees, Asia, Africa, and Europe, 1980–92**

# Military Trends

# Arms Trade Continues Decline Michael Renner

In 1991, worldwide arms exports declined by 36 percent, from $39.8 billion to $25.5 billion, according to the U.S. Arms Control and Disarmament Agency (ACDA).[1] The global arms trade surged from about $12 billion per year in the early sixties to $73 billion in 1984 (in 1991 dollars), and during the past three decades more than $1.2 trillion worth of military equipment has been shipped across national borders.[2]

Since the mid-eighties, however, a combination of factors has put apparently unrelenting downward pressure on the arms bazaar. (See Figure 1.) Data compiled by the Stockholm International Peace Research Institute—though not directly comparable—confirm these trends.[3] (See Figure 2.)

All publicly available data are rough estimates, not precise measurements. Government secrecy is a major reason for the lack of completely reliable data on the global arms trade. Arms transfers through licensed production in recipient countries, retrofitting and modernizing of existing weapons, small-weapons transactions, and deals on the grey and black markets elude any systematic accounting.

During the seventies and eighties, three quarters of the global arms flow went to developing countries; some 10–15 countries, most prominently India, Saudi Arabia, Iraq, Iran, and Afghanistan, accounted for the bulk of the Third World's imports.[4] According to U.S. government statistics, during those two decades Third World governments received approximately 20,000 tanks and self-propelled howitzers, 28,000 artillery pieces, 37,000 armed personnel carriers, 1,100 warships and submarines, 8,000 military aircraft (of which more than half were supersonic combat planes), 3,600 helicopters, and more than 50,000 missiles.[5]

Among the sellers, there is an even tighter concentration. The United States and the former Soviet Union accounted for more than two thirds of global arms exports.[6] With France, the United Kingdom, China, and Germany, six countries together accounted for close to 90 percent of the total during the past two decades.[7]

The reversal of the arms trade explosion since the mid-eighties is the product of a variety of factors. Rising debt and dire economic circumstances have put weapons out of reach for a large group of developing countries. Market saturation is a factor in other countries that had gone on buying sprees in earlier years. Furthermore, a series of long-standing conflicts around the world have come to an end, reducing the demand for arms. Expanded Third World capabilities to produce arms and to refurbish and upgrade existing weaponry, meanwhile, signal not a lessened appetite for arms but simply a switch from foreign to domestic sources.[8]

Strong economic growth allows many East Asian countries to lavish substantial resources on arms procurement. Oil-rich nations in the Middle East continue to be big military spenders. By contrast, African and South American countries have progressively reduced their imports—some because they enjoy more peaceful relations, others because of sheer economic necessity.[9]

Despite vigorous sales pitches, many suppliers have seen their sales drop. The most dramatic change has occurred in the former Soviet Union. According to Richard Grimmett of the Congressional Research Service (CRS), Soviet/Russian deliveries to the Third World plunged from $23 billion in 1988 to $2.3 billion in 1992 (in 1992 dollars).[10]

The United States has emerged as the world's principal arms supplier, accounting for 60 percent of sales to the Third World in 1992. The CRS compilation, however, does not include commercial deals—negotiated by the manufacturers themselves—because the data for such deliveries tend to be incomplete.[11]

The stiff competition means that exporters are willing to sell arms of growing sophistication to almost any country that can pay for them, and few are prepared to cut off deliveries to governments embroiled in violent conflict or abusing the human rights of their own people. Moreover, to win contracts that might be awarded to competitors, exporters are not only transferring weapons but also offering production technology that enables the recipients to build their own arms industries.[12]

EXPORTS OF CONVENTIONAL
WEAPONS, 1963–91

| YEAR | EXPORTS (bill. 1991 dollars) |
|------|------------------------------|
| 1963 | 12.9 |
| 1964 | 12.5 |
| 1965 | 14.4 |
| 1966 | 16.8 |
| 1967 | 18.4 |
| 1968 | 18.6 |
| 1969 | 19.6 |
| 1970 | 18.4 |
| 1971 | 19.0 |
| 1972 | 29.4 |
| 1973 | 35.4 |
| 1974 | 29.1 |
| 1975 | 28.4 |
| 1976 | 35.6 |
| 1977 | 45.4 |
| 1978 | 50.7 |
| 1979 | 54.9 |
| 1980 | 57.0 |
| 1981 | 66.6 |
| 1982 | 69.3 |
| 1983 | 67.7 |
| 1984 | 72.8 |
| 1985 | 63.1 |
| 1986 | 61.2 |
| 1987 | 68.7 |
| 1988 | 61.9 |
| 1989 | 54.3 |
| 1990 | 39.8 |
| 1991 | 25.5 |

SOURCE: U.S. Arms Control and
Disarmament Agency, *World
Military Expenditures and Arms
Transfers* (Washington, D.C.:
U.S. Government Printing
Office, various years).

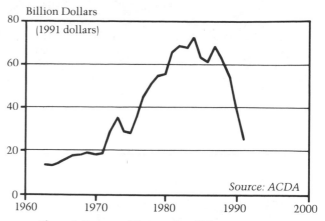

Figure 1: Exports of Conventional Weapons, 1963–91

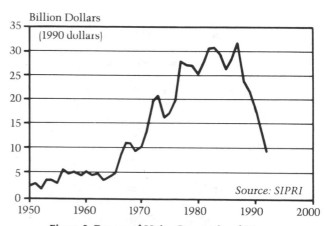

Figure 2: Exports of Major Conventional Weapons
to Third World, 1950–92*

* *Unlike ACDA data, the SIPRI valuation system is not
comparable to official economic statistics; SIPRI data
are not intended as precise measurements but rather
as a trend-measuring device.*

# U.N. Peacekeeping Expands                    Michael Renner

Expenditures for U.N. peacekeeping operations rose to a record $3 billion in 1993, up 69 percent from the previous year.[1] Historically, very modest sums of money have been devoted to such activities. But since 1987, spending has grown almost thirteenfold as the number, size, and complexity of peacekeeping missions have exploded. (See Figure 1.) From 1947 to 1993, the United Nations spent a cumulative $10 billion on peacekeeping.[2]

In 1991, according to the Independent Advisory Group on U.N. Financing, the world's governments spent $1,877 on their militaries for each $1 they spent on U.N. peacekeeping. In just the last two years that ratio has changed rapidly in favor of peacekeeping outlays, to within a range of 250:1 to 200:1.[3] Yet the world still spends less on the "Blue Helmets" during one year than on traditional military forces in a couple of days. Clearly, governments across the globe still believe their security interests are better served by clinging to military muscle than by constructing a cooperative, less-heavily armed security system.

During the first four decades of the United Nations, 18 missions were undertaken. From 1979 to 1987, no new operations began. But during the past six years—1988 to 1993—25 new missions sprang to life, including the three largest ever: in Cambodia, the former Yugoslavia, and Somalia.[4] Until 1987, the highest number of operations that were active in any given year was seven. Since then, however, this number skyrocketed to 22. With the exception of 1990, every one of these years saw the launching of several new missions. (See Figure 2.)

The escalation covered not only expenditures but also the number of people involved. In 1987, some 10,000 soldiers and civilians served with the Blue Helmets. By mid-1993, the number had swelled to about 85,000 (including almost 70,000 military personnel, 4,500 police, and more than 10,000 civilians); by the end of the year, it approached the 100,-000 mark.[5]

Even as the U.N.'s responsibilities have mushroomed, its members have effectively denied it the resources to cope with the challenges the peacekeepers now face. Many governments pay their share late, or only a portion of what they owe. Collectively, the member states' peacekeeping arrears grew from $19 million in 1975 to $261 million in 1980 and then to $993 million by the end of 1993.[6] (See Figure 3.) This did not even include the deficit of roughly $200 million that the Cyprus operation, financed until 1993 through voluntary contributions, incurred.[7]

When the U.N. is unable to cover its peacekeeping expenses, governments that contribute troops are left holding the bag; by October 1993, the U.N. owed them about $605 million.[8] This unhappy experience renders them increasingly reluctant to commit personnel or equipment to future missions. Forced to deplete its working capital fund and to juggle money among different accounts, the U.N. is teetering on the edge of financial collapse at a time when its services are in demand as never before.

It is possible that the peacekeeping wave has crested. Faced with difficulties, many governments are drawing back from rather than bolstering the United Nations. The Clinton administration has made a sharp retreat from its earlier commitment to building a multilateral peace system.[9] With the huge Cambodia operation over, and with many nations withdrawing their troops from Somalia, the personnel and financial resources invested in peacekeeping are likely to decline in 1994.[10]

Prospects for the third large operation, in the former Yugoslavia, are clouded. At the same time, however, other operations are being reinforced. And potential new missions are always waiting in the wings, even though they may not be nearly as large, and therefore attract much less public attention.[11] Less spectacular growth in coming years may help the United Nations remedy the current situation of being so overextended.

## U.N. PEACEKEEPING OPERATION EXPENDITURES, 1986–93

| YEAR | EXPENDITURE (mill. dollars) |
|---|---|
| 1986 | 242 |
| 1987 | 240 |
| 1988 | 266 |
| 1989 | 635 |
| 1990 | 464 |
| 1991 | 488 |
| 1992 | 1,802 |
| 1993 (prel) | 3,043 |

SOURCE: Field Operations Division, Department of Peace-keeping Operations, United Nations, New York, February 14, 1994.

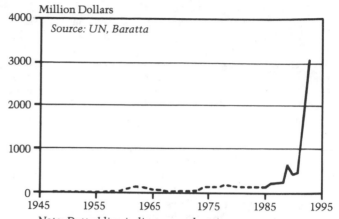

Note: Dotted line indicates rough estimates.

**Figure 1: U.N. Peacekeeping Expenditures, 1947–93**

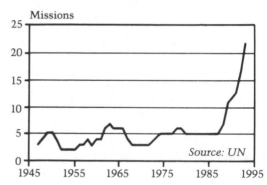

**Figure 2: Number of Peacekeeping Missions Per Year, 1947–93**

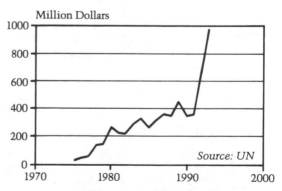

**Figure 3: Arrears of U.N. Members for Peacekeeping Expenses, 1975–93**

# Nuclear Arsenals Shrinking          Michael Renner

The number of nuclear warheads worldwide declined by almost 6 percent in 1993, from 52,875 to 49,910. Robert Norris and William Arkin estimate that the total number of warheads peaked at 69,480 in 1986.[1] (See Figure 1.) By far the greatest number are held by the United States and the former Soviet Union. (See Figure 2.) This count includes warheads that are deployed, placed in reserve, or retired awaiting dismantlement. In a reflection of the shift toward disarmament, in 1993 the last two categories accounted for almost half the total.[2]

During the past half-century, the United States, Soviet Union, China, the United Kingdom, and France together built some 128,000 nuclear warheads.[3] These five countries also manufactured more than 250 tons of weapons-grade plutonium and at least 1,300 tons of highly enriched uranium (HEU), though the two superpowers together accounted for more than 90 percent of the total.[4] Although the Soviet Union is believed to have kept intact 80–90 percent of the 55,000 warheads it manufactured (even long after they stopped being operational), the United States recycled its fissile materials from older into newer warheads; of some 70,000 warheads built, more than 53,000 were dismantled again.[5]

The end of the cold war brought about the conditions that now permit a reversal of the process—ending fissile materials production and nuclear warhead testing, dismantling a large portion of the existing arsenals, and safely disposing of the plutonium and HEU contained in the warheads.

The United States has stopped producing weapons plutonium and HEU; Russia will soon terminate its military fissile materials production; France has also stopped manufacturing plutonium and will end HEU production.[6] The Clinton administration has proposed a global treaty banning military plutonium and HEU production, but it would allow plutonium reprocessing for civilian purposes in Japan, France, and the United Kingdom to continue, provided it is subject to international inspection.[7]

After the breakup of the Soviet Union, Ukraine, Kazakhstan, and Belarus agreed to transfer all their nuclear weapons to Russia, where they would be dismantled.[8] Ukraine, however, while beginning to deactivate some missiles, has had second thoughts. Russia and Ukraine have been in a seemingly endless tug-of-war over the issue.[9] In January 1994, the U.S. government brokered an agreement that appears to move the two countries a big step closer to resolving their quarrel. Some details, however—including the precise timetable—remain unclear, as does the question of whether Ukraine's parliament will ultimately go along with the deal.[10]

The era of nuclear weapons test explosions appears to be rapidly drawing to a close (although government scientists are working feverishly to perfect technologies that will allow them to simulate explosions on their computer screens). The number of explosions conducted annually has decreased from 47 tests in 1987 to 1 in 1993. By far the largest number—143—were carried out in 1962. (See Figure 3.) A total of 2,037 test explosions were carried out between 1945 and 1993. More than half were undertaken by the United States; 715 by the former Soviet Union, 210 by France, 44 by Britain, 39 by China, and 1 by India.[11]

Despite pressure from their military establishments to resume testing, the governments of Russia, the United States, and France extended national moratoria originally adopted in 1991 and 1992.[12] Only the United Kingdom and China have refused to follow suit. But since the former has no test grounds of its own (it exploded its devices at the U.S. test site in Nevada), it has been forced by U.S. policy to suspend testing.[13]

With testing by four of the five declared nuclear powers suspended, there has been some progress toward a Comprehensive Test Ban Treaty. Many developing countries have made extension of the Nuclear Non-Proliferation Treaty—a decision to be made during a 1995 treaty review conference—conditional upon a treaty outlawing all testing.[14]

WORLD NUCLEAR ARSENALS, 1945–93

| YEAR | NUCLEAR WARHEADS (number) |
|---|---|
| 1945 | 2 |
| 1950 | 303 |
| 1955 | 2,490 |
| 1960 | 20,430 |
| 1961 | 25,700 |
| 1962 | 30,405 |
| 1963 | 34,080 |
| 1964 | 37,015 |
| 1965 | 39,050 |
| 1966 | 40,330 |
| 1967 | 41,685 |
| 1968 | 41,055 |
| 1969 | 39,600 |
| 1970 | 39,695 |
| 1971 | 41,365 |
| 1972 | 44,020 |
| 1973 | 47,745 |
| 1974 | 50,840 |
| 1975 | 52,325 |
| 1976 | 53,255 |
| 1977 | 54,980 |
| 1978 | 56,805 |
| 1979 | 59,120 |
| 1980 | 61,480 |
| 1981 | 63,055 |
| 1982 | 64,770 |
| 1983 | 66,980 |
| 1984 | 67,865 |
| 1985 | 68,590 |
| 1986 | 69,480 |
| 1987 | 68,835 |
| 1988 | 67,040 |
| 1989 | 63,650 |
| 1990 | 60,240 |
| 1991 | 55,775 |
| 1992 | 52,875 |
| 1993 (prel) | 49,910 |

SOURCE: *Bulletin of the Atomic Scientists,* December 1993.

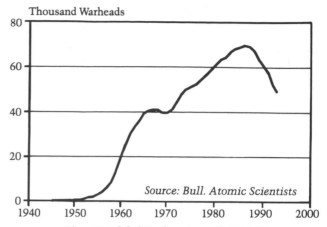

Figure 1: Global Nuclear Arsenal, 1945–93

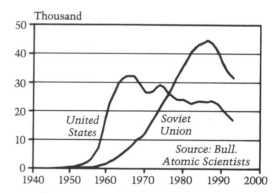

Figure 2: U.S. and Soviet Nuclear Warheads, 1945–93

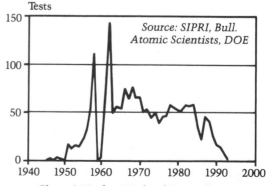

Figure 3: Nuclear Warhead Tests, 1945–93

Part TWO

# Special Features

# Environmental Features

# Paper Recycling on a Roll

Megan Ryan

As pressures on the world's forests build and as countries face mounting problems finding enough landfill space, interest in paper recycling continues to grow. In many nations, paper recycling efforts have been spurred by consumer demand for recycled paper products and legislative incentives. Other countries—most notably in Europe and East Asia—have been recycling large amounts of wastepaper for years because it has been cost-effective to do so.

Historically, many of the world's wastepaper recycling facilities have been in Europe and East Asia.[1] Mexico has also relied heavily on waste for its new paper production for many years. Countries with very high wastepaper use rates (that is, with waste making up a large share of total paper output) have tended to be fiber-poor and have found it cheaper to rely on waste than to import wood.[2] Although wastepaper use in fiber-rich nations such as the United States, Canada, and the Nordic countries has been growing in recent years, the rates are dramatically lower than in fiber-poor nations.[3] (See Table 1.)

| TABLE 1: WASTEPAPER USE RATES, SELECTED COUNTRIES, 1992 | |
| --- | --- |
| COUNTRY | SHARE[1] (percent) |
| Taiwan | 98 |
| Denmark | 97 |
| Mexico | 81 |
| Thailand | 80 |
| South Korea | 70 |
| Netherlands | 70 |
| Japan | 53 |
| Germany | 52 |
| United Kingdom | 60 |
| United States | 33 |
| Canada | 17 |
| Sweden | 14 |

[1]Amount of wastepaper used in production divided by total amount of paper and paperboard produced.
SOURCE: *Pulp and Paper*, October 1993.

Because most of the paper reprocessing capacity is located in Europe and Asia and most of the world's producers of surplus wastepaper are northern industrial countries, there is substantial trade in wastepaper. Globally, 17 percent of recovered wastepaper was traded in 1992—up from 15 percent in 1990.[4] The United States and Germany together account for 65 percent of 1992 wastepaper exports, with the United States exporting three times as much as Germany. Other net exporters included Belgium, Switzerland, the United Kingdom, and Denmark.[5]

Most of these exports were bound for Asia. The region imported almost 6.5 million tons of wastepaper in 1992, compared with 5.1 million tons in 1990.[6] Taiwan was the world's largest net importer—taking in almost 2 million tons. South Korea was the second largest, followed by Mexico, Italy, China, and Indonesia.[7]

In the United States, consumers are putting pressure on the paper industry to use more post-consumer wastepaper in new paper products. This pressure is sometimes being followed up with legislation to bolster recycling.

In 1993, President Clinton issued an executive order requiring that all paper purchased by the federal government contain 20 percent post-consumer recycled content by the end of 1994, increasing to 30 percent by 1998.[8] Although the government purchases less than 3 percent of the printing and writing paper in the country, this order is likely to have a broader effect on the paper industry as other purchasers adopt the government's standards.[9]

In Europe, paper recycling efforts have been focused largely on newsprint, corrugated cardboard, kraft paper, and other low grades of paper.[10] Legislative mandates have been targeted at the packaging component of the waste stream, which uses large amounts of these paper products. Belgium has mandated an "eco-tax" on paper board used for food packaging, but the tax is waived if the board is made from recycled material.[11] Germany has mandated an industry-funded take-back system for packaging waste that has recycling quotas for paper, cardboard, and other packaging material.[12] The law targets collection, however, and not recycled content.

Canada is trying a truth-in-advertising approach of setting out labelling standards for "recycled" paper. It has a national eco-labelling program for printing and writing paper. To use its symbol, paper must contain 10 percent post-consumer recycled materials and 50 percent total recycled materials, although the program is set up to raise this standard over time.[13]

Much of the paper currently called "recycled" is not really what the public understands this term to mean. It is simply paper waste produced during production itself, which is re-routed from one step in the process to another. It often includes high levels of commercial wastes, such as paper scraps from cutting envelopes or from punching holes out of notebook paper.[14] Much of this "wastepaper" has always been reused, because it has been cost-effective to do so.[15] In a typical recycled paper stock made by a U.S. manufacturer for magazines, for example, the total recycled content is 50 percent—but the post-consumer content is only 10 percent.[16]

Labelling standards and initiatives that target post-consumer content may help to make this distinction clearer to buyers, pushing the market toward recycled paper with higher post-consumer content.[17]

Although no global breakdown is available, paper recycling rates vary greatly by the type of product produced. Newsprint, paperboard, corrugated cardboard, and tissue tend to have relatively high amounts of post-consumer content.[18]

High-grade printing and writing paper, however, lags far behind.[19] Until recently, industry has not had the technology to make recycled paper that is uniformly smooth, clean, and white. Also, industry was concerned that recycled fibers could not meet high quality standards because recycled fibers are shorter and weaker than virgin fibers.[20]

In the past two or three years, however, the technologies for making high-grade paper with recycled stock have improved greatly. New methods of deinking, designing (crisscrossing and layering the fibers for maximum strength), and pulping have improved quality to the

point where recycled grades are virtually indistinguishable from their virgin counterparts.[21]

In the United States, these technological changes are increasing industry's interest in "mixed office paper." In the past, the paper industry has only accepted high-grade, carefully sorted papers as stock for recycled writing paper. Some new mills, however, can make high-grade paper out of a much wider mix of office paper discards.[22] This should increase the post-consumer content of high-grade paper.

Although capital costs for high-grade paper recycling are decreasing, they still represent additional costs for mills that have already invested in making paper from virgin pulp. However, legislative efforts and consumer concern—particularly in industrial countries—are likely to speed the development of these technologies by placing a premium on recycled pulp.[23]

Given consistent growth rates in wastepaper utilization almost everywhere, wastepaper recycling is likely to continue on its upward path.

# Coral Reefs in Decline                    Peter Weber

Coral reefs, which form in shallow tropical waters and are one of the world's most biologically diverse ecosystems, are in a steady state of decline around the world. A study from the World Conservation Union and the U.N. Environment Programme in the mid-eighties found that people had damaged or destroyed significant amounts of reef off the coasts of 93 countries.[1]

An analysis done by Clive Wilkinson of the Australian Institute of Marine Science indicates that to date people have directly or indirectly caused the death of 5–10 percent of the world's living reefs.[2] If current rates of degradation continue, another 30 percent could be lost in the next 10–20 years, and an additional 30 percent are in danger of severe deterioration in 30–40 years.

In both assessments, only reefs in remote regions were found to be generally healthy. The causes of degradation vary, but coastal populations and heavy coastal development are factors shared by all.[3] (See Table 1.) Reefs usually suffer from a mix of declining water quality, direct destruction, and depletion. Topping a long list of abuses is sedimentation from logging, farming, mining, dredging, and other coastal activities. Sediments can smother corals and block out sunlight, which they need for photosynthesis. (Although corals are animals, not plants, they get a large portion of their food from microscopic algae that live in their translucent tissues.)[4]

Deforestation is the most common source of sediments, and mangrove clearing is the most important type of forest loss. Mangroves along coastlines trap soils that would otherwise wash into the coastal waters onto reefs. When trees are cleared, they can no longer play this protective role. In the watershed of Bacuit Bay in the Philippines, logging increased erosion into the bay by more than 200 times.[5] The sediment plume over the reefs blocked out precious sunlight and smothered corals in a blanket of soil. In 1985, the first year of logging there, 5 percent of the corals in the bay died.[6] Similar scenarios of deforestation are found in most regions where reefs are deteriorating.

Coastal development, which helps drive this deforestation, is itself a major cause of reef decline. Sewage, industrial pollution, and urban runoff lower coastal water quality and harm reefs. Over half the world now lives in coastal regions, and as human numbers continue to grow this proportion is expected to increase. Already, more than 70 percent of the people in Southeast Asia live near the coast.[7] In the Philippines and Indonesia, coastal populations are growing by 4 percent or more a year, compared with rates of 3 percent or less for the uplands.[8] Along Africa's east coast, Kenya, Tanzania, Mozambique, and Madagascar are experiencing annual population growth rates of 3–4 percent.[9] As populations continue to grow, both land clearing and development will likely increase.

Too many fishers chasing too few fish is a nearly ubiquitous problem that can lead to a self-reinforcing cycle of degradation. Reef fish are prone to overfishing because like many slow-growing, long-lived animals, they have low natural fertility. When depleted, they are slow to repopulate the reef. As incomes fall, fishers are forced to pursue other sources of income, some of which can destroy reefs.

Although it is almost universally illegal, blast fishing still occurs in 40 countries throughout the Pacific, Southeast Asia, the Indian Ocean, and, to a lesser extent, the Caribbean. An explosion near a reef kills or stuns fish for divers to gather.[10] Reefs are also mined for building materials. In Sri Lanka and India, entire sections of reef have been removed to produce cement.[11]

Corals themselves are gathered and sold as part of the international trade of reef products. Worldwide, some 1.5 million kilograms of coral are harvested annually.[12] The Philippines accounts for more than a third of this, with Malaysia, Indonesia, New Caledonia, and Fiji supplying another third. Although a portion is sold to tourists domestically, most is exported.[13]

Tourism is often cited as a motivation for countries to protect their reefs from these various forms of destruction, yet the boom in this industry is also contributing to the degradation of reefs in various areas. In some instances,

TABLE 1. STATUS OF CORAL REEFS IN THE MAJOR REGIONS OF THE WORLD

| REGION (with estimated percentage of global reef area) | STATUS |
| --- | --- |
| Southeast Asia (30 percent) | In the primary countries, including the Philippines and Indonesia, 60–70 percent of the reefs are in poor condition. Deforestation, fishing with dynamite and poisons, and coral mining are the most severe causes of reef degradation. Overharvesting of reef species and pollution from coastal development also harm reefs. More than 70 percent of the population lives in the coastal region. |
| Pacific Ocean (25 percent) | Has largest area of reefs in good condition due to low populations and intensive management—both traditional and modern. Stresses on reefs include fishing with explosives, overharvesting of reef species, coral predators, land-based and coral mining, and pollution from coastal development. |
| Indian Ocean (24 percent) | Has lost over 20 percent of reefs due to coral mining, fishing with explosives, and coastal pollution. Excepting Australia's west coast and isolated islands in mid-ocean, reefs are heavily exploited for fish and other reef species. Coastal erosion is increasing due to degraded reefs. Region has some of the highest coastal population densities in the world. |
| Caribbean (9 percent) | Pollution from coastal development and deforestation, the primary causes of reef degradation, is exacerbated by low water circulation in the sea. Region has world's highest density of ocean cruises and coastal tourism. Worst damage is off countries with higher rates of population growth and poverty, such as Haiti, the Dominican Republic, and Jamaica. |
| Atlantic Ocean (6 percent) | Coastal development and tourism damage reefs in the northern Atlantic. The notable exception is Bermuda, where reefs are in protected marine reserves and fishing is regulated. In the southern Atlantic, off the coast of Brazil, deforestation, coral mining, and tourism threaten reefs. |
| Middle East (6 percent) | Low rainfall, low populations, and low tourism have preserved many of the reefs, particularly in the Red Sea. Shipping, oil spills, and water pollution from coastal cities are the notable stresses. |

SOURCE: Worldwatch Institute, based on sources documented in endnote 3.

tourists and divers walk on the reef, killing coral polyps. Anchors from both small boats and cruise ships can be even more destructive.

Ultimately, coral reefs are very sensitive to human disruption, and their current decline serves as an indicator of unsustainable development practices both in the water and on land.

# Conserving the Other Rain Forest           Derek Denniston

Although efforts to save the world's tropical rain forests have rightly received widespread attention, another type of rain forest is perhaps even more threatened. Now estimated to cover less than half their original area, coastal temperate rain forests are an exceptionally productive and biologically diverse ecosystem. They include some of the oldest and most massive tree species in the world, and constitute some of the largest remaining pristine landscapes in the temperate zone.[1]

Forest ecologists have found that three physical features are common to all coastal temperate rain forests: proximity to the ocean, the presence of mountains, and, as a result of the atmospheric interaction between the two, high rainfall throughout the year.[2] Thus these forests are distinguished by complex interactions between terrestrial, freshwater, estuarine, and marine ecosystems—especially through the cycling of water.[3]

Coastal temperate rain forests once covered 30–40 million hectares, an area roughly the size of Germany, or less than 0.3 percent of the earth's land area.[4] Since temperate forests now encompass about 2 billion hectares, the coastal rain forest type has always been rare.[5] It existed originally on the western margins of North America, New Zealand, Tasmania, Chile, Argentina, the Black Sea coast of Turkey and Georgia, Norway, Scotland, Ireland, and Iceland.[6] (See Table 1.)

A preliminary study by Ecotrust and Conservation International estimates that at least 55 percent of the world's coastal temperate rain forest has been logged or cleared for other uses.[7] The remaining area now spans about 14 million hectares, smaller than the state of Wisconsin.[8]

North America harbors the largest contiguous zone of this type of forest, stretching about 3,000 kilometers from the Alaska Peninsula south through British Columbia and Washington state to Oregon's Siuslaw River. In the southern hemisphere, Chile holds the largest zone, extending from Arauco south into Magellanes province.[9] On Tasmania, broad-leaved temperate rain forest has provided refuge for some of the oldest flora in Australia.[10] New Zealand's South Island also hosts a sizable area. In Europe, more than 99 percent of this forest has been cleared or converted into managed forests.[11]

University of Montana forest ecologist Paul Alaback has used the type, amount, and annual distribution of precipitation as well as a critical maximum summer temperature to classify three temperate rain forest types: seasonal, perhumid, and subpolar.[12] He defines temperate rain forests as ecologically distinguished by year-round precipitation that keeps them wet, such that the plant organisms are

## TABLE 1. STATUS OF UNLOGGED AND PROTECTED COASTAL TEMPERATE RAIN FOREST

| REGION | UNLOGGED | PROTECTED[1] |
|---|---|---|
| | (percent) | |
| Alaska | 89 | 36 |
| Argentina | ? | ? |
| British Columbia | 43 | 5? |
| Chile | 40 | 7? |
| Europe[2] | < 1 | 0 |
| New Zealand | 28 | 28 |
| Oregon | 4 | 2 |
| Tasmania | 85 | 60 |
| Washington | 25 | 21 |
| Total | 45 | 17 |

[1]Figures for protected areas are inflated due to the inclusion of unforested, alpine areas.  [2]Includes Iceland, Norway, Ireland, Scotland, Georgia, and Turkey.
SOURCE: Erin Kellogg, ed., "Coastal Temperate Rain Forests: Ecological Characteristics, Status and Distribution Worldwide" (a working manuscript), Occasional Paper Series No. 1, Ecotrust/Conservation International, Portland, Ore., June 1992.

not adapted to drought and do not naturally burn. Together, the absence of drought, rareness of fire, and cool summers generally distinguish temperate rain forests from all other temperate forests.[13]

Because of the maritime climactic influence, overabundant precipitation falls virtually year-round—often in the form of fog, drizzle, and light rain. Thus temperate rain forests have little variation in temperature, adding to the fertile growing conditions. The heavy rainfall and low temperatures also combine to produce some of the highest runoff rates in the temperate zone, leading to rapid rock weathering and soil formation, as well as frequent landslides and other forms of erosion.[14] Complex riparian networks add to the structural diversity of the forest.[15] Together with frequent coastal winds, these processes make temperate rain forests one of the most dynamic and productive ecosystems on earth.

No other terrestrial ecosystem produces as much living matter (biomass) per unit of area—as much as 500–2,000 tons per hectare (compared with about 100 in tropical rain forests).[16] Not surprisingly, coastal temperate rain forests host some of the oldest, largest trees in the world—such as an ancient Sitka spruce more than 95 meters tall and 3 meters thick at its base in the Carmanah Valley on Vancouver Island in British Columbia.[17] Indices for the biological diversity of lichen and bryophytes (mosses and liverworts) in these forests may be comparable with those of tropical rain forests.[18] Providing a steady supply of dissolved nutrients, particulate organic matter, and large woody debris, these forests also help sustain some of the world's most productive shellfish beds and spawning grounds for commercially valued fish species.[19]

The global demand for the wood products of these forests has been the primary force driving their loss. Among the most valuable timber species are South America's alerce and monkey puzzle and North America's Sitka spruce, yellow cypress (cedar), and Douglas fir.[20] Temperate rain forests have evolved and adapted to small-scale disturbances like erosion, landslides, and windthrows (a few trees blown over at a time). But large clear-cuts—virtually the only logging method used in North America—dramatically impair the ecological integrity of these complex, ancient forests.[21]

In Washington and Oregon, temperate rain forests have been harvested for more than a century, leaving only one entire large watershed unlogged.[22] Since 1950, more than half of the most productive rain forest in Alaska's Tongass National Forest has been clear-cut.[23] In Chile and New Zealand, much of the drier hardwood forests have been converted to exotic pine plantations. In Chile, much of the remaining rain forest is increasingly threatened by Japanese and other multinational companies seeking trees for pulping.[24]

On Vancouver Island, logging companies have already removed two thirds of the original ancient groves; most of what remains is fragmented or clinging to steep slopes, where road building and logging cause erosion, landslides, damage to fish-bearing streams, and soil degradation.[25] In the largest civil disobedience action in Canadian history, more than 850 protestors have been arrested since the summer of 1993 trying to halt logging in Vancouver Island's Clayoquot Sound.[26] Clayoquot's 4,000 square kilometers of interconnected marine, estuarine, and terrestrial ecosystems support abundant fish, seabirds, marine mammals, migratory waterfowl, and more than 100,000 shorebirds—as well as large predators, such as bears, cougars, and Orca whales.[27]

Protecting what remains of the world's coastal temperate rain forests will give scientists time to better understand the close relationships between wildlife and forests at the landscape scale.[28] The prospect of global climate change further underlines the need for comparative data on ecosystem processes along analogous climactic gradients, especially at the high latitudes—where the most pronounced changes are expected to occur.[29]

The time is short to continue identifying threatened areas, launch local conservation projects, and perform long-term monitoring and research on local, regional, and global levels. With pressures mounting to harvest or clear the remaining temperate rain forest, conserving what survives has become imperative.

# Energy Productivities Vary Widely     David Malin Roodman

Energy productivity—the amount of goods produced for each ton of oil or the equivalent in another energy source—has been improving in parts of the world where it is low, including heavily industrialized nations, but falling where it is high, particularly in the developing world.[1] Within these broad trends, there is considerable variation among countries with similar levels of affluence, suggesting that large, cost-effective productivity gains are within the reach of effective policy. Since fossil fuel use needs to fall in order to reach sustainable levels even as economic output is expected to double in the next 25 years, increasing energy productivity will be a key to future environmental sustainability.[2]

Energy productivity usually falls in countries beginning to industrialize—such as the United States in the nineteenth century or developing countries today.[3] But after several decades, the trend reverses. In both phases, changing energy productivity indicates profound economic changes as well, although not necessarily more or less wasteful use of energy, so comparisons between different economies can mislead.

In the majority of nations today—developing ones, that is—energy productivity is falling because recorded energy use is rising even faster than gross domestic product (GDP). For example, energy use in Brazil grew 223 percent between 1970 and 1992 while economic output grew only 155 percent, resulting in an energy productivity decline of 21 percent, to $5,650 per ton of oil equivalent. Similarly, it fell 27 percent in India, to $4,690. And in Egypt, productivity declined 45 percent, to $3,080.[4] (See Figure 1.)

These declines may reflect the early growth of energy-intensive industries such as mining, and a concentration on building massive infrastructures such as roads.[5] An apparently rapid rise in energy use can also result from a shift away from energy sources that do not appear in national accounts (because they are often not bought and sold for money) toward ones that do: from fuelwood to coal for cooking, for example, from clotheslines to laundromats, or from bicycles to buses. Increasing personal uses of commercial energy, such as for home heating or driving, have a similar effect since they increase energy use while contributing little economic production. Finally, the declines in developing countries may also reflect true energy inefficiency. The buildings and transportation systems there are generally inefficient by world standards, often relying on outdated and poorly maintained equipment.[6]

In countries where industrialization began earliest, however, energy productivity is now

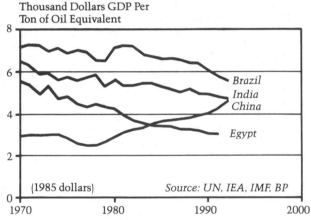

Thousand Dollars GDP Per Ton of Oil Equivalent

(1985 dollars)     Source: UN, IEA, IMF, BP

**Figure 1: Energy Productivity for Selected Developing Countries, 1970–92**

rising. In the United States, after remaining stable from 1950 to 1977 at about $1,750 per ton of oil equivalent, productivity began rising, reaching $2,400 in 1990.[7] West Germany's grew even more impressively, dipping nearly to the U.S. level in 1951, at $1,880, but climbing to $3,310 at the time of unification with East Germany in 1991.[8] Japan's climb has also been dramatic. After decades of the steady decline characteristic of industrializing economies, energy productivity in Japan began to rise sharply in 1975, so that by 1992 it had grown to $4,330 per ton of oil equivalent—almost

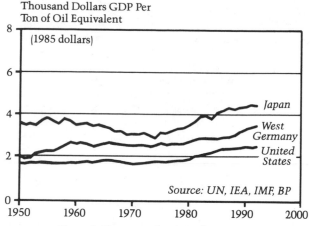

Thousand Dollars GDP Per Ton of Oil Equivalent

(1985 dollars)

Japan

West Germany

United States

Source: UN, IEA, IMF, BP

**Figure 2: Energy Productivity for Selected Industrial Countries, 1950–92**

double the level in the United States.[9] (See Figure 2.)

As with developing countries, several factors contribute to the trend in richer nations. The demand for energy-intensive goods such as refrigerators and cars has slowed. New economic growth has increasingly come from less energy-intensive activities such as education and health care, while energy-intensive industries such as steelmaking have shifted to developing countries.[10] And the commercialization of work traditionally done by women, such as house cleaning and child care, may not increase energy use, but it does increase measured GDP and thus energy productivity.

Nevertheless, the energy efficiency of everything from cars to light bulbs has improved substantially in industrial countries since the oil crises of the seventies. Technological improvements can explain about half the energy productivity increase in Japan between 1973 and 1988, and more than three quarters of it in the United States and West Germany, according to one study.[11]

The formerly communist countries of Europe break the patterns found elsewhere. While supporting material standards of living well below those of their more capitalist neighbors, they have used much more energy, resulting in energy productivity levels that are less than half those of other industrial countries. Central planners have seen energy more as a commodity whose production should be maximized than as a resource whose consumption should be minimized. Under such a system, building designers, factory operators, and consumers were largely insulated from the consequences of wastefulness. Energy productivity in this part of the world can be expected to rise substantially as it modernizes.[12]

Similarly, China has been far less efficient than comparable developing countries. In 1970, it extracted only $2,980 of GDP from each ton of oil equivalent of energy used.[13] The level languished there until the first market reforms of the late seventies, when it commenced a climb that continues today, having reached $4,590 in 1992.[14]

These trends raise two major environmental questions. The first is whether energy productivity in countries now home to three quarters of the world's people can avoid sinking as low as it did in industrial countries before it improved. If developing countries were to experience moderate economic growth while their energy productivities fell to the level West Germany registered in 1951, global energy use would double in 20 years.[15] This would accelerate the problems of global warming risks, acid rain, urban smog, and all the environmental side effects of damming rivers, pumping oil, and mining coal. However, it is just as plausible that they will follow a less energy-intensive path.

Equally relevant is the question of whether energy productivity in the most industrialized countries—which still account for more than half the world's energy use—will continue to rise. Since the collapse of world oil prices in 1986, energy productivity growth has tapered noticeably in both Japan and the United States, opening up the chance that it could stop rising altogether. This would make it practically impossible to reduce industrial-world carbon emissions anytime soon.

# Birds Are in Decline                    Howard Youth

Keeping an eye on birds is no longer just a flight of fancy. The world's 9,600 plus bird species are superlative indicators of environmental change. They occur in all regions, respond quickly to environmental change, and are among the easiest creatures to track and study. (Even the more elusive species tend to have loud calls.) Much like the canaries that coal miners carried into the mines to test for dangerous air, drops in the world's bird species flag environmental dangers that imperil us as well as them. Some 70 percent (about 6,600) of the world's bird species are declining, including 1,000 that are in imminent danger of extinction.[1] (See Table 1.)

Birds serve not only as beacons of change, however. They are themselves part of the vital life-support system that maintains the health of ecosystems. For example, owls, hawks, and eagles keep small rodent populations in check, while hummingbirds pollinate flowering shrubs, cacti, and trees. Some trees, such as those in the nutmeg family, rely upon hornbills and a few other large fruiteaters to disperse their seeds through droppings.[2]

Threats to birds are often multiple. Many species are simultaneously jeopardized by habitat destruction and overhunting, trapping, pesticides, oil spills, acid rain, or introduced birds or animals that outcompete or prey on them. A few species—the common pigeon, cattle egret, and common backyard birds, for instance—have prospered in disturbed habitats, giving the impression that birds are abundant. But most species are not. Satellite imagery reveals that expansive habitats are being carved into patchworks, leaving only fragments within which birds must struggle to survive.

The last large pockets of tropical forest—home to at least 3,500 bird species—are being whittled away even as new species are being discovered.[3] Temperate and boreal forests are disappearing, especially in the former Soviet Union, where once-protected areas are now vulnerable. On remaining grasslands in Pakistan, India, Spain, Portugal, and other countries, the disappearance of plentiful bustards and other birds is a swan song for wilderness, as is the decline of the ostrich-like rhea for the South American pampas.[4]

Wetlands—rich areas for bird breeding, resting, and feeding—have become rare commodities. In the United States, for example, only 53 percent of the country's wetlands remain, a fact reflected in the steady decline of waterfowl dependent on these areas: surveys reveal a 30-percent drop in the populations of 10 of North America's most common duck species, from 37 million in 1955 to 26 million in 1992.[5] Entire mosaics of ecosystems—woodland, wetland, grassland—are being submerged by massive dam projects such as those proceeding in northwest India and Quebec.

While habitat loss is one of the most visible threats, many birds are simultaneously suffering chemical contamination. DDT, though banned in the seventies in many western countries, remains a cheap and widely used

---

### TABLE 1. STATUS OF THE WORLD'S BIRD POPULATIONS[1]

| STATUS OF SPECIES | BIRD SPECIES (number) |
|---|---|
| Stable or Increasing | 3,000 |
| In Decline | 5,000 |
| Nearly Threatened with Extinction | 600 |
| Threatened with Extinction | 1,000 |
| Total | 9,600 |

[1]These numbers are only approximations, since classification and status of species are in constant flux. In addition, many areas remain poorly surveyed. These numbers are based on 1988 data currently being reanalyzed based on new developments in bird taxonomy; new analysis is expected to put the number of threatened species at around 1,300, while near-threatened species may rise to 1,000.

SOURCES: Worldwatch estimates based on Nigel Collar, BirdLife International, Cambridge, U.K., private communication, February 9, 1994.

pesticides in many developing nations.

Often chemicals are scrutinized only after thousands of birds die. Doses of fenitrothion that were used to battle locusts in Africa during 1986 and 1987 killed most birds the pesticide contacted.[6] And an agricultural pesticide called carbofuran, which was spread on fields in granulated form, is now being phased out by the U.S. Environmental Protection Agency after it killed tens of thousands of birds.[7]

Water, the staff of life for all species, today is often an agent of death to birds. Toxic residues from farms and factories often wash into wetlands. High levels of mercury (an industrial effluent) and selenium (a mineral that builds up to toxic levels in agricultural runoff) have been found in 150,000 dead grebes that washed up on shores of southern California's Salton Sea, a drainage area for three polluted rivers.[8] Oil spills—regular occurrences around the world—also have a major effect on bird populations; the Exxon Valdez oil spill alone killed about 300,000 birds.[9]

Scientists study habitats as far south as Argentina for clues in the decline of many familiar North American birds. At least half the neotropical migrants, the 250 species breeding in North America but wintering in points south, have declined significantly in recent years.[10] Habitat damage both north and south, as well as heavy pesticide use, are likely to blame. Today's populations of forest-living tropical migrants—which feed predominantly upon insects, including such pests as the spruce budworm, tent caterpillar, and gypsy moth—have probably dropped 75 percent since Europeans settled in North America.[11]

Compounding the varied dangers birds face is the problem of unrestricted hunting and trapping in many countries. In Malta, about 3 million transiting birds are shot each year for fun or food; about 700,000 "protected" birds are annually shot in Greece; and 50 million songbirds are served up as bite-sized delicacies in Italy alone each year.[12]

Bird species also succumb to the pressure wrought by animal agents introduced, unwittingly or not, by humans. For example, the brown tree snake, an escapee from cargo shipments from New Guinea or the Solomon Is-

lands, has devastated the endemic birds on the Pacific island of Guam and has recently been discovered at airports in Hawaii.[13] A study in Victoria, Australia, found that domestic cats there killed 14 million small animals a year, including members of 67 native bird species.[14] A similar study in Wisconsin found that the state's 1 million cats may nab hundreds of millions of birds and small animals each year, and British researchers pin 20 million bird deaths on house cats.[15]

Though many species of birds have benefited from nature reserves that have been set aside to protect their habitats, these areas constitute a mere 4.9 percent of the total land area, and enforcement of protection laws there is often lax.[16] A 1991 U.S. Fish and Wildlife Service study found activities harmful to wildlife—from military bombing and mining to logging—were occurring on 60 percent of the country's 470 refuges.[17]

Human-caused bird extinctions are not new, they are just increasing. Since the seventeenth century some 150 species and subspecies have been lost, including North America's passenger pigeon—one of the world's most abundant birds until deforestation and overhunting wiped it out by 1920.[18] Some of the more recent losses include the Atitlan grebe in Guatemala in 1987, Mexico's imperial woodpecker (last seen in 1958), and possibly the Bachman's warbler (last seen in 1981), which bred in southeast U.S. swamp forest and wintered in Cuba before virtually all the evergreen forest there was converted to sugarcane fields.[19]

The rate of extinctions is poised to accelerate, as encroachments into localized species' ranges continue. A BirdLife International study published in 1992 revealed that 20 percent of all bird species were confined to 2 percent of the earth's surface in 221 pockets of endemism, areas where large numbers of other endemic animals and plants also occur.[20] Two thirds of these areas fall in the tropics, and many remain unprotected.

Melodious songs and flashy colors are not all that is being lost as birds decline. The disappearance of bird species sounds an alarm that environmental life-support systems are faltering, and that our future is also at stake.

# Social
## Features

# Traffic Accidents Taking Many Lives     Hal Kane

In many countries that are free of war, the largest cause of violent death is traffic fatalities.[1] In the European Union, car accidents kill four times as many people as homicides do; in North America, the figure is more than twice as many.[2] In many Latin American countries, car accidents take several times as many lives.[3]

A veteran soldier might laugh if told that driving is dangerous. Yet car accidents took nearly as many American lives in 1993 alone as the Vietnam War did over a decade.[4] A survey of 100 countries that report such data found that about 350,000 people die every year after being struck by automobiles. Including the remaining 90 or so countries in such a survey might bring the total to nearly a half-million.[5]

In Portugal, with one of the highest traffic fatality rates (see Table 1), car accidents annually take twice as many lives as colon cancer, breast cancer, or prostate cancer. Almost 3 percent of all deaths in Portugal occur in car accidents.[6] Even in Japan, which has a relatively low traffic fatality rate, accidents on the road take more than twice as many lives as breast cancer and four times as many as prostate cancer.[7] In the United States, in the early nineties, they killed far more people than AIDS did.[8]

Moreover, young people have more car accidents than almost any other age group, so traffic mishaps take an especially high toll when measured in lost years of life. Diseases, by contrast, the largest killer worldwide, take a heavier toll on older people and so reduce life expectancy less. In most countries, industrial and developing alike, those aged 15–24 are the most prone to traffic accidents. The 25- to 34-year-olds are usually next. At almost all ages, men are much more prone to car accidents than women are.[9]

The magnitude of the menace posed by car accidents depends on two factors. The first is the amount of driving done in a society. The second is the safety of its cars and roads and the driving habits of its people (along with the medical care received by the injured). Those two factors interact to affect traffic fatality rates: in some wealthy countries with rela-

tively safe roads and cars, the mortality rate is high because many people drive every day. In many poor countries with hazardous, poorly maintained roads and cars, on the other hand, the number of lives lost remains small because few people drive. Examples of the latter include Congo, Albania, and Thailand.[10]

The most effective way to prevent these accidental deaths is to drive less. Unfortunately, in 1991 cars in what was then the European Community travelled more than twice as many kilometers as they did in 1970; those in North America travelled almost twice as

TABLE 1. THE TOLL IN HUMAN LIVES OF DRIVING, SELECTED COUNTRIES, CIRCA 1990

| COUNTRY | DEATHS (per 100,000 people a year) |
|---|---|
| Latvia | 34 |
| Estonia | 31 |
| Portugal | 29 |
| Saudi Arabia | 23 |
| Poland | 20 |
| United States | 17 |
| Mexico | 17 |
| France | 16 |
| Canada | 14 |
| Bulgaria | 13 |
| Australia | 12 |
| Japan | 12 |
| Thailand | 11 |
| Zambia | 10 |
| Brazil | 10 |
| Israel | 9 |
| Morocco | 8 |
| India | 7 |
| Sweden | 7 |
| Congo | 4 |

SOURCES: International Road Federation, *World Road Statistics 1987–91* (Washington, D.C.: 1992); WHO, *World Health Statistics 1992* (Geneva: 1993); data are for 1989, 1990, or 1991, depending on the country.

many; and vehicles in all industrial countries together covered 6.9 trillion kilometers in 1991 compared with 3.3 trillion in 1970.[11]

During the last few decades, many industrial countries and some developing ones have witnessed a trend toward dispersed communities characterized by subdivisions, high-rise office buildings, and shopping malls connected by highways. In such places, many people cannot go to the grocery store, to their workplaces, or to a friend's home without driving. Attempts to cut traffic fatality rates will be stifled by such land use patterns.

Public transport systems such as trains and subways can reduce traffic deaths. Their safety records are far better than those of cars. But their development is being discouraged by the sprawl of subdivisions, where no single fixed point would serve as a central station. Funding and public support for public transit have been lacking in many regions where fatalities could be avoided.

The second way to reduce deaths on the road is to design cars as well as roads for safer use. With mandatory seat belt laws and slower speed limits in the United States, for example, traffic fatality rates have dropped by a quarter since 1970.[12] Even though the number of miles driven rose sharply during that period, fewer than 40,000 Americans died from car accidents in 1992, compared with almost 55,000 in 1970.[13] Scandinavian countries are famous for their strict and successful laws designed to prevent drunken driving, and their mortality rates from driving are among the lowest in the world.[14]

By preventing car accidents, safety precautions for driving already may save more years of life than many medical procedures, including some cancer and heart disease treatments. If these safety restrictions receive support from the public, automakers, and politicians, they will continue to be among the most successful public health initiatives ever taken. Many emergency room doctors have underlined the fact that it is far more efficient to fight drunken driving than to try to put people back together once they arrive in the hospital.[15]

Many fatalities are caused by poor driving.

Even when they stay within the speed limit or the law, many people drive recklessly. Accidents stem from one of two factors: either the layout of roads and the number and placement of cars is such that accidents are unavoidable, or one or more people drive in ways that allow an accident to happen. Around growing urban areas, commuters spend hours every day behind the wheel; these frequent drivers often have difficulty thinking of themselves as handling a deadly weapon.

Traffic fatalities affect the way we live. Protecting children from traffic, for example, means limiting where they are allowed to play. Especially in cities where streets run close by front doors, the danger posed by cars sometimes means some children must stay inside, or wait to be taken to a park to play.

Injuries on the road that do not lead to death also drive up health care costs and reduce productivity. In the United States, 3.6 million people are hurt in cars every year—some 1.5 percent of the population, or one in 70.[16] In Belgium, more than 88,000 people were injured in 1990 by cars—almost 1 percent of the population.[17] And in Germany, almost a half-million people are hurt each year.[18] Most of those injuries are minor. But a number require months or years in a hospital and involve incapacitation.

Getting people to drive more carefully or to drive less will fight one of the most deadly public health epidemics of our time. Traffic fatalities can be reduced. It will require fighting drunk driving, increasing the use of seat belts, accepting speed limits, enhancing road quality, raising the use of public transport, and introducing many other technological improvements. And most of all, it will involve designing communities that are less dependent on cars.

# Life Expectancy Lengthens

Hal Kane

Now at 65 years, the average human life expectancy has increased by almost 20 years since mid-century.[1] (See Table 1.) No other period in history registered such an improvement. Life expectancy data are an indicator of more than just longer lives; they also signal improvements in sanitation, water supplies, health education, literacy, food security, the spread of basic nursing services, immunizations, and human rights.

One of the first and most basic changes that lengthens life expectancy is the supply of clean water. It was not until the middle of the nineteenth century in Europe that life expectancies first began to climb, and that often coincided with improvements in safe water supply. Lyon in France, for example, improved water and sanitation in 1844, and people started living longer. Less than a decade later, Paris followed suit; through continual extension of safe water supplies and sanitation, it witnessed extensions of life span. When Marseilles began its water improvements around 1885, life spans there too began to lengthen.[2]

That history is typical of many of today's industrial countries, which escaped low life expectancies during the middle and end of the last century. Up until the 1830s, for example, even in industrial countries people died on average by the age of 40. Yet for developing countries, life expectancy did not pass 40 years until the mid-forties of this century.[3] (And even in the nineties, more than half the Africans south of the Sahara, almost half of all Southeast Asians, 30 percent of South Asians, and nearly 20 percent of Latin Americans lacked safe water according to the U.N. Development Programme.)[4] Today, life expectancy is 63 in developing countries and 74 in industrial ones.[5]

A second, equally critical trend for longevity is the spread of immunizations. UNICEF reports that by late 1990 its world goal of having 80 percent of all children immunized had been reached. Some 3 million child deaths have been avoided annually as a result. For the Third World, widespread immunization is recent: less than 20 years ago, rates there were 10–20 percent.[6]

Other bases of longevity include adequate and balanced diets, such as the elimination of vitamin A and iodine deficiencies, and access to oral rehydration pills for sick children, who often die of dehydration otherwise.

Behind all the trends that raise life expectancy are education and political participation. Especially for women who take care of family needs and children, the ability to make decisions about household spending, nutrition, and health care is critical. Among women who become literate, the ability to care for their children rises dramatically, and survival of children along with it.[7] When it comes to nutrition, Harvard Professor Amartya Sen has observed that no democratic country with a relatively free press has ever suffered a major famine. For countries like India that must care for large numbers of people living in poverty, Sen argues that a free press and the ability of people to express their needs has helped derail tragedies.[8]

The results of investments in health can be seen in comparisons of average lifetimes between countries. Kerala, India, with a gross national product of less than $400 per person, enjoys average life spans of 73 years for women and 67.5 years for men—almost as high as in wealthier countries—largely as a result of a government and a community that put an unusually high value on public health.[9] Other poor countries have done as well. China, despite having to cope with the largest population in the world, targeted simple health services, nutrition, and sanitation; life expectancy there rose from 41 at the beginning of the fifties to 71 today—the vital statistics of an affluent industrial country.[10] Similarly, although Cuba has no great wealth and little economic success, people there live on average to the age of 76—as long as in the United States.[11]

In contrast to these records, some wealthier countries have done worse. Saudi Arabia's oil money helped boost its average income to $7,000 a person, but people there only live to an average age of 69—no older than the average Sri Lankan, who earns less than $500 per year.[12] Sri Lankans, it turns out, have social support services comparable to those of many

TABLE 1. LIFE EXPECTANCIES AT BIRTH IN THE 21 MOST
POPULOUS COUNTRIES, 1950 AND 1993

| COUNTRY | 1950 (years) | 1993 (years) | INCREASE (percent) |
|---|---|---|---|
| Slowly Growing Countries | | | |
| Russia[1] | 64 | 69 | 8 |
| United States | 69 | 75 | 9 |
| Japan | 64 | 79 | 23 |
| United Kingdom | 69 | 76 | 10 |
| Germany | 68 | 75 | 10 |
| Italy | 66 | 77 | 17 |
| France | 67 | 77 | 15 |
| Quickly Growing Countries | | | |
| Philippines | 48 | 64 | 33 |
| Nigeria | 37 | 53 | 43 |
| Ethiopia & Eritrea | 33 | 46 | 39 |
| Iran | 46 | 62 | 35 |
| Pakistan | 39 | 56 | 44 |
| Bangladesh | 37 | 53 | 43 |
| Egypt | 42 | 60 | 43 |
| Turkey | 44 | 66 | 50 |
| Indonesia | 38 | 59 | 55 |
| India | 39 | 59 | 51 |
| Brazil | 51 | 67 | 31 |
| China | 41 | 70 | 71 |
| World | 46 | 65 | 41 |
| Industrial Countries | 66 | 74 | 12 |
| Developing Countries | 41 | 63 | 54 |

[1]Soviet Union for 1950 number; recent reports from Russia put the 1993 figure
much lower.
SOURCES: United Nations, *World Population Prospects, The 1992 Revision* (New
York: 1993); Population Reference Bureau, *1993 World Population Data Sheet*
(Washington, D.C.: 1993).

tries. And after 40 years of age, survival rates fall faster in Harlem than in Bangladesh: while fewer than 40 percent of black men in Harlem survive to their sixty-fifth year, more than half the men in Bangladesh do.[14]

Today's Russia offers an alarming picture. Longevity there is thought to be declining sharply as the health care system collapses along with the economy and as pollution of air and water worsens. The Russian government reported a life expectancy of 66 years overall but of just 59 years for men.[15] This contrasts with the figure of 69 years overall previously used by the United Nations.

Due to a different set of health problems, countries like Thailand and Uganda may be following that same downward path of longevity. An estimated 1–1.5 million Ugandans are infected with HIV, and estimates of AIDS cases there range from 100,000 to 300,000, for example.[16] In Thailand, 2–4 million people may be infected with HIV by decade's end.[17]

Saudis. On the other hand, in Gabon, where oil money raised per capita incomes to more than six times those in Sri Lanka, the average life expectancy is 54 years and health services are lacking.[13]

There are also sharp differences in longevity among different groups in the same country. In the Harlem district of New York City, for example, the percentage of black men who live to see their fortieth birthday is the same as in Bangladesh, one of the world's poorest coun-

In industrial countries that already have high longevity levels, life can be lengthened even more through a shift in emphasis from curative to preventive medicine—heading off heart disease and cancer before they develop. And in developing countries, basic sanitation projects and improved nursing care and nutrition can continue to expand lifetimes.

# NOTES

## GRAIN HARVEST
## PLUMMETS (pages 26–27)

1. U.S. Department of Agriculture (USDA), *World Grain Situation and Outlook*, Washington, D.C., November 1993; USDA, "Production, Supply, and Demand View" (electronic database), Washington, D.C., November 1993.
2. USDA, *Situation and Outlook*, op. cit. note 1; USDA (electronic database), op. cit. note 1.
3. USDA, *Situation and Outlook*, op. cit. note 1.
4. Ibid.
5. USDA (electronic database), op. cit. note 1.
6. USDA, *Situation and Outlook*, op. cit. note 1; USDA (electronic database), op. cit. note 1.
7. USDA, *Situation and Outlook*, op. cit. note 1; USDA (electronic database), op. cit. note 1.
8. USDA, *Situation and Outlook*, op. cit. note 1; USDA (electronic database), op. cit. note 1; U.S. Bureau of the Census, "Midyear Population and Average Annual Growth Rates for the World: 1950–1995" (unpublished printout), Suitland, Md., March 25, 1993.
9. USDA, *Situation and Outlook*, op. cit. note 1; USDA (electronic database), op. cit. note 1.
10. Worldwatch calculation based on USDA, *Situation and Outlook*, op. cit. note 1; USDA (electronic database), op. cit. note 1.
11. Chicago Board of Trade, personal communication, November 5, 1993; "Worry About Rice Supplies Lifts Prices to 5 1/2 Year High," *New York Times*, October 29, 1993.

## SOYBEAN CROP DOWN (pages 28–29)

1. U.S. Department of Agriculture (USDA), "Production, Supply, and Demand View" (electronic database), Washington, D.C., November 1993.
2. Ibid.
3. USDA, *World Agricultural Production*, Washington, D.C., October 1993.
4. USDA, *World Oilseed Database* (unpublished printout) (Washington, D.C.: 1992); USDA, op. cit. note 1.
5. USDA, op. cit. note 1.
6. USDA, *Oil Crops Situation and Outlook Yearbook*, July 1993; USDA, op. cit. note 1.
7. USDA, op. cit. note 1.
8. Ibid.
9. USDA, *World Oilseed Situation and Outlook*, December 1993; USDA, op. cit. note 1.
10. USDA, op. cit. note 9; USDA, op. cit. note 1.
11. USDA, op. cit. note 9; USDA, op. cit. note 1.
12. USDA, op. cit. note 1.
13. USDA, *World Grain Database* (unpublished printout) (Washington, D.C.: 1992); USDA, op. cit. note 1.
14. USDA, op. cit. note 13; USDA, op. cit. note 1.

## MEAT PRODUCTION
## INCREASES SLIGHTLY (pages 30–31)

1. U.S. Department of Agriculture (USDA), "Production, Supply, and Demand View" (electronic database), Washington, D.C., November 1993.
2. USDA, *Dairy, Livestock, and Poultry: World Livestock Situation*, Washington, D.C., October 1993.
3. Ibid.
4. USDA, *World Agricultural Production*, Washington, D.C., August 1993; USDA, *Dairy, Livestock, and Poultry: World Poultry Situation*, Washington, D.C., January 1993.
5. USDA, *World Agricultural Production*, Washington, D.C., October 1993.
6. USDA, op. cit. note 2; USDA, August 1993, op. cit. note 4; USDA, January 1993, op. cit. note 4.

7. U.N. Food and Agriculture Organization (FAO), *1948–1985 World Crop and Livestock Statistics* (Rome: 1987); FAO, *FAO Production Yearbooks* (Rome: 1988–91); USDA, op. cit. note 2.
8. Conversion ratio for grain to beef based on Allen Baker, Feed Situation and Outlook staff, Economic Research Service (ERS), USDA, Washington, D.C., private communication, April 27, 1992; pork data from Leland Southard, Livestock and Poultry Situation and Outlook staff, ERS, USDA, Washington, D.C., private communication, April 27, 1992.
9. Feed-to-poultry conversion ratio derived from data in Robert V. Bishop et al., *The World Poultry Market—Government Intervention and Multilateral Policy Reform* (Washington, D.C.: USDA, 1990).
10. USDA, August 1993, op. cit. note 4; USDA, January 1993, op. cit. note 4.
11. USDA, op. cit. note 2.
12. Ibid.
13. Ibid.

## FISH CATCH STABLE (pages 32–33)

1. 1992 and 1993 data and revisions to 1983, 1986, and 1987 catches from Maurizio Perotti, fishery statistician, Fishery Information, Data and Statistics Service, Fisheries Department, U.N. Food and Agriculture Organization (FAO), Rome, private communication, December 20, 1993.
2. FAO, "Marine Fisheries and the Law of the Sea: A Decade of Change," Fisheries Circular No. 853, Rome, 1993.
3. Ibid., with Worldwatch estimate of growth rate.
4. Ibid.
5. Ibid.
6. FAO, *Yearbook of Fishery Statistics: Catches and Landings* (Rome: various years); 1992–1993 data from Perotti, op. cit. note 1; population data from U.S. Bureau of Census.
7. M. Nerens, Fish Utilization and Marketing Services, Fisheries Industries Division, FAO, Rome, private communication, November 11, 1993.
8. Lennox Hinds, "World Marine Fisheries," *Marine Policy*, September 1992.
9. Mark Clayton, "Hunt for Jobs Intensifies as Fishing Industry Implodes," *Christian Science Monitor*, August 25, 1993.
10. FAO, op. cit. note 2.
11. Ibid.
12. David Pilling, "Heeding the Call of the Deep," *Financial Times*, September 29, 1993.
13. Alison Maitland, "Hook, Line and Sinker," *Financial Times*, November 24, 1993.
14. First U.N. resolution against driftnets from "United Nations: General Assembly Resolution on *Large-Scale Pelagic Driftnet Fishing and Its Impact on Living Marine Resources of the World's Oceans and Seas* (passed December 22, 1989)," *International Legal Materials*, November 1990; 1990 and 1991 U.N. resolutions and moratorium from Mike Hagler, Greenpeace International, Devonport, Auckland, Australia, private communication, October 1, 1993.
15. Hagler, op. cit. note 14, and Gerald Leape, Greenpeace, Washington, D.C., private communication, October 13, 1993.

## AQUACULTURE OUTPUT UP (pages 34–35)

1. U.N. Food and Agriculture Organization (FAO), *Yearbook of Fishery Statistics: Catches and Landings 1991* (Rome: 1993); FAO, "Aquaculture Production 1985–1991," Fisheries Circular No. 815, Revision 5, Rome, 1993; FAO, "Aquaculture Production 1984–1990," Fisheries Circular No. 815, Revision 4, Rome, 1992.
2. FAO, "Aquaculture Production 1985–1991," op. cit. note 1.
3. Ibid.
4. Ibid.
5. Ibid.
6. Ibid.
7. Conversion ratio for grain to beef based on Allen Baker, Feed Situation and Outlook staff, Economic Research Service (ERS), U.S. Department of Agriculture (USDA), Washington, D.C., private communication, April 27, 1992.
8. Conversion ratio for grain to pork based on Leland Southard, Livestock and Poultry Situation and Outlook staff, ERS, USDA, Washington, D.C., private communication, April 27, 1992.
9. Conversion ratio for grain to poultry derived from data in Robert V. Bishop et al., *The World Poultry Market—Government Intervention and Multilateral Policy Reform* (Washington, D.C.: USDA, 1990); poultry data from Linda Bailey, Livestock and Poultry Situation staff, ERS, USDA, Washington, D.C., private communication, April 27, 1992, and from various issues of *Feedstuffs*.
10. Fish conversion from Ross Garnaut and Guonan Ma, *Grain In China* (Canberra: Commonwealth of Australia, East Asia Analytical Unit Department of Foreign Affairs and Trade, Australian Government Publishing Service, 1992).
11. Carole Sugarman, "Aquaculture & Drugs: Wondering How Much is Too Much," *Washington Post*, August 14, 1991; Tim Coone, "Salmon Farms Blamed for Parasite Problem," *Financial Times*, August 6,

1992; Stephanie Pain, "Pesticide Causes Cataracts in Salmon," *New Scientist*, August 26, 1989.

12. Omar Sattaur, "The Threat of the Well-bred Salmon," *New Scientist*, April 29, 1989.

13. "The Goo Factor: Salmon Farming," *The Economist*, August 10, 1991.

14. Tarlochan Singh, "Mangroves and Aquaculture—Striking a Balance," *Infofish International*, May 1987; Crispina A. Saclauso, "Brackishwater Aquaculture: Threat to the Environment?" *Naga, The ICLARM Quarterly*, International Center for Living Aquatic Resource Management, Philippines, July 1989.

15. FAO, *FAO Production Yearbook 1991* (Rome: 1993).

16. Worldwatch Institute calculation based on feed-to-fish conversion ratio of approximately 2 kilograms of feed to 1 kilogram of fish and on growth in aquaculture production of approximately 1 million tons a year.

## GRAIN STOCKS DROP (pages 36–37)

1. U.S. Department of Agriculture (USDA), *World Grain Situation and Outlook*, Washington, D.C., November 1993.

2. Ibid.

3. Ibid.

4. USDA, "Production, Supply, and Demand View," (electronic database), Washington, D.C., November 1993.

5. Ibid.

6. Ibid.

7. Chicago Board of Trade, personal communication, November 5, 1993; "Worry About Rice Supplies Lifts Prices to 5 1/2 Year High," *New York Times*, October 29, 1993.

8. USDA, op. cit. note 1.

9. Ibid.

10. USDA, *World Grain Situation and Outlook*, Washington, D.C., October 1993.

11. USDA, *World Grain Database* (unpublished printout) (Washington, D.C.: 1993).

12. K.F. Isherwood and K.G. Soh, "Short Term Prospects for World Agriculture and Fertilizer Use," 19th Enlarged Council Meeting, International Fertilizer Association, Paris, November 22, 1993.

## WORLD GRAIN YIELD DROPS (pages 40–41)

1. U.S. Department of Agriculture (USDA), "Production, Supply, and Demand View" (electronic database), Washington, D.C., November 1993.

2. Ibid.

3. USDA, *World Grain Database* (unpublished printout) (Washington, D.C.: 1992); USDA, op. cit. note 1.

4. USDA, op. cit. note 3; USDA, op. cit. note 1.

5. USDA, op. cit. note 3; USDA, op. cit. note 1.

6. From historical data in Lester R. Brown, *Man, Land, and Food* (Washington, D.C.: USDA, 1963); USDA, op. cit. note 1.

7. USDA, op. cit. note 1.

8. Ibid.

9. Ibid.

10. Ibid.; irrigated area figures from "Thirsty Fields: Asia's Rice Lands," *Asiaweek*, May 26, 1993.

11. U.N. Food and Agriculture Organization, *Fertilizer Yearbooks* (Rome: various years).

12. Worldwatch calculation based on ibid. and on K.F. Isherwood and K.G. Soh, "Short Term Prospects For World Agriculture and Fertilizer Use," 19th Enlarged Council Meeting, International Fertilizer Industry Association, Paris, November 22, 1993.

13. USDA, op. cit. note 1.

## FERTILIZER USE KEEPS DROPPING (pages 42–43)

1. K.F. Isherwood and K.G. Soh, "Short Term Prospects For World Agriculture and Fertilizer Use," 19th Enlarged Council Meeting, International Fertilizer Association, Paris, November 22, 1993.

2. U.N. Food and Agriculture Organization (FAO), *Fertilizer Yearbook* (Rome: various years).

3. Isherwood and Soh, op. cit. note 1; U.S. Bureau of the Census, "Midyear Population and Average Annual Growth Rates for the World: 1950–1995" (unpublished printout), Suitland, Md., March 25, 1993.

4. Isherwood and Soh, op. cit. note 1.

5. Ibid.

6. Ibid.; FAO, op. cit. note 2.

7. Isherwood and Soh, op. cit. note 1.

8. Ibid.; FAO, op. cit. note 2.

9. Isherwood and Soh, op. cit. note 1.

10. Ibid.

11. Ibid.

12. Ibid.

13. Ibid.

14. Ibid.

15. Ibid.

## IRRIGATION EXPANSION SLOWING (pages 44–45)

1. Sandra Postel, *Last Oasis: Facing Water Scarcity* (New York: W.W. Norton & Company, 1992).

2. U.N. Food and Agriculture Organization, *FAO Production Yearbook 1991* (Rome: 1991).

3. Sandra Postel, "Water and Agriculture," in Peter H. Gleick, ed., *Water in Crisis: A Guide to the World's Fresh Water Resources* (New York: Oxford University Press, 1993).
4. Daniel P. Beard, "Blueprint for Reform: The Commissioner's Plan for Reinventing Reclamation," Bureau of Reclamation, U.S. Department of Interior, Washington, D.C., November 1993.
5. Dina L. Umali, *Irrigation-Induced Salinity: A Growing Problem for Development and Environment* (Washington, D.C.: World Bank, 1993).
6. Ibid.
7. Shawki Barghouti and Guy Le Moigne, "Irrigation and the Environmental Challenge," *Finance & Development*, June 1991.
8. Postel, op. cit. note 1.
9. R.P.S. Malik and Paul Faeth, "Rice-Wheat Production in Northwest India," in Paul Faeth, ed., *Agricultural Policy and Sustainability: Case Studies from India, Chile, the Philippines, and the United States* (Washington, D.C.: World Resources Institute, 1993).
10. Patrick E. Tyler, "China Lacks Water to Meet its Mighty Thirst," *New York Times*, November 7, 1993.
11. "1992 Annual Transactions Review: Drought Stimulates Contractual Innovation," *Water Strategist* (Claremont, Calif.: Stratecon, Inc.), January 1993.
12. "Aftermath of Congressional Water War: Restructuring the CVP," *Water Strategist*, January 1993.
13. Robert Reinhold, "U.S. Proposes to Divert Fresh Water to Save Imperiled Delta in California," *New York Times*, December 16, 1993.
14. Postel, op. cit. note 1.

## OIL PRODUCTION FLAT (pages 48–49)

1. "Worldwide Production Falls as Market Plays its Wild Cards," *Oil & Gas Journal*, December 27, 1993.
2. British Petroleum, *BP Statistical Review of World Energy* (London: 1993).
3. Ibid.
4. Ibid.
5. U.S. Department of Energy, Energy Information Administration, *Monthly Energy Review December 1993* (Washington, D.C.: 1993).
6. Ibid.
7. Ibid. The figures used here exclude natural gas liquids from the calculation of oil import dependence.
8. *OGJ Newsletter*, December 13, 1993.
9. "Worldwide Production Falls," op. cit. note 1.
10. Worldwatch Institute estimates based on various sources.
11. Worldwatch Institute estimate based on Tom Boden,

Oak Ridge National Laboratory, Oak Ridge, Tenn., private communication and electronic database, July 28, 1992.
12. James MacKenzie, *Driving Forces* (Washington, D.C.: World Resources Institute, 1991).

## WIND POWER RISES (pages 50–51)

1. Estimates by Paul Gipe and Associates, Tehachapi, Calif., January 31, 1994.
2. Ibid.
3. Ibid.
4. Daniel Kaplan, "Wind Power Becalmed in Altamont Pass?" *The Energy Daily*, December 16, 1993.
5. Ros Davidson, "Environmentalists Say Stop," *Windpower Monthly*, October 1993.
6. "BRPU Competition Lowers Cost of Electricity," *Coalition Energy News*, Winter 1994.
7. American Wind Energy Association, private communication, February 25, 1994.
8. D.L. Elliott, L.L. Wendell, and G.L. Gower, *An Assessment of the Available Windy Land Area and Wind Energy Potential in the Contiguous United States* (Richland, Wash.: Pacific Northwest Laboratory, 1991).
9. Electric Power Research Institute (EPRI), *European Wind Technology* (Palo Alto, Calif.: 1993).
10. Gipe, op. cit. note 1.
11. EPRI, op. cit. note 9.
12. Ibid.
13. *Windpower Monthly*, various issues.
14. Susan Hock, Robert Thresher, and Tom Williams, "The Future of Utility-Scale Wind Power," in *Advances in Solar Energy: An Annual Review of Research and Development* (Boulder, Colo.: American Solar Energy Society, 1992).
15. EPRI, op. cit. note 9.
16. Hock, Thresher, and Williams, op. cit. note 14.
17. Harvey Sachs and Frank Muller, "Technology Policy and Wind Power in the U.S. Utility Sector," presented at Windpower 92 Conference, Seattle, Wash., October 19–21, 1992.

## NUCLEAR POWER CLIMBS (pages 52–53)

1. Installed nuclear capacity is defined as reactors connected to the grid as of December 31, 1993, and is based on Worldwatch Institute database compiled from Mycle Schneider and Assad Kondakji, WISE-Paris, private communication and electronic file, January 14, 1994, from Nuclear Engineering International, *The World Nuclear Industry Handbook* (London: 1994), from "World List of Nuclear Power Plants," *Nuclear News*, March 1994, from Interna-

tional Atomic Energy Agency, *Nuclear Power Reactors in the World* (Vienna: 1993), from Greenpeace International, WISE-Paris, and Worldwatch Institute, *The World Nuclear Industry Status Report: 1992* (London: 1992), and additional press clippings and private communications.

2. Worldwatch database, op. cit. note 1.
3. Ibid.
4. Ibid.
5. Ibid.
6. British Petroleum, *BP Statistical Review of World Energy* (London: 1993).
7. Worldwatch database, op. cit. note 1.
8. Lydia Popova, Socio-Ecological Union, Moscow, private communication and printout, February 4, 1994; "Chernobyl Plant to Remain Open, Two-Year-Old Ban on New Nuclear Units Lifted," *International Environment Reporter*, November 3, 1993.
9. Worldwatch database, op. cit. note 1.
10. Ibid.
11. Yurika Ayukawa, Citizens' Nuclear Information Center, Tokyo, private communication and printout, January 11, 1994; Gregg M. Taylor, "Taipower Resumes Project; Improves Operating Plants," *Nuclear News*, October 1992.
12. "Guangdong-1 Criticality; New Qinshan Construction," *Nuclear News*, September 1993.
13. Megan Ryan, "Snake Oil and Nuke Plants," *World Watch*, March/April 1994.
14. Worldwatch database, op. cit. note 1.
15. Ibid.
16. Ibid.; Barbara Martocci, Tennessee Valley Authority, Watts Bar, Tenn., private communication, January 12, 1994; U.S. Department of Energy, Energy Information Administration, *Commercial Nuclear Power* (Washington, D.C.: U.S. Government Printing Office, 1990).
17. Paul C. Parshley, Deborah F. Grosser, and Daria A. Roulett, "Should Investors Be Concerned About Rising Nuclear Plant Decommissioning Costs?" Electric Utilities Commentary, Shearson Lehman Brothers, New York, January 6, 1993; Mo Ying W. Seto et al., "Nuclear Power—A Current Risk Assessment," Moody's Special Comment, New York, April 1993.

## SOLAR CELL GROWTH
## SLOWS (pages 54–55)

1. Paul D. Maycock, "1993 World Module Shipments," *PV News*, February 1994.
2. Ibid.
3. Ibid.
4. Ibid.
5. Neville Williams, Solar Electric Light Fund, Wash-

ington, D.C., private communication, January 14, 1994.
6. Frank Muller and Harvey M. Sachs, Center for Global Change, "Renewable Energy and Pollution Prevention in Southern California," a report for the South Coast Air Quality Management District, January 1993.
7. Ted Kennedy, Meridian Corp., Alexandria, Va., private communication and printout, December 22, 1993.
8. "Bayenwerk Offers Shares," *Renewable Energy Report*, supplement to the *European Energy Report*, December 10, 1993; "European Conference Hopes New Charter Will Boost Photovoltaics Along Swiss Model," *European Energy Report*, October 30, 1992; Ronal W. Larson, Frank Vignola, and Ron West, "Economics of Solar Energy Technologies," American Solar Energy Society, Boulder, Colo., December 1992.
9. Koichi Yamanashi, executive managing director, New Energy Foundation, Tokyo, private communications, December 16, 1993, and February 17, 1994.
10. Ibid.; "MITI to Subsidize Home Photovoltaics," *The Quad Report*, Washington, D.C., November 1993.
11. "UPVG Directors Tentatively Approve $510M, Six-Year, 50-MWp Program," *The Solar Letter*, July 9, 1993.
12. Ibid.
13. Donald Osborn, Solar Program, Sacramento Municipal Utility District, Sacramento, Calif., private communication, February 22, 1994.
14. Paul Maycock, "Boomer's Corner," *PV News*, May 1993; "PV Efficiencies to Rise Sharply, Costs to Crumble by 2010: Maycock," *The Solar Letter*, July 23, 1993.

## NATURAL GAS PRODUCTION
## EXPANDS (pages 56–57)

1. 1973–91 figures from U.S. Department of Energy (DOE), Energy Information Agency (EIA), *Annual Energy Review 1992* (Washington, D.C.: U.S. Government Printing Office, 1993); 1950–1972 and 1992 figures are Worldwatch estimates based on ibid., on American Petroleum Institute (API), *Basic Petroleum Data Book* (Washington, D.C.: September 1993), and on United Nations, *World Energy Supplies 1950–1974* (New York: 1976); 1993 figure is a Worldwatch estimate based these sources, on Ray Thomas, Department of Natural Resources, Ottawa, Ont., Canada, private communication, February 23, 1994, on Matthew Sagers, PlanEcon, Inc., Washington, D.C., private communications, February 24, 1994, and on DOE, EIA, *Monthly Energy Review February 1994* (Washington, D.C.: 1994).

2. David Knott, "Natural Gas Demand Surges Among European Customers," *Oil & Gas Journal*, December 27, 1993.

3. British Petroleum (BP), *BP Statistical Review of World Energy* (London: 1993); "German Energy Use Drops But Decline Slows in East," *European Energy Report*, January 1994.

4. Worldwatch Institute based on various sources.

5. Government of Thailand, *Thailand National Report to the United Nations Conference on Environment and Development* (Bangkok: 1992); "A Spat Between Neighbours," *Asiaweek*, April 1, 1992.

6. Feng Liu et al., "An Overview of Energy Supply and Demand in China," Lawrence Berkeley Laboratory, Berkeley, Calif., May 1992.

7. Daniel A. Dreyfus, "The Pacific Rim and Global Natural Gas," *Energy Policy*, February 1993.

8. Ibid.

9. "LNG Versus an Asian Grid," *Energy Economist*, June 1992.

10. "Special Report: Gas Fired Powerplants," *Power Magazine*, February 1993.

11. James S. Cannon, *Paving the Way to Natural Gas Vehicles* (New York: Inform, 1993).

12. AGA Planning and Analysis Group, "Projected Natural Gas Demand from Vehicles under the Mobile Source Provisions of the Clean Air Act Amendments," Washington, D.C., January 30, 1991.

13. Alan Smith, Brooklyn Union Gas, Brooklyn, N.Y., private communication, December 7, 1993.

14. Worldwatch Institute estimates based on gas resource estimates cited here and on the expectation that the recent 3.5-percent annual growth rate in world gas production will continue.

## COAL USE DECLINES (pages 58–59)

1. United Nations, *World Energy Supplies* (New York: various years); United Nations, *Yearbook of World Energy Statistics* (New York: 1983); United Nations, *Energy Statistics Yearbook* (New York: various years); 1992 figure is a Worldwatch estimate, based on UN and on British Petroleum (BP), *BP Statistical Review of World Energy* (London: 1993); 1993 figure is a Worldwatch estimate based on UN, on BP, on U.S. Department of Energy (DOE), Energy Information Administration (EIA), *Monthly Energy Review February 1994* (Washington, D.C.: 1994), on Lisa Shapiro, Department of Natural Resources, Ottawa, Ont., Canada, private communication, February 22, 1994, on "German Energy Use Drops But Decline Slows in East," *European Energy Report*, January 1994, on Roberto C. Chiarotti, World Coal Institute, London, private communication and printout, February 22,

1994, on Matthew Sagers, PlanEcon, Inc., Washington, D.C., private communication, February 18, 1994, on J.F. Erasmus, Department of Mineral and Energy Affairs, Johannesburg, South Africa, private communication, February 25, 1994, and on "China Forecasts Slower Growth Rate For Coal Use in '94," *China Daily*, December 14, 1993.

2. BP, op. cit. note 1.

3. Former East Germany is included under former Eastern bloc in 1991 and 1992, and figures for it are Worldwatch estimates, based on United Nations, *Energy Statistics Yearbook*, op. cit. note 1, and on "German Energy Use Drops," op. cit. note 1.

4. United Nations, 1991 *Energy Statistics Yearbook*, op. cit. note 1; includes former East Germany.

5. Worldwatch estimates based on United Nations, *World Energy Supplies*, op. cit. note 1, on BP, op. cit. note 1, and on D.O. Hall, King's College London, private communication and printout, March 7, 1994.

6. DOE, EIA, *Annual Energy Review 1992* (Washington, D.C.: 1993).

7. BP, op. cit. note 1.

8. Jonathan E. Stinton, ed., *China Energy Databook* (Berkeley, Calif.: Lawrence Berkeley Laboratory, 1992).

9. Charles D. Masters, David H. Root, and Emil D. Attanasi, "World Resources of Crude Oil and Natural Gas," *Proceedings of the Thirteenth World Petroleum Congress* (Chichester, U.K: John Wiley & Sons, 1991); BP, op. cit. note 1.

10. M.J. Chadwick and M. Hutton, *Acid Depositions in Europe: Environmental Effects, Control Strategies, and Policy Options* (Stockholm: Stockholm Environment Institute, 1991).

11. Chris Neme, *Electric Utilities and Long-Range Transport of Mercury and Other Toxic Air Pollutants* (Washington, D.C.: Center for Clean Air Policy, 1991).

12. Satinath Sarangi and Carol Sherman, "Piparwar: White Industries' Black Hole," *The Ecologist*, March/April 1993; D.D. Dharmadhikari et al., "Impact of Coal Mining on Heavy Metals in Water," *Asian Environment*, Third Quarter 1992.

13. Gregg Marland, "Carbon Dioxide Emission Rates for Conventional and Synthetic Fuels," *Energy*, Vol. 8, No. 12, 1983.

14. Worldwatch Institute estimate based on Tom Boden, Oak Ridge National Laboratory, Oak Ridge, Tenn., private communication and electronic database, July 28, 1992.

15. I.M. Smith and K.V. Thambimuthu, "Greenhouse Gas Emissions and the Role of Coal," *World Energy Council Journal*, December 1992.

## COMPACT FLUORESCENTS FLOURISH (pages 60–61)

1. Evan Mills, Lawrence Berkeley Laboratory, Berkeley, Calif., private communication, February 3, 1993; 1993 from Nils Borg, National Board for Industrial and Technical Development, Stockholm, Sweden, private communication, March 14, 1994.
2. Worldwatch estimate, based on 1,000-megawatt generating capacity, 15-watt CFLs replacing 60-watt incandescents, and 15-percent decay in existing CFL stock per year.
3. Mills, op. cit. note 1.
4. Worldwatch, based on Mills, op. cit. note 1.
5. Michael Siminovitch, Lawrence Berkeley Laboratory, Berkeley, Calif., private communication, February 4, 1993.
6. Worldwatch estimates of net present value of the payback from replacing a 60-watt, 1,000-hour incandescent bulb with a 15-watt, 10,000-hour CFL, using a 5-percent annual rate of return on five-year savings and a price of 75¢ for incandescent bulbs. Electricity prices from International Energy Agency (IEA), *Energy Prices and Taxes, Third Quarter, 1992* (Paris: Organisation for Economic Co-operation and Development (OECD), 1992). The Japanese price (and thus the net savings) is taken in U.S. dollars, corrected for purchasing power parities.
7. "Shedding Light on the Compact Fluorescent," *EPRI Journal*, March 1993.
8. David Malin Roodman, "Power Brokers: Managing Demand for Electricity," *World Watch*, November/December 1993.
9. Linda Bromley, U.S. Department of Energy, Washington, D.C., private communication, December 13, 1993; Plexus Research, Inc. and Scientific Communications, Inc., *1992 Survey of Utility Demand-Side Management Programs*, Vol. 1 (Palo Alto, Calif.: Electric Power Research Institute, 1993).
10. Roodman, op. cit. note 8.
11. Warren C. Liebold and Lindsay Audin, "Compact Fluorescents, Radioisotopes and Solid Waste," *ACEEE 1992 Summer Study on Energy Efficiency in Buildings: Proceedings* [*Environment*: Vol. 9] (Washington, D.C.: American Council for an Energy-Efficient Economy, 1992). The solid and toxic waste impacts depend heavily on the mix of fuels that would have been used to generate the saved electricity, which will vary from region to region. The figures cited here assume the overall fuel mix of the United States.
12. Share of electricity generated from coal from IEA, *World Energy Outlook* (Paris: OECD, 1993).
13. Liebold and Audin, op. cit. note 11.
14. IEA, op. cit. note 12; Green Seal, "Proposed Environmental Standard for Compact Fluorescent Lamps," Washington, D.C., 1992.

## CFC PRODUCTION CONTINUES TO DROP (pages 64–65)

1. Mack McFarland, E.I. Du Pont de Nemours, Wilmington, Del., private communication, March 8, 1994.
2. U.N. Environment Programme, "Montreal Protocol on Substances that Deplete the Ozone Layer," Nairobi, 1987.
3. Joseph C. Farman et al., "Large Losses of Total Ozone in Antarctica Reveal Seasonal $CLO_x/NO_x$ Interaction," *Nature*, May 16, 1985.
4. William K. Stevens, "Peril to Ozone Hastens a Ban on Chemicals," *New York Times*, November 26, 1992; "Ministers Approve Stepped Up Timetable to Phase Out Ozone Depleting Substances," *International Environment Reporter*, January 13, 1993.
5. Figure 2 from Michael Prather and Mack McFarland, E.I. Du Pont de Nemours, Wilmington, Del., private communication, March 18, 1994. It uses measured data through 1991 and projections thereafter. The top curve assumes continued growth of 3 percent per year. The next assumes compliance with the original Montreal Protocol, with 3-percent growth of ozone-depleting substances not controlled by the agreement. The third assumes compliance with the London agreements, with HCFC phaseout by 2040. The bottom curve assumes global compliance with the Copenhagen agreements.
6. Regulation EC 3952, Brussels, December 1992.
7. U.N. Environment Programme, "Draft Report of the Fifth Meeting of the Parties to the Montreal Protocol on Substances that Deplete the Ozone Layer," Bangkok, November 17–19, 1993.
8. Ibid.
9. Ibid.
10. R. Monastersky, "Antarctic Ozone Level Reaches New Low," *Science News*, October 16, 1993.
11. Ibid.
12. Pamela S. Zurer, "Ozone Depletion's Recurring Surprises Challenge Atmospheric Scientists," *Chemical and Engineering News*, May 24, 1993.
13. Ibid.
14. Ibid.

## GLOBAL TEMPERATURE RISES SLIGHTLY (pages 66–67)

1. James Hansen and Sergej Lebedeff, "Global Trends of Measured Surface Air Temperature," *Journal of Geophysical Research*, Vol. 92, November 1987; Helene Wilson and James Hansen, NASA Goddard Institute for Space Studies and Columbia University, New York, private communication, February 18, 1994.
2. Wilson and Hansen, op. cit. note 1; "Global and Hemispheric Anomolies," in Thomas A. Boden, Robert J. Sepanski, and Frederick W. Stoss, eds., *Trends '91: A Compendium of Data on Global Change* (Oak Ridge, Tenn.: Oak Ridge National Laboratory, 1991).
3. P.D. Jones and T.M.L. Wigley, "Satellite Data Under Scrutiny," *Nature*, April 19, 1990.
4. Richard A. Kerr, "Pinatubo Global Cooling on Target," *Science*, January 29, 1993.
5. Wilson and Hansen, op. cit. note 1.
6. Ibid.
7. Ibid.
8. Ibid.; Kerr, op. cit. note 4.
9. Intergovernmental Panel on Climate Change (IPCC), *Climate Change 1992: The IPCC Supplementary Report* (Cambridge: Cambridge University Press, 1992).
10. Kerr, op. cit. note 4; IPCC, *Climate Change: The IPCC Scientific Assessment* (Cambridge: Cambridge University Press, 1990).
11. Charles D. Keeling and Timothy Whorf, Scripps Institution of Oceanography, La Jolla, Calif., private communications, February 26, 1993, and February 14, 1994.
12. Worldwatch estimate based on World Resources Institute, *World Resources 1992–93* (New York: Oxford University Press, 1993), on R.A. Houghton et al., "The Flux of Carbon from Terrestrial Ecosystems to the Atmosphere in 1980 Due to Changes in Land Use: Geographic Distribution of the Global Flux," *Tellus*, February/April 1987, on Gregg Marland et al., *Estimates of $CO_2$ Emissions from Fossil Fuel Burning and Cement Manufacturing, Based on the United Nations Energy Statistics and the U.S. Bureau of Mines Cement Manufacturing Data* (Oak Ridge, Tenn.: Oak Ridge National Laboratory, 1989), and on British Petroleum, *BP Statistical Review of World Energy* (London: 1993).
13. IPCC, op. cit. note 9.
14. IPCC, op. cit. note 10.

## CARBON EMISSIONS UNCHANGED (pages 68–69)

1. Carbon emissions figures are from C.D. Keeling, Scripps Institution of Oceanography, "Global Historical $CO_2$ Emissions," in Thomas A. Boden et al., *Trends '93* (Oak Ridge, Tenn.: Oak Ridge National Laboratory, in press); 1992 figures are Worldwatch estimates based on Keeling, on Gregg Marland et al., *Estimates of $CO_2$ Emissions from Fossil Fuel Burning and Cement Manufacturing, Based on the United Nations Energy Statistics and the U.S. Bureau of Mines Cement Manufacturing Data* (Oak Ridge, Tenn.: Oak Ridge National Laboratory, 1989), and on British Petroleum (BP), *BP Statistical Review of World Energy* (London: 1993); 1993 figure is a Worldwatch estimate based on BP, op. cit. in this note, on United Nations, *1991 Energy Statistics Yearbook* (New York: 1993), on U.S. Department of Energy, Energy Information Administration, *Monthly Energy Review February 1994* (Washington, D.C.: 1994), on Lisa Shapiro and Ray Thomas, Department of Natural Resources, Ottawa, Ont., Canada, private communications, February 22 and 23, 1994, on "German Energy Use Drops But Decline Slows in East," *European Energy Report*, January 1994, on Roberto C. Chiarotti, World Coal Institute, London, private communication and printout, February 22, 1994, on Matthew Sagers, PlanEcon, Inc., Washington, D.C., private communications, February 18 and 24, 1994, on J.F. Erasmus, Department of Mineral and Energy Affairs, Johannesburg, South Africa, private communication, February 25, 1994, on "China Forecasts Slower Growth Rate For Coal Use in '94," *China Daily*, December 14, 1993, and on "Worldwide Production Falls as Market Plays its Wild Cards," *Oil & Gas Journal*, December 27, 1993.
2. R.A. Houghton et al., "The Flux of Carbon from Terrestrial Ecosystems to the Atmosphere in 1980 Due to Changes in Land Use: Geographic Distribution of the Global Flux," *Tellus*, February/April 1987.
3. "Final Conference Statement: Scientific/Technical Sessions," Second World Climate Conference, Geneva, November 7, 1990.
4. Worldwatch estimate based on World Resources Institute, *World Resources 1992–93* (New York: Oxford University Press, 1993).
5. R.M. Rotty and G. Marland, "Carbon Dioxide Production from Fossil Fuels and Cement, 1860–1982" (electronic database), Oak Ridge National Laboratory, Oak Ridge, Tenn., 1984.
6. Lee Schipper and Stephen Meyers, *Energy Efficiency*

*and Human Activity: Past Trends, Future Prospects* (Cambridge: Cambridge University Press, 1992).

7. Keeling, op. cit. note 1; Worldwatch estimate based on ibid., on BP, op. cit. note 1, on Marland et al., op. cit. note 1, on Sagers, op. cit. note 1, and on "Worldwide Production Falls," op. cit. note 1.

8. Worldwatch estimates based on Keeling, op. cit. note 1, on BP, op. cit. note 1, and on Marland et al., op. cit. note 1.

9. Worldwatch estimates based on Keeling, op. cit. note 1, on BP, op. cit. note 1, and on Marland et al., op. cit. note 1.

10. International Energy Agency, *World Energy Outlook* (Paris: Organisation for Economic Co-operation and Development, 1993).

11. Worldwatch estimates based on Keeling, op. cit. note 1, on BP, op. cit. note 1, and on Marland et al., op. cit. note 1.

12. Boden et al., op. cit. note 1; Population Reference Bureau, *1993 World Population Data Sheet* (Washington, D.C.: 1993).

13. "World Status: The Climate Change Treaty," *Energy Economist*, June 1992.

14. David Malin Roodman, "Pioneering Greenhouse Policy," *World Watch*, July/August 1993.

15. Intergovernmental Panel on Climate Change, *Climate Change: The IPCC Scientific Assessment* (Cambridge: Cambridge University Press, 1990).

## WORLD ECONOMY EXPANDING (pages 72–73)

1. International Monetary Fund (IMF), *World Economic Outlook, October 1993* (Washington, D.C.: 1993).

2. Ibid.; U.S. Bureau of the Census, "Midyear Population and Average Annual Growth Rates for the World: 1950–1995" (unpublished printout), Suitland, Md., March 25, 1993.

3. IMF, op. cit. note 1.

4. Ibid.

5. Ibid.; Ferdinand Protzman, "Recession in Germany Appears to Bottom Out," *New York Times*, December 8, 1993.

6. IMF, op. cit. note 1.

7. Ibid.; Charles Wolf Jr., "How China Grew Overnight," *Wall Street Journal*, November 16, 1993; Michael Holman, "Africa: Enfeebled Giant Burdened by Debt," *Financial Times*, October 24, 1993.

8. IMF, op. cit. note 1.

9. Ibid.; Stephen Fidler, "Latin America: The Floodgates Have Opened," *Financial Times*, October 24, 1993.

10. IMF, op. cit. note 1; Patrick E. Tyler, "Chinese End Austerity Drive In Favor of Yet More Growth," *New York Times*, November 23, 1993.

11. IMF, op. cit. note 1.

12. Ibid.; Stefan Wagstyl, "India: Infrastructure Tops Agenda," *Financial Times*, October 24, 1993.

13. IMF, op. cit. note 1.

14. Ibid.

15. Ibid.

16. Ibid.

17. Ibid.

18. Ibid.

19. Ibid.

## THIRD WORLD DEBT STILL RISING (pages 74–75)

1. Worldwatch calculation, based on International Monetary Fund (IMF), *World Economic Outlook,* October 1993, and on World Bank, private communication and unpublished printout from the database of the *World Debt Tables 1993–94* (Washington, D.C.: World Bank, 1994), February 2, 1994.

2. Ibid.; Ruth Leger Sivard, *World Military and Social Expenditures 1991* (Washington, D.C.: World Priorities, 1991).

3. World Bank, op. cit. note 1; Third World gross domestic product figures from World Bank, unpublished printout, August 24, 1992; Third World growth for 1993 from IMF, op. cit. note 1.

4. IMF, op. cit. note 1.

5. World Bank, op. cit. note 1.

6. IMF, op. cit. note 1.

7. Raundi Halvorson-Quevedo and Isabelle Joumard, "Is the Debt Crisis Coming to an End?" *OECD Observer*, October/November 1993.

8. Ibid.

9. Ibid.

10. Ibid.

11. Worldwatch calculation, op. cit. note 1.

12. UNICEF, *Adjustment with a Human Face: Protecting the Vulnerable and Promoting Growth* (Oxford: Clarendon Press, 1987); Wilfrido Cruz and Robert Repetto, *The Environmental Effects of Stabilization and Structural Adjustment Programs: The Philippines Case* (Washington, D.C.: World Resources Institute, 1992).

## TRADE CONTINUES TO CLIMB (pages 76–77)

1. Trade data and Table 1 based on International Monetary Fund (IMF), *International Financial Statistics Yearbook*, various years; current dollars were cal-

culated using the IMF's export unit value index; 1993 estimate generated using IMF, *World Economic Outlook*, October 1993.

2. Worldwatch estimate based on IMF, *International Financial Statistics Yearbook* (Washington, D.C.: 1993), and on IMF, *World Economic Outlook*, op. cit. note 1.

3. General Agreement on Tariffs and Trade (GATT) Secretariat, ''GATT: What It Is, What It Does,'' Geneva, 1991.

4. Estimate cited in Organisation for Economic Co-operation and Development, *Assessing the Effects of the Uruguay Round* (Paris: 1993).

5. Craig Dunlap, ''Clinton Signs the Nafta Into Law; Eyes Turn Toward GATT, Caribbean,'' *Journal of Commerce,* December 9, 1993.

6. ''Southeast Asia Joins the Bloc Party: Six Nations Figure Best Trade Defense is a Zone of Their Own,'' *Washington Post*, November 10, 1992; Steven Holmes, ''Pacific Nations Willing to Cut Tariffs,'' *New York Times*, November 20, 1993.

7. Figure 2 based on IMF, op. cit. note 2, using the export unit value index as the deflator series.

8. GATT, *International Trade 91–92* (Geneva: 1993).

9. Ibid.

10. United Nations Development Programme, *Human Development Report 1991* (New York: Oxford University Press, 1991).

11. Hilary F. French, *Costly Trade-Offs: Reconciling Trade and the Environment*, Worldwatch Paper 113 (Washington, D.C.: Worldwatch Institute, March 1993).

12. Governments of Canada, the United Mexican States, and the United States of America, ''North American Agreement on Environmental Cooperation,'' final draft, September 13, 1993.

13. Barbara Verhoeve, Graham Bennett, and David Wilkinson, Institute for European Environmental Policy, ''Maastricht and the Environment,'' Arnhem and London, August 1992.

14. Frances Williams, ''GATT Support on Environmental Links,'' *Financial Times*, January 27, 1994.

## GLOBAL PAPER PRODUCTION KEEPS GROWING (pages 78–79)

1. 1993 data from *Pulp and Paper* (Pulp and Paper International, Miller Freeman Inc., Brussels), January 1994; 1950–92 from U.N. Food and Agriculture Organization (FAO), *Forest Products Yearbook 1950* through *1991* (Rome: 1952–93).

2. FAO, *Yearbooks*, op. cit. note 1.

3. FAO, *FAO Forest Products Yearbook 1991* (Rome: 1993).

4. Alan Thein Durning, *Saving The Forests: What Will It*

*Take?* Worldwatch Paper 117 (Washington, D.C.: Worldwatch Institute, December 1993).

5. Ed Ayres, ''Literacy Gaining Slowly,'' in Lester R. Brown, Hal Kane, and Ed Ayres, *Vital Signs 1993* (New York: W.W. Norton & Company, 1993).

6. Durning, op. cit. note 4.

7. Ed Ayres, ''Whitewash: Pursuing the Truth About Paper,'' *World Watch*, September/October 1992.

8. Bill Richardson, ''Why Clinton Should Take Chlorine Out of Paper 'Pool','' *Christian Science Monitor*, October 4, 1993.

9. Christopher Brown-Humes, ''Run-of-the-Mill Debates,'' *Financial Times*, October 20, 1993.

10. Ibid.

11. Mary Ceser, Senior Consultant, Jaakko Pöyry Consulting Inc., Tarrytown, N.Y., private communication, February 18, 1994.

12. *Pulp and Paper* (Pulp and Paper International, Miller Freeman Inc., Brussels), October 1993.

13. Ed Ayres, ''Making Paper Without Trees,'' *World Watch*, September/October 1993.

14. Ibid.

15. Ed Ayres, ''Paper Production Continues Growth,'' in Lester R. Brown, Hal Kane, and Ed Ayres, *Vital Signs 1993* (New York: W.W. Norton & Company, 1993).

16. Bernard Simon, ''Newsprint Set to Crumble as Demand Falls,'' *Financial Times*, December 1, 1993.

## ROUNDWOOD PRODUCTION UNABATED (pages 80–81)

1. Philip Wardle, U.N. Food and Agriculture Organization (FAO), Rome, private communication, February 17, 1994.

2. 1950–60 from FAO, *Forest Products Yearbook, 1950* through *1960* (Rome: 1952–62); 1961–91 from FAO, AGROSTAT-PC 1993 (electronic database), Rome, 1993.

3. FAO, *Yearbooks*, op. cit. note 2; FAO (electronic database), op. cit. note 2.

4. Wardle, op. cit. note 1.

5. Nancy Chege, ''Not-Yet-Fossil Fuel,'' *World Watch*, September/October 1993.

6. Ibid.

7. FAO, *Yearbooks*, op. cit. note 2; FAO (electronic database), op. cit. note 2.

8. Willem Floor and Robert van der Plas, *$CO_2$ Emissions by the Residential Sector: Environmental Implications of Inter-fuel Substitution*, Industry and Energy Department Working Paper 51 (Washington, D.C: World Bank, 1992).

9. FAO, *Yearbooks*, op. cit. note 2; FAO (electronic database), op. cit. note 2.

10. FAO, *Yearbooks*, op. cit. note 2; FAO (electronic database), op. cit. note 2.
11. FAO, *Yearbooks*, op. cit. note 2; FAO (electronic database), op. cit. note 2.
12. FAO, *Yearbooks*, op. cit. note 2; FAO (electronic database), op. cit. note 2.
13. Sandra Postel and John C. Ryan, "Reforming Forestry," in Lester Brown et al. *State of the World 1991* (New York: W.W. Norton & Company, 1991).
14. Ibid.
15. John Young, *Global Network: Computers in a Sustainable Society*, Worldwatch Paper 115 (Washington, D.C: Worldwatch Institute, September 1993).
16. John Zarocostas, "Timber Trade In Asia Guilty of Destruction, Report Says," *Journal of Commerce*, January 20, 1994.
17. Claude Martin, *The Rainforests of West Africa* (Basel, Switzerland: Birkhäuser Verlag, 1991).

## GOLD PRODUCTION AT RECORD HIGH (pages 82–83)

1. Gold production from U.S. Bureau of Mines (BOM), *Mineral Commodity Summaries 1994* (Washington, D.C.: U.S. Government Printing Office, 1994).
2. Gold mining waste is a Worldwatch Institute estimate, based on global average ore grade estimate in Donald G. Rogich, "Trends in Material Use: Implications for Sustainable Development," Division of Mineral Commodities, BOM, Washington, D.C., unpublished, April 1992; 690 million tons of gold mining waste would make 3.2 million loads for the huge (218-ton payload, 13 meters long) dump trucks often used at large mines; the line of trucks would stretch for nearly 41,000 kilometers, slightly more than the circumference of the earth; truck size and capacity from Pete Holman, Caterpillar, Peoria, Ill., private communication, March 1993.
3. John E. Young, "For the Love of Gold," *World Watch*, May/June 1993.
4. Real price of gold calculated using price figures from International Monetary Fund (IMF), *International Financial Statistics* (Washington, D.C.), various issues, and price deflators from U.S. Department of Commerce, *Survey of Current Business* (Washington, D.C.), various issues; gold production from John Lucas, BOM, Washington, D.C., private communication, February 8, 1994, and BOM, op. cit. note 1.
5. Lucas, op. cit. note 4; BOM, op. cit. note 1.
6. Lucas, op. cit. note 4; BOM, op. cit. note 1.
7. "Guyana's Gold Diggers Dredge Up Trouble," *New Scientist*, November 10, 1990; Marc J. Dourojeanni and Maria Tereza Jorge Padua, "Gold Rush and Environment in the Brazilian Amazon," Inter-American Development Bank, Washington, D.C., unpublished, undated; Alexander Gurov, "Gold Rush in Kalimantan," *Asia and Africa Today*, No. 2, 1990; Paul Jourdan, Institute of Mining Research, Harare, Zimbabwe, private communication, April 12, 1991; Melvyn Westlake and Robin Stainer, "Rising Gold Fever," *South*, March 1989; "Gold Rush Ruin for Grasslands," *China Daily*, July 13, 1989.
8. Lucas, op. cit. note 4; BOM, op. cit. note 1.
9. James Coates, "Cyanide Propels Latest Nevada Gold Rush," *Journal of Commerce*, February 7, 1992.
10. BOM, *Minerals Yearbook* (Washington, D.C.: U.S. Government Printing Office, various years).
11. George Laycock, "Going for the Gold," *Audubon*, July 1989; Kenneth Gooding, "Miners Dig Deep to Give Birds a Safer Passage," *Financial Times*, December 15, 1990; Coates, op. cit. note 9; U.S. Congress, Office of Technology Assessment (OTA), *Background Paper: Managing Industrial Solid Wastes From Manufacturing, Mining, Oil and Gas Production, and Utility Coal Combustion* (Washington, D.C.: 1992).
12. Dourojeanni and Padua, op. cit. note 7; David Cleary, *Anatomy of the Amazon Gold Rush* (Iowa City: University of Iowa Press, 1990); Olaf Malm et al., "Mercury Pollution Due to Gold Mining in the Madeira River Basin, Brazil," *Ambio*, February 1990; Jerome A. Nriagu et al., "Mercury Pollution in Brazil," *Nature*, April 2, 1992; Christine Lamb, "Quicksilver Flows in the Jungle," *Financial Times*, October 9, 1991.
13. Goldfields Mineral Services, *Gold 1993* (London: 1993).
14. Ibid.
15. Ibid.
16. BOM, op. cit. note 1.
17. Ibid.

## BICYCLE PRODUCTION RISES AGAIN (pages 86–87)

1. Bicycle figure is author's estimate, based on *Interbike Directory 1994* (Newport Beach, Calif.: Primedia, Inc., 1994; automobile figure from American Automobile Manufacturers Association, *AAMA Motor Vehicle Facts & Figures '93* (Detroit, Mich.: 1993).
2. "Ways to Turn the Wheels of the Bicycle Industry," *China Daily*, March 14, 1990.
3. Guangzhou's intentions from Peter Lim, "Chinese City to Ban Bikes," *The Mercury* (Hobart, Tasmania), April 8, 1993; Shanghai from Bronwen Maddox, "It Will Get Worse," *Financial Times*, November 18, 1993.

4. Susan V. Lawrence, "Imagine L.A. Banning the Automobile," *U.S. News & World Report*, September 27, 1993.
5. For an extensive overview, see Michael Replogle, *Non-Motorized Vehicles in Asian Cities*, World Bank Technical Paper Number 162 (Washington, D.C.: 1992).
6. Information on bicycling to rail stations is from Michael Replogle and Harriet Parcells, "Linking Bicycle/Pedestrian Facilities with Transit," report prepared for the U.S. Federal Highway Administration, Washington, D.C., September 1992.
7. Ibid.
8. Ibid.
9. Current number of U.S. bicycle commuters from 1992 Harris Poll cited in J.C. McCullagh, "The 50 State Solution," *Bicycling*, June 1992; tripling is a Worldwatch estimate based on Bicycle Institute of America (BIA), *Bicycling Reference Book 1993–1994 Edition* (Washington, D.C.: 1993).
10. BIA, op. cit. note 9.
11. U.S. Department of Transportation, "Bicycle and Pedestrian Provisions Under the Intermodal Surface Transportation Efficiency Act (ISTEA) of 1991," Federal Highway Administration, Washington, D.C., 1992. See also Andy Clarke, "A Bicyclist's Guide to ISTEA," in *Bicycling Reference Book 1993–1994 Edition* (Washington, D.C.: BIA, 1993).
12. Manuel Alepuz, "Bicycles Overtake Bus Travel in Havana," *The Urban Age*, Fall 1993.
13. Lima from ibid.; Rio from "César Maia Quer Trazer da China Bicicletas e Expandir Ciclovias," *Cidade* (Rio de Janeiro), January 11, 1993.

## AUTO PRODUCTION
## FALLS (pages 88–89)

1. Production in 1950–90 from Motor Vehicle Manufacturers Association (MVMA), *Facts & Figures '92* and *World Motor Vehicle Data*, 1991 ed. (Detroit, Mich.: 1991); 1991 production from Kevin Done, "World Car Industry: The Engine Overheats," *Financial Times*, October 10, 1992; 1992 production from Kevin Done, "West European Car Sales To Slide," *Financial Times*, August 23, 1993; production for 1993 in United States, Japan, Europe, and the world from *Automotive News*, various issues, January and February 1994 (preliminary estimates).
2. Population growth from United Nations, *World Population Prospects, 1992 Revision* (New York: 1993).
3. "Auto Sales Off in Europe," *New York Times*, January 12, 1994.
4. Krystal Miller and Jacqueline Mitchell, "After Years

of Growth in U.S. Car Market, Japanese Surge is Over," *Wall Street Journal*, March 4, 1993.
5. P.T. Bangsberg, "China Expects to See 15% Growth This Year In Motor Vehicle Output," *Journal of Commerce*, January 20, 1994; "India Carmakers Expect to Break Production Record This Fiscal Year," *Journal of Commerce*, December 30, 1993; Brazilian Car Output Returns to Fast Lane," *Journal of Commerce*, June 4, 1993.
6. Ed Ayres, "Breaking Away," *World Watch*, January/February 1993.
7. "Start Your Engines: Continent of a Billion Cars," *Asiaweek*, February 24, 1993.
8. Ibid.; "More Want Cars Instead of Motorbikes in Guangdong," *China Daily*, July 24, 1993.
9. Decline of per capita food is from Lester R. Brown, "Facing Food Insecurity," in Lester R. Brown et al., *State of the World 1994* (New York: W.W. Norton & Company, 1994); land required for highways is from Ayres, op. cit. note 6.
10. James J. MaKenzie, Roger C. Dower, and Donald D.T. Chen, *The Going Rate: What It Really Costs to Drive* (Washington, D.C.: World Resources Institute, 1992).
11. Ibid.
12. Optimism of U.S. industry from *Automotive News*, December 1993, quoted in "Detroit's Output to Pass Japan's, Magazine Says," *Journal of Commerce*, December 21, 1993; adoption of lean production from Wilton Woods, "The World's Top Automakers Change Lanes," *Fortune*, October 4, 1993.

## RESISTANCE TO PESTICIDES
## GROWING (pages 92–93)

1. Jodie S. Holt and George P. Georghiou, University of California at Riverside, private communication, March 9, 1992, with an update on insects from Mark E. Whalon, Department of Entomology, Michigan State University, Ann Arbor, private communication, February 14, 1994. Resistance data is collected on an ad hoc basis by interested researchers; new weed resistance data is expected to be available by the end of 1994.
2. James R. Cate and Maureen Kuwano Hinkle, *Integrated Pest Management: The Path of a Paradigm* (Washington, D.C.: National Audubon Society, 1993).
3. Insect losses and most destructive pests from David Pimentel et al., "Environmental and Economic Impacts of Reducing U.S. Agricultural Pesticide Use" in David Pimentel, ed., *CRC Handbook of Pest Management in Agriculture* (Boca Raton, Fla.: CRC Press,

1991), and from David Pimentel, private communications, March 6, 1992, and January 13, 1994.

4. Whalon, op. cit. note 1.

5. Cate and Hinkle, op. cit. note 2.

6. Anna Maria Gillis, "The Magnificent Devastator Gets Around," *BioScience*, June 1993; "World Potato Supply Threatened by Disease Outbreak: More Chemical Spraying Likely," news release, International Potato Center, Lima, Peru, October 21, 1993.

7. Arnold L. Aspelin, Arthur H. Grube, and Robert Torla, *Pesticide Industry Sales and Usage* (Washington, D.C.: Office of Pesticide Programs, Environmental Protection Agency, 1992).

8. Fred Gould, "The Evolutionary Potential of Crop Pests," *American Scientist*, November-December 1991.

9. Carol Mallory-Smith of the Department of Plant, Soil, and Entomological Sciences at the University of Idaho is heading up the study of the Herbicide Resistant Weeds Committee for the Weed Science Society of America.

10. Jeffrey L. Fox, "Insect Resistance to Bt Delta-Endotoxin," synopsis of Bt Resistance Workshop, sponsored by the National Audubon Society, October 21, 1991; Ann Gibbons, "Moths Take the Field Against Biopesticide," *Science*, November 1, 1991.

11. Nancy Long, "Pesticide Management Techniques Help Indonesian Farmers," *Front Lines*, December 1991. Recent studies indicate that some farmers may be circumventing the government ban.

## SULFUR AND NITROGEN EMISSIONS RESUME RISE (pages 94–95)

1. Dr. J. Dignon, Lawrence Livermore National Laboratory, Livermore, Calif., unpublished data series, private communication, February 23, 1994.

2. Ibid.

3. "The Price of Pollution," *Options* (International Institute for Applied Systems Analysis), September 1990.

4. World Health Organization and U.N. Environment Programme, *Assessment of Urban Air Quality* (Nairobi: Global Environment Monitoring System, 1988).

5. Thomas Crocker of the University of Wyoming, as described in James S. Cannon, *The Health Costs of Air Pollution* (New York: American Lung Association, 1985).

6. David Lascelles, "The High Cost of Cleaning Up," *Financial Times*, May 26, 1993.

7. "Energy and the Environment," *The Economist*, August 31, 1991.

8. "Nitrogen Oxide Levels Reaches Second Worst Level," (Tokyo) *Kyodo*, December 18, 1990, as reprinted in *JPRS Report: Environmental Issues*, January 29, 1991.

9. "Energy and the Environment," op. cit. note 7.

10. Sultan Hameed and Jane Dignon, "Global Emissions of Nitrogen and Sulfur Oxides in Fossil Fuel Combustion 1970–1986," *Journal of the Air & Waste Management Association*, February 1991.

11. Ibid.

12. Ibid.

13. Ibid.

14. Ibid.

15. Ibid.

16. Ibid.

## POPULATION INCREASE DROPS SLIGHTLY (pages 98–99)

1. U.S. Bureau of the Census, Center for International Research, Suitland, Md., private communication, January 24, 1994.

2. Ibid.

3. Ibid.

4. Ibid.

5. United Nations, Department of International Economic and Social Affairs, *Long-range World Population Projections: Two Centuries of Population Growth, 1950–2150* (New York: 1992).

6. Population Reference Bureau (PRB), *1993 World Population Data Sheet* (Washington, D.C.: 1993).

7. Bureau of the Census, op. cit. note 1; PRB, op. cit. note 6.

8. PRB, op. cit. note 6.

9. Ibid.

10. Nicholas D. Kristoff, "China's Crackdown on Births: A Stunning, and Harsh, Success," *New York Times*, April 25, 1993.

11. Ibid.

12. John M. Goshko, "Planned Parenthood Gets AID Grant," *Washington Post*, November 23, 1993.

## OVERALL CIGARETTE PRODUCTION RISES (pages 100–01)

1. U.S. Department of Agriculture (USDA), Economic Research Service (ERS), Washington, D.C., unpublished printouts and private communications, December 2, 1993, and February 2, 1994.

2. USDA, ERS, Washington, D.C., printout and private comunication, December 22, 1993.

3. USDA, op. cit. note 1.

4. Ibid.

5. Ibid.
6. "Philip Morris Buys Stake in Czech Firm," *Journal of Commerce*, March 5, 1993; "Philip Morris to Buy Share of Lithuania Firm," *Journal of Commerce*, March 23, 1993; Elisabeth Rubinfien and Laurie Hays, "Foreign Investment in Russia Picks Up As Privatization, Reform Ease the Way," *Wall Street Journal*, March 1, 1993; "US, Russian Firms Form Cigarette Venture," *Journal of Commerce*, August 4, 1993.
7. USDA, op. cit. note 1.
8. Ibid.
9. Ibid.
10. Ibid.
11. Statement of Roger Herdman, acting director, Maria Hewitt, senior analyst, and Mary Laschober, analyst, all from Health Program, Office of Technology Assessment, on "Smoking-Related Deaths and Financial Costs: Office of Technology Assessment Estimates for 1990," Hearing On Preventive Health: An Ounce of Prevention Saves a Pound of Cure, Special Committee on Aging, U.S. Senate, Washington, D.C., May 6, 1993.
12. Ibid.
13. "Report Links One Form of Leukemia to Smoking," *New York Times*, September 20, 1993; "Smoking Tied to Leukemia Risk," *New York Times*, February 23, 1993; K.A. Fackelmann, "Mom's Smoking Linked to Hearing Defect," *Science News*, July 10, 1993.
14. Cancer deaths from World Bank, *World Development Report 1993* (New York: Oxford University Press, 1993).
15. Ibid.
16. Ibid.
17. Ibid.
18. Ibid.
19. David Sweanor, Non-Smokers' Rights Association of Canada, Ottawa, Ont., private communication, March 1993.

## HIV/AIDS CASES RISING STEADILY (pages 102–03)

1. World Health Organization (WHO), Global Programme on AIDS, "The Current Global Situation of the HIV/AIDS Pandemic," 1993 and 1994 editions, Geneva; Global AIDS Policy Coalition (GAPC), Harvard School of Public Health, Boston, Mass., private communication, February 24, 1994.
2. WHO 1994, op. cit. note 1; GAPC, op. cit. note 1; WHO, Global Programme on AIDS, "Current and Future Dimensions of the HIV/AIDS Pandemic: A Capsule Summary," Geneva, 1992; Jonathan Mann,

Daniel Tarantola, and Thomas W. Netter, eds., *AIDS in the World* (Cambridge, Mass.: 1992). WHO's estimates and projections are on the low end of the spectrum, and, in the organization's own words, "should be considered conservative" (WHO 1992). The higher estimates come from GAPC, an organization founded by Jonathan Mann, former head of WHO's Global Programme on AIDS. Estimates from GAPC are used for the table and figures because WHO does not release historical estimates.
3. WHO 1992, op. cit. note 2; Mann, Tarantola, and Netter, op. cit. note 2; U.S. Bureau of the Census, Center for International Research, private communication, Suitland, Md., November 2, 1993.
4. WHO 1994, op. cit. note 1; GAPC, op. cit. note 1.
5. WHO 1994, op. cit. note 1.
6. WHO 1993 and 1994, op. cit. note 1; GAPC, op. cit. note 1; WHO 1992, op. cit. note 2.
7. WHO 1992, op. cit. note 2; UNICEF, *Children and AIDS: An Impending Calamity* (New York: 1990).
8. WHO 1993 and 1994, op. cit. note 1; GAPC, op. cit. note 1.
9. WHO 1994, op. cit. note 1; WHO 1992, op. cit. note 2; Population Reference Bureau (PRB), *1993 World Population Data Sheet* (Washington, D.C.: 1993).
10. Ronald K. St. John, "The World-Wide AIDS Epidemic: A Crisis in Public Health," in Virginia Polytechnic Institute and State University, *AIDS: The Modern Plague, Volume Two of The President's Symposium* (Blacksburg, Va.: 1991).
11. "U.N. Agency Reports AIDS Virus Spreading Very Quickly in Africa," *New York Times*, December 13, 1993.
12. UNICEF, op. cit. note 7.
13. WHO 1992, op. cit. note 2.
14. Ibid.
15. William Branigin, "Asia Faced With AIDS Catastrophe," *New York Times*, December 2, 1993; Mann, Tarantola, and Netter, op. cit. note 2.
16. WHO 1992, op. cit. note 2.
17. Ibid.
18. WHO 1994, op. cit. note 1; GAPC, op. cit. note 1; PRB, op. cit. note 9.

## IMMUNIZATION RATES SOAR (pages 104–05)

1. UNICEF and World Health Organization, New York and Geneva, private communications, February 17, 1994.
2. UNICEF, *The State of the World's Children 1993* (New York: Oxford University Press, 1993).
3. Ibid.
4. Ibid.

5. Ibid.

6. Ibid.

7. Ibid.

8. World Bank, *World Development Report 1993* (New York: Oxford University Press, 1993).

9. UNICEF, *The Progress of Nations* (New York: 1993).

10. George Will, "The Disease of Violence," *Washington Post*, November 29, 1992.

11. Isao Arita, "A Crisis to Be Overcome," *World Health*, March/April 1993.

12. World Bank, op. cit. note 8.

13. Harry Hull, "Polio Eradication is in Sight," *World Health*, March/April 1993.

14. Terrel M. Hill, "The Promise of CVI," *World Health*, March/April 1993.

15. Robert J. Kim-Farley, "Expanded Programme on Immunizations: Achievements and Challenges," *World Health*, March/April 1993.

## REFUGEE FLOWS SWELLING (pages 106–07)

1. Worldwatch estimate, based on data from U.N. High Commissioner for Refugees (UNHCR), Geneva, private communication, March 16, 1994.

2. UNHCR, *The State of the World's Refugees: The Challenge of Protection* (New York: Penguin Books, 1993).

3. Ibid.

4. Ibid.

5. Ibid.

6. Ibid.

7. Roger Winter, "The Year in Review," *1993 World Refugee Survey* (Washington, D.C.: U.S. Committee for Refugees, 1993).

8. "Refugees on Move in Azerbaijan War," *New York Times*, October 16, 1993.

9. Raymond Bonner, "Asian Republic Still Caught in Web of Communism," *New York Times*, October 13, 1993.

10. Valery Tishkov, "The Russians are Leaving," *Development* (Journal of SID), Vol. 1, 1993.

11. Winter, op. cit. note 7.

12. Population Reference Bureau, *World Population Data Sheet 1993* (Washington, D.C.: 1993).

13. "Soil Loss Accelerating Worldwide: Hinders Effort to Feed Earth's Growing Population," U.N. Food and Agriculture Organization, Rome, press release, July 13, 1993.

## ARMS TRADE CONTINUES DECLINE (pages 110–11)

1. U.S. Arms Control and Disarmament Agency (ACDA), *World Military Expenditures and Arms Transfers 1991–1992* (Washington, D.C.: U.S. Government Printing Office, 1994).

2. ACDA, *World Military Expenditures and Arms Transfers* (Washington, D.C.: U.S. Government Printing Office, various editions); conversion into 1991 U.S. dollars by author.

3. Stockholm International Peace Research Institute (SIPRI), *SIPRI Yearbook 1993: World Armaments and Disarmament* (Oxford: Oxford University Press, 1993); Gerd Hagmeyer-Geverus, SIPRI, Stockholm, private communication, January 20, 1994. The SIPRI data cover aircraft, armor and artillery, guidance and radar systems, missiles, and warships. They do not include ammunition, support equipment, services and components, whereas ACDA does (as well as a broader array of weapons than SIPRI). ACDA and SIPRI also differ substantially in the methods used to assign a monetary value to traded items and their sources of information. Readers are advised to consult the sources referenced for precise definitions of the scope of transfers covered and the methodologies applied.

4. Nicole Ball, *Briefing Book on Conventional Arms Transfers* (Boston: Council for a Livable World Education Fund, 1991).

5. Calculated from Richard F. Grimmett, "Conventional Arms Transfers to the Third World, 1985–1992," *CRS Report to Congress*, Congressional Research Service (CRS), Library of Congress, Washington, D.C., July 19, 1993, and from Richard F. Grimmett, "Trends on Conventional Arms Transfers to the Third World by Major Supplier, 1977–1984," *CRS Report to Congress*, CRS, Library of Congress, Washington, D.C., April 19, 1985.

6. ACDA, op. cit. note 2.

7. Ibid.

8. Ball, op. cit. note 4.

9. Ian Anthony et al., "Arms Production and Arms Trade," in SIPRI, op. cit. note 3; Grimmett, "Arms Transfers, 1985–1992," op. cit. note 5.

10. Grimmett, "Arms Transfers, 1985–1992," op. cit. note 5.

11. Ibid.; U.S. Department of Defense, *Foreign Military Sales, Foreign Military Construction Sales and Military Assistance Facts, as of September 30, 1992* (Washington, D.C.: Defense Security Assistance Agency, undated).

12. Michael T. Klare, "Who's Arming Who? The Arms Trade in the 1990s," *Technology Review*, May/June 1990; U.S. Congress, Office of Technology Assessment, *Global Arms Trade* (Washington, D.C.: U.S. Government Printing Office, 1991).

## U.N. PEACEKEEPING EXPANDS (pages 112–13)

1. Amir Dossal, Field Finance and Budget Section, Field Operations Division, Department of Peacekeeping Operations, United Nations, New York, private communication, February 15, 1994.

2. Calculated from ibid., from Joseph Preston Baratta, *International Peacekeeping: History and Strengthening* (Washington, D.C.: Center for UN Reform Education, 1989), and from U.N. Department of Public Information, *United Nations Peace-keeping* (New York: 1993).

3. Independent Advisory Group on U.N. Financing, *Financing an Effective United Nations* (New York: Ford Foundation, 1993). The ratio given here should be understood to be no more than a rough indicator, since military spending is shrouded in secrecy in many countries.

4. Calculated from U.N. Department of Public Information, "United Nations Peace-Keeping Operations: Information Notes," 1993: Update No. 2, New York, November 1993, from Baratta, op. cit. note 2, and from William J. Durch and Barry M. Blechman, *Keeping the Peace: The United Nations in the Emerging World Order* (Washington, D.C.: The Henry L. Stimson Center, 1992).

5. Roger Hill, "Preventive Diplomacy, Peace-making and Peace-keeping," in Stockholm International Peace Research Institute (SIPRI), *SIPRI Yearbook 1993: World Armaments and Disarmament* (Oxford: Oxford University Press, 1993), for 1987 and 1992 data; June 1993 from "UN Operations: Not Only Expanding, but Breaking New Ground," *UN Chronicle*, September 1993; end of 1993 calculated from U.N. Department of Public Information, op. cit. note 4.

6. Calculated from U.N. Secretariat, "Status of Contributions" (issued monthly), New York, various editions.

7. U.N. Department of Public Information, "United Nations Peace-Keeping Operations: Information Notes," New York, September 1992.

8. U.N. Secretariat, "Improving the Financial Situation of the United Nations, Financing an Effective United Nations: A Report of the Independent Advisory Group on United Nations Financing, Report of the Secretary-General," New York, November 2, 1993.

9. Michael Renner, "Clinton Retreats from U.N. Peace System," *The New Economy*, Summer 1993; Eric Schmitt, "U.S. Set to Limit Role of Military in Peacekeeping," *New York Times*, January 29, 1993; Edward Mortimer, "Washington Casts Cloud Over UN Peacekeeping," *Financial Times*, January 11, 1994;

Daniel Williams and Ann Devroy, "U.S. Limits Peace-Keeping Role," *Washington Post*, November 25, 1993; Barton Gellman, "U.S. Reconsiders Putting GIs Under U.N.," *Washington Post*, September 22, 1993.

10. The Security Council voted in February 1994 to reduce the maximum authorized strength of U.N. peacekeepers in Somalia from 30,000 to 22,000; a further reduction to 15,000 is planned. Donatella Lorch, "Rising Violence in Somalia Throws U.N.'s Role into Question," *New York Times*, January 10, 1994; "United Nations Votes to Cut Somalia Peacekeeping Force," *New York Times*, February 5, 1994.

11. For example, the 1,260-strong peacekeeping force in Rwanda is to be doubled, and the observer mission in South Africa is being bolstered by 1,800 persons dispatched to monitor the forthcoming elections; "U.N. to Send 1,800 Observers," *New York Times*, January 15, 1994; "More U.N. Troops for Rwanda," *New York Times*, January 7, 1994. On the other hand, in November 1993 the Security Council rejected a request for a small peacekeeping force in Burundi; Mortimer, op. cit. note 9.

## NUCLEAR ARSENALS SHRINKING (pages 114–15)

1. Robert S. Norris and William M. Arkin, "Estimated Nuclear Stockpiles 1945–1993," *Bulletin of the Atomic Scientists*, December 1993.

2. Ibid.

3. Ibid.

4. Ibid.

5. Ibid.; amount of fissile materials from David Albright, Frans Berkhout, and William Walker, *World Inventory of Plutonium and Highly Enriched Uranium 1992* (Oxford: SIPRI and Oxford University Press, 1993).

6. Robert S. Norris and William M. Arkin, "Russian (C.I.S.) Strategic Nuclear Forces, End of 1992," *Bulletin of the Atomic Scientists*, March 1993; Robert S. Norris and William M. Arkin, "Estimated CIS (Soviet) Nuclear Stockpile (July 1992)," *Bulletin of the Atomic Scientists*, July/August 1992.

7. Michael R. Gordon, "U.S. Hopes to Curb A-Arms By Restricting Fuel Output," *New York Times*, July 28, 1993; "Multilateral Convention Proposed for a Cut-Off of Fissionable Material," *Disarmament Newsletter* (U.N. Centre for Disarmament Affairs), November 1993; "Comm I Consensus on CTB, Fissionable Ban," *Disarmament Times*, November 23, 1993.

8. Michael Renner, "Nuclear Arsenal Decline on Hold," in Lester R. Brown, Hal Kane, and Ed Ayres,

*Vital Signs 1993* (New York: W.W. Norton & Company, 1993).

9. Michael R. Gordon, "U.S. Says Ukraine Has Begun Dismantling Nuclear Missiles," *New York Times*, July 28, 1993; Robert Seely, "Ukraine Deactivates 17 Missiles in Goodwill Gesture Toward U.S. and Russia," *Washington Post*, December 21, 1993; "Warnings from Massandra," *Economist*, September 11, 1993.

10. R.W. Apple, Jr., "Ukraine Gives in on Surrendering its Nuclear Arms," *New York Times*, January 11, 1994; "Ukrainian Parliament Edges Closer to Atomic Disarmament," *New York Times*, February 4, 1994; Institute for Defense and Disarmament Studies (IDDS), *Arms Control Reporter 1994* (Cambridge, Mass.: 1994), sheets 611.B.836-.839.

11. Ragnhild Ferm, "Nuclear Explosions, 1945–92," in Stockholm International Peace Research Institute (SIPRI), *SIPRI Yearbook 1993: World Armaments and Disarmament* (Oxford: Oxford University Press, 1993); Steven A. Holmes, "World Moratorium on Nuclear Tests Broken by China," *New York Times*, October 6, 1993; U.S. Department of Energy, Nevada Operations Office, Office of External Affairs, "Announced United States Nuclear Tests: July 1945 through December 1992," May 1993; "Summary List of Previously Unannounced Tests," in U.S. Department of Energy, "Openness Press Conference: Fact Sheets," Office of the Press Secretary, Washington, D.C., December 7, 1993.

12. Fred Hiatt, "Russia Extends Test Ban," *Washington Post*, October 14, 1992; R. Jeffrey Smith, "President Extends Moratorium on Underground Nuclear Tests," *Washington Post*, July 4, 1993; David Buchan, "Mitterand Risks Paris Split on N-Weapons Tests," *Financial Times*, October 7, 1993.

13. Holmes, op. cit. note 11; British position from IDDS, *Arms Control Reporter 1993* (Cambridge, Mass.: 1993), sheets 603.B.253 and .254.

14. William Epstein, "CTB: Two Paths, One Goal," *Bulletin of the Atomic Scientists*, October 1993; Michael Wilkenson, "Forum on CTB, NPT, Fissionable Ban," *Disarmament Times*, November 23, 1993; Jim Wurst, "Countdown to the NPT Continues," *BASIC Reports*, February 3, 1994.

## PAPER RECYCLING ON A ROLL (pages 120–21)

1. Mary Cesar, Senior Consultant, Jaakko Pöyry Consulting, Tarrytown, N.Y., private communication, February 18, 1994.

2. Ibid.

3. *Pulp and Paper* (Pulp and Paper International, Miller Freeman, Inc., Brussels), October 1993. Wastepaper utilization rate is defined as the total amount of wastepaper a country uses in its production process, divided by the total amount of paper and paperboard produced. If 50 tons of wastepaper were used to make 100 tons of paper, the utilization rate would be 50 percent. It differs from a recovery rate in that it does not include wastepaper that is exported.

4. Calculated using Pulp and Paper International's figure for world imports of wastepaper divided by its recovery figure; *Pulp and Paper*, op. cit. note 3, and *Pulp and Paper* (Pulp and Paper International, Miller Freeeman, Inc., Brussels), October 1992.

5. *Pulp and Paper*, op. cit. note 3.

6. Ibid.; *Pulp and Paper*, op. cit. note 4.

7. *Pulp and Paper*, op. cit. note 3.

8. Bureau of National Affairs, "Executive Order on Federal Procurement, Recycling, Waste Prevention Signed By President Clinton October 20, 1993," Washington, DC.

9. John Holusha, "White House Issues an Order to Bolster Recycling of Paper," *New York Times*, October 21, 1993.

10. Don Marikovics, Premier Papers, Merrick, N.Y., private communication, February 24, 1994.

11. "Belgian Greens Exact Promise for Measure to Impose Eco-Tax on Wide Range of Products," *International Environment Reporter*, February 10, 1993.

12. Ordinance on the Avoidance of Packaging Waste of 12 June 1991.

13. John Polak, Director, Environmental Choice Program, Environment Canada, Ottawa, Ont., private communication, February 24, 1994.

14. Ibid.

15. Ed Ayres, "Whitewash: Pursuing the Truth About Paper," *World Watch*, September/October 1992.

16. Ibid.

17. Some commercial paper waste, although pre-consumer, is difficult to recycle; see Recycling Advisory Council, *Final Report on Recycled Paper Definitions, Standards, Measurement and Labeling Guidelines* (Washington, D.C.: 1992). For a discussion of some of the disputed issues pertaining to content standards, see Mary Cesar, "Recycled Content Guidelines for Paper: Too Many Cooks Spoil the Pot," *Resource Recycling*, November 1993.

18. Steve Apotheker, "The New Tissue Industry: Recycled on a Roll," *Resource Recycling*, November 1993; Steve Apotheker, "It's Black and White and Recycled All Over," *Resource Recycling*, July 1993; Steve Apotheker, Resource Recycling, private communication, February 18, 1994.

19. Apothaker, private communication, op. cit. note 18.

20. Ayres, op. cit. note 15.
21. Ibid.
22. "More Mixing, Better Paper Diversion," *BioCycle*, August 1993.
23. Robert Steuteville, "Capital Intensive Pulping," *Biocycle*, November 1993.

## CORAL REEFS IN DECLINE (pages 122–23)

1. Susan M. Wells, *Coral Reefs of the World* (Cambridge: International Union for Conservation of Nature and Natural Resources and U.N. Environment Programme, 1988); for a summary, see Susan M. Wells, "Coral Reefs: Undersea Gardens Lose Their Sheen," *International Wildlife*, March/April 1990.
2. Clive R. Wilkinson, "Coral Reefs Are Facing Widespread Extinctions: Can We Prevent These Through Sustainable Management Practices?" Proceedings 7th International Coral Reef Symposium, Guam, June 1992.
3. Table 1 based on S.V. Smith, "Coral-Reef Area and the Contributions of Reefs to Processes and Resources of the World's Oceans," *Nature*, May 18, 1978 (for area estimates); Wilkinson, op. cit. note 2; Clive Wilkinson, Australian Institute of Marine Science, Townsville, Australia, private communications, August and October 1992; Wells, *Coral Reefs*, op. cit. note 1; World Conservation Monitoring Centre, *Global Biodiversity: Status of the Earth's Living Resources* (London: Chapman & Hall, 1992); "The Status of Living Coastal Resources of ASEAN Countries: Reports Presented at the 4th Management Committee Meeting of the ASEAN-Australia Marine Science Project: Living Coastal Resources, Bali, January 29-February 1, 1992," *ASEAN Marine Science* (Newsletter of the ASEAN-Australia Marine Science Project, Townsville, Australia), April 1992; Thia-Eng Chua and Daniel Pauly, eds., *Coastal Area Management in Southeast Asia: Policies, Management Strategies and Case Studies*, Proceedings of the ASEAN/US Policy Workshop on Coastal Area Management, Johore Bahru, Malaysia, October 25–27, 1988 (Manila, Philippines: International Center for Living Aquatic Resources Management, 1989); Charles Birkeland, "Caribbean and Pacific Coastal Marine Systems: Similarities and Differences," *Nature & Resources*, Vol. 26, No. 2, 1990; North Rohan Gunasekera, "Threat to Sri Lanka's Coral Reefs," *Panoscope*, September 1990; "Coastal Belt Coral Reefs Threatened," Colombo Sri Lanka Broadcasting Corporation International Service, July 28,1991, in *JPRS Report:*

*Environmental Issues*, August 22, 1991; Paul Dutton, "WWF Master Plan to Preserve Bazaruto Archipelago," *World Wildlife Fund News*, January/February 1991; Tim MacClanahan, "Triggerfish: Coral Reef Keystone Predator," *Swara* (East African Wildlife Society, Nairobi, Kenya), May/June 1992; "Corals in Death Throes," *Down to Earth*, June 30, 1992; Kenneth Brower, "State of the Reef," *Audubon*, March 1989; Carlos Goenaga, "The State of Coral Reefs in the Wider Caribbean," *Interciencia*, January/February 1991; F. Gable, "Caribbean Coastal and Marine Tourism: Coping with Climate Change and its Associated Effects," in Marc L. Miller and Jan Auyong, *Proceedings of the 1990 Congress on Coastal and Marine Tourism*, Vol. I (Newport, Ore.: National Coastal Resources Research & Development Institute, 1991); Zvy Dubinsky, Bar-Ilan University, Ramat Gan, Israel, private communication, September 18, 1992.
4. B.G. Hatcher et al., "Review of Research Relevant to the Conservation of Shallow Tropical Marine Ecosystems," *Oceanography and Marine Biology Annual Review*, Vol. 27, 1989, pp. 337–414.
5. Gregor Hodgson and John A. Dixon, *Logging Versus Fisheries and Tourism in Palawan: An Environmental and Economic Analysis*, Occasional Paper No. 7 (Honolulu, Hawaii: East-West Environmental and Policy Institute, 1988).
6. Ibid.
7. Chua and Pauly, op. cit. note 3.
8. Don Hinrichsen, *Our Common Seas: Coasts in Crisis* (London: Earthscan Publications Ltd., 1990).
9. Population Reference Bureau, *1993 World Population Data Sheet* (Washington, D.C.: 1993).
10. Wells, *Coral Reefs*, op. cit. note 1.
11. Ibid; Wilkinson, op. cit. note 3.
12. U.N. Food and Agriculture Organization, *FAO Production Yearbook: Fishery Statistics, Commodities, 1989* (Rome: 1990).
13. Ibid.; Mark Derr, "Raiders of the Reef," *Audubon*, March/April 1992.

## CONSERVING THE OTHER RAIN FOREST (pages 124–25)

1. A. Lara and R. Villaba, "A 3620-Year Temperature Record from *Fitzroya cupressoides* Tree Rings in Southern South America," *Science*, May 21, 1993; Jerry F. Franklin and R.H. Waring, "Distinctive Features of the Northwestern Coniferous Forest: Development, Structure, Function," in R.H. Waring (ed.), *Forests: Fresh Perspectives from Ecosystem Analysis*, Proceedings of the 40th Annual Colloquium (Corvallis: Oregon State University, 1980).

2. Some forest ecologists define temperate rain forests strictly by annual rainfall to include some isolated patches in interior, mid-mountain regions. Rain forests with high rainfall stemming only from mountainous features without any marine influence tend to have continental climates with hot summers and strong seasonal variation in precipitation. Because they are primarily disturbed by fire, these forests do not share the disturbance regimes or evolutionary processes of coastal temperate rain forests. While tropical mountain cloud forests also exhibit many similar ecological characteristics, they tend to have less accumulated organic matter, are less productive, and have shorter trees. Paul Alaback, "Comparative Ecology of Temperate Rainforests of the Americas Along Analogous Climactic Gradients," *Revista Chilena de Historia Natural*, Vol. 64, pp. 399–412, 1991.

3. Erin Kellogg, ed., "Coastal Temperate Rain Forests: Ecological Characteristics, Status and Distribution Worldwide" (a working manuscript), Occasional Paper Series No. 1, Ecotrust/Conservation International, Portland, Ore., June 1992.

4. Paul Alaback, "Endless Battles, Verdant Survivors," *Natural History*, August 1988; James Weigand, "Coastal Temperate Rain Forests: Definition and Global Distribution With Particular Emphasis on North America," prepared for Ecotrust/Conservation International, unpublished, 1990; Kellogg, op. cit. note 3. All figures on the original and current area of coastal temperate rain forests are preliminary, rough estimates that are currently under revision.

5. U.N. Economic Commision for Europe/Food and Agriculture Organization, *The Forest Resources of the Temperate Zones: The UN-ECE/FAO 1990 Forest Resource Assessment, Vol 1: General Forest Resource Information* (New York: United Nations, 1992).

6. In this list, Ireland is the sole exception to the presence of high mountains; Kellogg, op. cit. note 3.

7. Many researchers consider this estimate conservative; Kellogg, op. cit. note 3.

8. Ibid.

9. Ibid.

10. Working Group for Rain Forest Conservation, *The Rain Forest of Tasmania* (Hobart, Australia: Forestry Commission/Tasmania, 1987).

11. Kellogg, op. cit. note 3.

12. Alaback defines seasonal rain forest as having a mean annual temperature (MAT) above 9 degrees Celsius and less than 10 percent annual rainfall during summer; perhumid as MAT 7 degrees Celsius and 10–20 percent annual rainfall during summer; and boreal as MAT below 6 degrees Celsius and more than 20 percent annual rainfall during summer. Paul Alaback, "Biodiversity Patterns in Relation to Climate for the Rainforests of the West Coast of North America," in R. Lawford, P. Alaback, and E.R. Fuentes, eds., *High Latitude Rainforests of the West Coast of the Americas: Climate, Hydrology, Ecology and Conservation* (New York: Springer-Verlag, in press).

13. Alaback, op. cit. note 2.

14. Highest runoff rates from F. Di Castri, *Bioclimatologia de Chile* (Santiago: Vicerrectoria Academica de la Universidad Catolica de Chile, 1976); E.B. Alexander, "Rates of Soil Formation: Implications for Soil-Loss Tolerance," *Soil Science*, January 1988; D.M. Bishop and M.E. Stevens, "Landslides on Logged Areas in Southeast Alaska," U.S. Forest Service Res Pap NOR-1, Pacific Northwest Research Station, Juneau, Alaska, 1964; Thomas Veblen et. al., "Forest Dynamics in Southcentral Chile," *Journal of Biogeography*, Vol. 8, pp. 211–47, 1981. All the above as cited in Alaback, op. cit. note 2.

15. Spencer B. Beebe and Edward C. Wolf, "The Coastal Temperate Rain Forest: An Ecosystem Management Approach," in Keith Moore, *An Inventory of Watersheds in the Coastal Temperate Forests of British Columbia* (Queen Charlotte City, B.C., and Portland, Ore.: Earthlife Canada Foundation and Ecotrust/Conservation International, 1991).

16. G.L. Atjay, P. Ketner, and P. Duvingneaud, "Terrestrial Primary Production and Phytomass," in B. Bolin et al., eds., *The Global Carbon Cycle*, SCOPE Report 13 (New York: John Wiley, 1979); Franklin and Waring, op. cit. note 1.

17. Randy Stoltmann, *Guide to Record Trees of British Columbia* (North Vancouver, B.C.: Western Canada Wilderness Committee/Lynn Canyon Ecology Center, 1992).

18. Overall species diversity is highest in the tropical rain forest. Edward O. Wilson, *The Diversity of Life* (Cambridge, Mass.: Harvard University Press, 1992); Alaback, op. cit. note 12; T.D. Schowalter, "Canopy Arthropod Community Structure and Herbivory in Old-growth and Regenerating Forests in Western Oregon," *Canadian Journal of Forest Research*, March 1989.

19. Kellogg, op. cit. note 3.

20. Ibid.

21. Alaback, op. cit. note 2.

22. "Large" is defined as larger than 10,000 hectares, from Beebe and Wolf, op. cit. note 15; Erin Kellogg, director, policy and comunications, Ecotrust, Portland, Ore., private communication, February 24, 1994.

23. John Ryan, "Plight of the Other Rain Forest," *World Watch*, May/June 1989.

24. Paul Alaback, assistant professor, College of Forestry, University of Montana, Missoula, private communication, February 24, 1994.

25. Sierra Club of Western Canada, "Ancient Rainforests at Risk," Final Report of the Vancouver Island Mapping Project, Vancouver, B.C., July 30, 1993.

26. Amy Simpson, Friends of Clayoquot Sound, Tofino, B.C., private communication, February 16, 1994.

27. Clayoquot Biosphere Project, "Conserving the Rain Forests of Home," Tofino, B.C., 1992.

28. Alaback, op. cit. note 24.

29. Paul Alaback and Michael McClellan, "Effects of Global Warming on Managed Coastal Ecosystems of Western North America," in H.A. Mooney, E. Fuentes, and B.I. Kronberg, eds., *Earth System Response to Global Change: Contrasts Between North and South America* (San Diego, Calif.: Academic Press, 1993).

## ENERGY PRODUCTIVITIES VARY WIDELY (pages 126–27)

1. Energy productivity is defined here as the ratio of gross domestic product (GDP) (converted to 1985 dollars relative to purchasing power parities) to commercial fuels consumed, excluding sources such as fuelwood that are often not bought and sold on the market.

2. International Energy Agency (IEA), *World Energy Outlook* (Paris: Organisation for Economic Co-operation and Development (OECD), 1993).

3. Amulya K.N. Reddy and José Goldemberg, "Energy for the Developing World," *Scientific American*, September 1990.

4. United Nations, *World Energy Supplies 1950–1974* (New York: 1976); IEA, "Energy Balances in Non-OECD Countries 1960–1991" (electronic database), OECD, Paris, 1993; 1992 figures are Worldwatch estimates based on British Petroleum (BP), *BP Statistical Review of World Energy 1993* (London: 1993), and on IEA; GDP data through 1990 from Robert Summers and Alan Heston, "The Penn World Table (Mark 5): An Expanded Set of International Comparisons, 1950–1988," *Quarterly Journal of Economics*, May 1991 and electronic database; 1991 and 1992 GDPs are Worldwatch estimates based on ibid. and on International Monetary Fund (IMF), *World Economic Outlook*, October 1993; Egypt numbers are for 1970–91 and are from United Nations, *World Energy Supplies 1973–1978* (New York: 1979), from United Nations, *1981 Yearbook of World Energy Statistics*

(New York: 1983), and from United Nations, *1985 Energy Statistics Yearbook* (New York: various years).

5. Reddy and Goldemberg, op. cit. note 3.

6. Michael Philips, *The Least Cost Energy Path For Developing Countries* (Washington, D.C.: International Institute for Energy Conservation, 1991).

7. United Nations, *World Energy Supplies 1950–1974*, op. cit. note 4; IEA, *Energy Balances of OECD Countries* (Paris: OECD, various years); GDP data through 1990 from Summers and Heston, op. cit. note 4; 1991 and 1992 GDPs are Worldwatch estimates based on ibid. and on IMF, op. cit. note 4.

8. United Nations, *World Energy Supplies 1950–1974*, op. cit. note 4; IEA, op. cit. note 7; 1992 figures are Worldwatch estimates based on BP, op. cit. note 4, and on IEA; GDP data through 1990 from Summers and Heston, op. cit. note 4; 1991 and 1992 GDPs are Worldwatch estimates based on ibid. and on IMF, op. cit. note 4.

9. United Nations, *World Energy Supplies 1950–1974*, op. cit. note 4; IEA, op. cit. note 7; 1992 figures are Worldwatch estimates based on BP, op. cit. note 4, and on IEA; GDP data through 1990 from Summers and Heston, op. cit. note 4; 1991 and 1992 GDPs are Worldwatch estimates based on ibid. and on IMF, op. cit. note 4.

10. Peter Gray, *Comparing National Energy Efficiencies* (Washington, D.C.: Environmental Law Institute, 1991).

11. Lee Schipper and Stephen Meyers, *Energy Efficiency and Human Activity: Past Trends, Future Prospects* (Cambridge: Cambridge University Press, 1992).

12. U.S. Congress, Office of Technology Assessment, *Energy Efficiency Technologies for Central and Eastern Europe* (Washington, D.C.: 1993).

13. United Nations, *World Energy Supplies 1950–1974*, op. cit. note 4; IEA, op. cit. note 4; GDP data through 1990 from Summers and Heston, op. cit. note 4; 1991 GDP, Worldwatch estimates based on ibid. and on IMF, op. cit. note 4.

14. United Nations, *World Energy Supplies 1950–1974*, op. cit. note 4; IEA, op. cit. note 4; 1992 figures are Worldwatch estimates based on BP, op. cit. note 4, and on IEA; GDP data through 1990 from Summers and Heston, op. cit. note 4; 1991 and 1992 GDPs are Worldwatch estimates based on ibid. and on IMF, op. cit. note 4.

15. Worldwatch estimate based on Summers and Heston, op. cit. note 4, on BP, op. cit. note 4, and on "low-growth" economic projection from IEA, op. cit. note 2.

16. Christopher Flavin and Alan B. Durning, *Building on Success: The Age of Energy Efficiency*, Worldwatch Paper 82 (Washington, D.C: Worldwatch Institute, March 1988).

## BIRDS ARE IN DECLINE (pages 128–29)

1. Nigel Collar, BirdLife International, Cambridge, U.K., private communication, February 9, 1994; Nigel Collar and P. Andrew, *Birds to Watch, The ICBP World Checklist of Threatened Birds* (Washington, D.C.: Smithsonian Institution Press, 1988).
2. Ragupathy Kannan, Department of Biological Sciences, University of Arkansas, Fayetteville, private communication, January 11, 1994.
3. Nigel Collar, BirdLife International, Cambridge, U.K., private communication, March 31, 1992.
4. Collar and Andrew, op. cit. note 1; Warren B. King (compiler), *Endangered Birds of the World: The ICBP Bird Red Data Book* (Washington, D.C.: Smithsonian Institution Press, 1981).
5. Thomas R. Dahl, *Wetlands: Losses in the United States, 1780s to 1980s* (Washington, D.C.: U.S. Department of the Interior, Fish and Wildlife Service, 1990); loss in duck species derived from D.F. Caithamer et al., *Trends in Duck Breeding Populations, 1955–1992* (Laurel, Md.: Office of Migratory Bird Management, U.S. Fish and Wildlife Service, 1992).
6. Humphrey Crick, "Poisoned Prey in the Heart of Africa," *New Scientist*, November 24, 1990.
7. National Audubon Society, *American Birds*, Fall 1992.
8. Joel Bourne, "The Salton Sea's Fatal Shore," *Defenders*, May/June 1992.
9. Ibid.
10. John Terborgh, *Where Have All the Birds Gone?* (Princeton, N.J.: Princeton University Press, 1989).
11. Ibid.
12. Malta from National Audubon Society, *American Birds*, Winter 1991; Greece from National Audubon Society, *American Birds*, Summer 1992; Italy from Richard L. Hudson, "Tough Bird Laws Mean Little When It's Time for Dinner," *Wall Street Journal*, January 18, 1990.
13. National Audubon Society, op. cit. note 7.
14. National Audubon Society, *American Birds*, Winter 1991.
15. Conservation Fund, *Common Ground*, November/December 1991.
16. John C. Ryan, *Life Support: Conserving Biological Diversity*, Worldwatch Paper 108 (Washington, D.C.: Worldwatch Institute, April 1992).
17. Ruth Norris, "A Prescription for Refuges," *Defenders*, May/June 1992.
18. Loss since 1600 from King, op. cit. note 4.
19. Roger T. Peterson et al., *Save the Birds* (Boston: Houghton Mifflin Co., 1989).
20. C.J. Bibby et al., *Putting Biodiversity on the Map: Priority Areas for Global Conservation* (Cambridge: International Council for Bird Preservation, 1992).

## TRAFFIC ACCIDENTS TAKING MANY LIVES (pages 132–33)

1. World Health Organization (WHO), *1992 World Health Statistics Annual* (Geneva: 1993).
2. United Nations Development Programme, *Human Development Report 1993* (New York: Oxford University Press, 1993).
3. WHO, op. cit. note 1; important exceptions include Mexico and northeastern Brazil.
4. U.S. Bureau of the Census, *Statistical Abstract of the United States 1993* (Washington, D.C.: U.S. Government Printing Office, 1993).
5. Worldwatch Institute calculation based on International Road Federation, *World Road Statistics 1987–1991* (Washington, D.C.: 1992), and on WHO, op. cit. note 1. Most countries with large car fleets, such as those in Europe and North America, were included; China, however, was not.
6. WHO, op. cit. note 1. Note that countries that score low in this table are not necessarily safe to drive in; they may have a high fatality rate per mile driven, but fewer people who drive, and hence a lower auto fatality rate.
7. Ibid.
8. Bureau of the Census, op. cit. note 4.
9. WHO, op. cit. ote 1; Bureau of the Census, op. cit. note 4.
10. International Road Federation, op. cit. note 5.
11. Organisation for Economic Co-operation and Development, *OECD Environmental Data: Compendium 1993* (Paris: 1993).
12. U.S. Department of Transportation, Federal Highway Administration, *Highway Statistics 1991* (Washington, D.C.: U.S. Government Printing Office, various years).
13. Ibid.
14. International Road Federation, op. cit. note 5.
15. Hal Kane, "Backstage at the Emergency Room," *The Ann Arbor Observer*, December 1988.
16. International Road Federation, op. cit. note 5.
17. Ibid.
18. Ibid.

## LIFE EXPECTANCY LENGTHENS (pages 134–35)

1. United Nations, *World Population Prospects, The 1992 Revision* (New York: 1993).

## Notes

2. World Bank, *World Development Report 1992* (New York: Oxford University Press, 1992).

3. Ibid.

4. United Nations Development Programme, *Human Development Report 1993* (New York: Oxford University Press, 1993).

5. Population Reference Bureau, *1993 World Population Data Sheet* (Washington, D.C.: 1993).

6. UNICEF, *The State of the World's Children 1993* (New York: Oxford University Press, 1993).

7. Shea O. Rustein, "Levels, Trends and Differentials in Infant and Child Mortality in the Less Developed Countries," presented at seminar on Child Survival Interventions: Effectiveness and Efficiency, The Johns Hopkins University School of Hygiene and Public Health, Baltimore, Md., June 20–22, 1991, cited in W. Henry Mosley and Peter Cowley, *The Challenge of World Health* (Washington, D.C.: Population Reference Bureau, 1991).

8. Amartya Sen, "The Economics of Life and Death," *Scientific American*, May 1993.

9. Ibid.

10. United Nations, op. cit. note 1.

11. Ibid.

12. Sen, op. cit note 8.

13. Ibid.

14. Ibid.

15. John Lloyd, "Russia Faces Population Crisis," *Financial Times*, February 14, 1994.

16. World Bank, *World Development Report 1993* (New York: Oxford University Press, 1993).

17. Ibid.

# THE VITAL SIGNS SERIES

*Some topics are included each year in* Vital Signs; *others, particularly those in Part Two, are included only in certain years. The following is a list of the topics covered thus far in the series, with the year or years each appeared indicated in parentheses. See page 8 for information on ordering the Worldwatch Database Diskette.*

## Part One: KEY INDICATORS

FOOD TRENDS
    Grain Production (1992, 1993, 1994)
    Soybean Harvest (1992, 1993, 1994)
    Meat Production (1992, 1993, 1994)
    Fish Catch (1992, 1993, 1994)
    Grain Stocks (1992, 1993, 1994)
    Grain Used for Feed (1993)
    Aquaculture (1994)

AGRICULTURAL RESOURCE
TRENDS
    Grain Area (1992, 1993)
    Fertilizer Use (1992, 1993, 1994)
    Irrigation (1992, 1994)
    Grain Yield (1994)

ENERGY TRENDS
    Oil Production (1992, 1993, 1994)
    Wind Power (1992, 1993, 1994)
    Nuclear Power (1992, 1993, 1994)
    Solar Cell Production (1992, 1993, 1994)
    Natural Gas (1992, 1994)
    Energy Efficiency (1992)
    Geothermal Power (1993)

Coal Use (1993, 1994)
Hydroelectric Power (1993)
Carbon Use (1993)
Compact Fluorescent Lamps (1993, 1994)

ATMOSPHERIC TRENDS
    CFC Production (1992, 1993, 1994)
    Global Temperature (1992, 1993, 1994)
    Carbon Emissions (1992, 1994)

ECONOMIC TRENDS
    Global Economy (1992, 1993, 1994)
    Third World Debt (1992, 1993, 1994)
    International Trade (1993, 1994)
    Steel Production (1993)
    Paper Production (1993, 1994)
    Advertising Expeditures (1993)
    Roundwood Production (1994)
    Gold Production (1994)

TRANSPORTATION TRENDS
Bicycle Production (1992, 1993, 1994)
Automobile Production (1992, 1993, 1994)
Air Travel (1993)

ENVIRONMENTAL TRENDS
Pesticide Resistance (1994)
Sulfur and Nitrogen Emissions (1994)

SOCIAL TRENDS
Population Growth (1992, 1993, 1994)
Cigarette Smoking (1992, 1993, 1994)

Infant Mortality (1992)
Child Mortality (1993)
Refugees (1993, 1994)
HIV/AIDS Incidence (1994)
Immunizations (1994)

MILITARY TRENDS
Military Expenditures (1992)
Nuclear Arsenal (1992, 1994)
Arms Trade (1994)
Peace Expenditures (1994)

# Part Two: SPECIAL FEATURES

ENVIRONMENTAL
FEATURES
Bird Populations (1992, 1994)
Forest Loss (1992, 1994)
Soil Erosion (1992)
Steel Recycling (1992)
Nuclear Waste (1992)
Water Scarcity (1993)
Forest Damage from Air Pollution (1993)
Marine Mammal Populations (1993)
Paper Recycling (1994)
Coral Reefs (1994)
Energy Productivity (1994)

ECONOMIC FEATURES
Wheat/Oil Exchange Rate (1992, 1993)
Trade in Arms and Grain (1992)
Cigarette Taxes (1993)
U.S. Seafood Prices (1993)

SOCIAL FEATURES
Income Distribution (1992)
Maternal Mortality (1992)
Access to Family Planning (1992)
Literacy (1993)
Fertility Rates (1993)
Traffic Accidents (1994)
Life Expectancy (1994)

MILITARY FEATURES
Nuclear Arsenal (1993)
U.N. Peacekeeping (1993)